CW00927364

ANGLING ESSAYS

GRAHAM MARSDEN

First published in June 2011

ISBN NUMBER 978-0-9567015-7-2

Designed and published by mpress (Media) LTD.

Unit Four, Ashton Gate, Harold Hill, Romford, RM3 8UF

FOR ANNE

I owe a debt of thanks to my wife Anne for allowing me the time to fish, the time to spend writing and processing photographs, and just for putting up with me when I'm deep in thought and oblivious to matters more important.

Acknowledgements

My thanks go to Mark Wintle for contributing the roach chapter and for checking my manuscript for typos and other errors. Thanks also to Gary Knowles for the perch chapter and for continuing to prove that not all the country's top big fish anglers live further south than Cheshire.

I've already dedicated this book to my wife Anne, but I'll thank her again as Brownie Points are always useful.

Finally, thanks to Cliff and Paul Moulder of Mpress Media who know how to design and publish a book for anglers, and who always consulted me and kept me informed as my book progressed through the various stages of design, set-up and publishing.

Contents

Graham Marsden

Introduction

Glancing behind me I could see my footprints where they'd flattened the dew-soaked grass. On my left the river flowed quietly, barely competing with the early morning birdsong and the soft sound of my tread. In the distance I could see the swim I was heading for and quickened my pace, excited anticipation fighting with my desire to tread quietly and leave the fish undisturbed. Barbel were my target and already, in my mind's eye, I could see a big double engulfing my bait and I eagerly looked forward to the exhilaration of a great battle. Yet, as appealing as that was, most of what I wanted from fishing was all around me, the natural beauty of the countryside and a sense of wellbeing just by being there, and being part of it.

That's just one of many reasons for going fishing, but few people who have never wet a line wonder just what we anglers see in it. And unless someone has tried it, for a few weeks at least, then no angler is ever going to convince a non-angler that it is perhaps the most satisfying recreation known to man. Let's be fair though, we anglers don't have exclusivity in feeling like that; golfers, cricketers, rock climbers, possibly even Morris

Dancers, and a host of other participants in other activities, will feel like that about their chosen escape.

Another thing that makes it difficult to describe what we get out of fishing is the absolute fact that it means different things to different people. My reason for going fishing could be vastly different to someone else's reason. With no desire to be pretentious though, being as this is my book and presumably you've bought it to read what I have to say about fishing, I'll tell you why I regularly take up rod and line, and have done at least once or twice every week for the past 60-odd years. By letting you know my reasons for fishing it will give you as good a clue as any as to the underlying theme of this book.

I could try to convince you that I go fishing because it appeals to my hunting instinct, that inbuilt urge in man to hunt for food, and I suppose there is a generous element of that. My primary reason though, for loving fishing, is much simpler than that, and I've already mentioned the key word: *escape*.

Fishing has, for as long as I can remember, offered me an escape from the involvement with, and responsibility of, everyday life. That involvement could have been traumatic at the time or simply tedious; it didn't matter, fishing took me away from it and offered me peace and tranquillity, or excitement if I needed it. I could be investigative, introspective, laid back, active or just taking time out to daydream about winning the lottery. Fishing provides an opportunity for all those things; all you need to do is choose the species, the method and the venue to go with the mood.

For me, most of my fishing adventures have been seen as a challenge, a determination to catch the biggest fish a particular water could offer. I invariably chose fairly local waters that produced the biggest specimens of a particular species. Any species was fair game for me providing it grew to specimen proportions in waters that were within about 50 miles of my home. The only species I didn't spend much time hunting, or at least not as much time as I spent seeking other species, were roach and perch. I just didn't have them available to me in realistic numbers. For that reason the roach chapter in this book has been written by Mark Wintle (author of 'Big Roach', Mpress), and the perch chapter by Gary Knowles, both of whom know their species extremely well and have caught more than their fair share of specimens. I have also left eels out of the book, even though I have caught them to over 6lb and at one time just loved fishing for them. However, they never have been a popular species and even less so today as they have unfortunately declined in numbers. Grayling are also absent, but again, they are not a hugely popular species with coarse anglers; more a fly fisherman's species. I fly fish too, but this book is big enough and lines have to be drawn somewhere.

Whatever species I've fished for I've gone after them with drive and determination. Both during fishing and in between fishing sessions I've studied the species I was targeting at the time, theorising different approaches and methods and then putting them into practice at the next available opportunity. I have never been happy to sit back and accept failure as being 'just another bad day when the fish were not feeding'. There always had to be a reason and I would chase that reason like an addict chases his next fix. Of course, like any other angler, I had my fair share of blank sessions, sometimes more than what I thought was my fair share when things were not going according to plan. Without any false modesty though, I'm considered to be a successful angler.

I've written articles in most of the UK's angling press for the last 40-odd years, and written in every issue of the now defunct Coarse Fisherman magazine (in its various guises) for over 30 years. That's over 360 articles in one magazine alone. I've also written regularly for Europe's biggest selling fishing magazine, Germany's Blinker, and other foreign publications. I'm not telling you this for bragging rights, but to point out that the great majority of those articles were based on my approach to fishing, not about any step by step guide to catching fish, but the deeper, more thoughtful aspects of angling upon which my attitude to angling was always based.

This book follows the same style, thoughts and philosophy found in many of those articles, with the sincere wish that I can pass on some of the things that have caught me fish over a great many years and, not the least important, some of the humour that always accompanied my angling adventures. What you won't see in this book are any step-by-step guides about how to tie hooks and shot floats, but that doesn't mean you will not learn anything about fishing. I hope the book will help you to learn the greatest lesson of all; how to think for yourself. If it goes some way to entertaining you and to inspiring you to think more deeply about your fishing and that in turn leads you to better and, most important, more enjoyable fishing, I will have achieved what I set out to do.

Chapter 1

Fish Facts

Feeding habits and other fishy behaviour – sorting fact from fiction

KNOW YOUR FISH - FISH SIGNS

An angler stands at the water's edge, a hand held across his brow, shielding his eyes from the sun as he looks through polarizing spectacles across the expanse of seemingly featureless water. He is looking intently at the surface for signs of fish.

The fish themselves could be there; leaping, rolling, splashing, swirling, tail-waving, or merely dimpling the surface. The angler, experienced as he is, knows that each of those movements tell him something about what the fish is doing, or about to do.

Leaping

Fish that jump through the surface, often completely clearing it, are almost always feeding, or about to feed, even when this happens in weak winter sunshine. These fish are using energy, and energy requires fuel, which in this case is food. Energetic leaping is a sure sign that the fish are fit and healthy, and fit and healthy fish feed most often. Leaping carp, in particular, are feeding carp.

Rolling

Fish that are seen rolling - and bream, tench, crucian carp, roach and barbel are especially prone to this - are also feeding, or about to feed. For years the rolling of bream was always referred to as the 'pre-feed roll', although we now know that bream roll during feeding too.

When you spot fish rolling at the surface, make sure it is a true roll; a genuine porpoise-like roll that slices through the surface like a hot knife through butter. Otherwise, a less 'stylish' roll may be no more than a sign that the fish are simply playing around, as most creatures do occasionally.

A carp swirls at the surface.

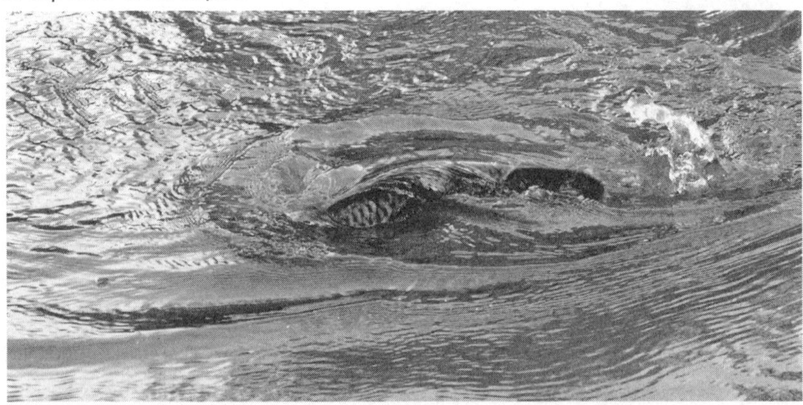

Splashing and Swirling

Erratic splashing and swirling at the surface is the least promising sign that fish are feeding, for it is just as likely the fish are playing, or spawning if it is the time of year for that activity. If pairs, or groups of fish, are seen splashing and cavorting together, then they are almost certainly spawning. Don't ignore splashing and swirling fish, however, for at the very least it tells you exactly where the fish are, and that alone is worth knowing. Furthermore, any splash or swirl could be a striking pike, which is good news for the pike angler, and at least you know there must be smaller fish around for the pike to strike at.

Tail-waving

This is an absolutely sure sign that fish are feeding at that very moment. They are in shallow water 'standing' on their heads, feeding, tails to heaven, waving clear of the surface.

Dimpling

Those tiny circles that appear and swell at the surface are the best sign of all that fish are feeding, especially if the appearance of a dimple is accompanied by a distinct sucking sound, known by carp men as a 'cloop'! It means the fish, most often rudd and carp, and chub on the river, are sucking insects or other edible items from the surface.

If there are no signs of fish actually at the surface, then the angler looks for signs on the surface that tell him fish are feeding on the bottom right at that moment. These include mud clouds, bubbles, and weed movement.

Mud clouds

Mud clouds needn't be muddy patches in otherwise clear water. Very often they are darker muddy patches in muddy water, and need a keen eye to spot them. Any area where the water is even slightly less clear than the surrounding area is worth investigating.

Bubbles

Bubbles at the surface probably cause more confusion amongst anglers than any other surface sign. Large bubbles that explode haphazardly can usually be ignored. They are simply the result of marsh gas breaking free of the bottom.

Genuine fish-feeding bubbles are tiny, hardly more than pin-head size, formed by the marsh gas being filtered through the fish's gill rakers. They erupt in regular patterns and in trails as the fish moves across the bottom, lingering here and there to feed. Carp and tench are especially prone to causing bubbles when feeding, and bream to a slightly lesser extent.

Weed Movement

Not a sure sign that fish are feeding: in spring to early summer the movement could be caused by spawning fish. But weed movement is always worth investigating, it could just be fish grubbing in the roots for something tasty. At the very least it indicates that fish are present.

ALL FISH ARE PREDATORS

In spite of the fact that pike and perch, for instance, are known as predatory fish, all fish have predatory instincts. Even the humble roach will devour a smaller fish given the opportunity. And you have only to keep tropical fish to see what predatory little devils they all are at times. But what has puzzled me as much as anything is the way we anglers usually ignore the opportunity to catch 'non-predatory' fish on fish baits.

Many years ago I caught an 11lb carp that regurgitated two small tench in the landing net, and over the years I've witnessed bream grabbing leger weights as they were being retrieved; tench coughing up hundreds of bream fry, as well as catching lots of chub on minnows and small gudgeon. There have been instances of all coarse fish taking spinners that were meant for trout, perch or pike. On the continent they will use a lure to catch any fish without giving it a second thought. My German angling friend Ralf Nauen goes plugging for chub just as though it is the most natural thing to do. Which of course it is in his country. But how many anglers have you seen plugging for chub, or any other species come to that, apart from our recognised predators; perch, pike, and zander? Not many, I'll bet. And I'm no different than most.

I think the main reason is due to the fact that we, as a nation, are not as tuned in to fishing with artificials as are most other angling nations. Lure fishing is a major branch of angling in most of the rest of the world, but especially in Europe and the USA, whereas in Britain it is still very much a minority branch of angling. Although this seems to be changing as each year goes by. Some of us, including myself, have used live and dead fish to catch fish other than pike, perch and zander, but the trouble is that a fish bait poses so many problems.

The main one being that to fish a legered or float-fished baitfish for anything other than pike you have to dispose of the wire trace in order to present the bait effectively. Which means, of course, that when a pike does pick up the bait it severs the line with its teeth. There are other ways and means of deterring pike when fishing a fish bait, but none that are totally reliable. And I hate the thought of a pike swimming off with my hook and a length of line trailing from it. When fishing a moving bait you can get away with a wire trace for any species, for the fish does not have time to make any inspections or trial tastings before it closes its mouth around the bait.

Although I don't rate fish baits any higher than any other big bait for picking out the better specimens of the so-called non-predatory species, I do think there are times when they will catch more big fish than any other bait, and that being so then they have to be considered as an alternative bait much the same as any bait choice.

The sardine on snap tackle that barbel couldn't resist.

An incident that happened a few years ago gave me a lot of fuel for thought.

Myself and two mates, John Charlesworth and Dave Colclough, were fishing the river Severn. Dave and I were fishing for barbel, using the conventional method of swimfeeder with caster and hemp, with a 14's hook baited with two casters. John was pike fishing, using a sardine on a snap tackle. The three of us sat in a line, in one big swim, no more than two yards apart. Dave was in the middle and me on the right, both of us fishing slightly downstream. John, on the left, was fishing straight out, perhaps very slightly upstream, and closer to the margin.

The barbel swim is an old favourite of ours, a swim that, on the right day, can produce a good bag of barbel of a decent average size. Not a swim that you would choose to try to catch a really big individual specimen, but an excellent one for introducing someone like Dave, who had limited experience of barbel at the time, to the delights of Severn barbel fishing. I'd had barbel to over 8lb out of the swim, but that was an exception. What makes it a good swim is the number of barbel in the 5lb to 6lb bracket you can catch when the swim is on top form. It is a big swim that can accommodate two anglers with ease, three, if, as was the case with John, one fishes away from the usual barbel area, which is about two thirds of the way across.

That day was not the right day for a good catch. I netted a couple of 4 to 5-pounders almost straight away, then Dave had a smaller one, and then we found we were struggling to get a bite. Over two hours went by without anything more than a tremble on the rod tips, which we put down to dace. A change to a 4lb bottom and a 16's hook didn't make any difference.

Without any preamble, John's drop-off indicator did just that, and the alarm sounded as line was pulled steadily from the spool. He struck, and the rod bent into a fish. 'It's not a big one,' John said, as he had a glimpse of it below the surface, 'but it's a lively bugger for a jack!'

And so it was, kicking and splashing like a good 'un. It was only when he was drawing it over the net we realised it wasn't a jack at all but a barbel of about 5lbs, and when we got it on the bank we could hardly believe it when we saw it was hooked cleanly in the top lip by the bottom treble of the snap tackle. The whole, eight inch long sardine, had disappeared, probably slipping the hooks during the commotion on the way to the net. We were still looking at each other in amazement as John slipped the fish back into the water, and I realised that I had been so stunned by the capture I hadn't thought about grabbing a shot of the fish with the treble in place to record this unusual event.

John cast another sardine to the same spot while Dave and I carried on trying to catch barbel on conventional tactics and baits. If I remember correctly Dave and I caught another small one apiece later in the afternoon, but what I do remember quite clearly is that John had three more runs on a sardine, runs that went at exactly the same pace as the barbel run, but which he missed each time he struck. Each time the bait came back intact, with not a tooth mark to be seen. I was convinced at the time, and still am, that barbel were responsible, and that perhaps if John had modified his tackle and bait to better accommodate barbel he may have caught several of them. Of course, chub could have been responsible, but the swim is noted for barbel, and chub are the exception in that swim rather than the rule.

But that is just one story amongst many that most experienced anglers could recite regarding 'non-predatory' fish eating other fish. But like most other anglers I have never followed up such an incident. I have never returned to that spot, or any other spot come to that, and tried to catch barbel on a live or dead fish. Mainly because of the risk of hooking pike with inadequate tackle, and not having a great deal of faith in consistently hooking barbel on stronger tackle utilising a wire trace. But perhaps at that time, in particular, there was an excellent opportunity to catch barbel on a lure.

Are we missing out on some exceptional sport because we, as a nation, are intrinsically bait fishermen? I rather think we are at times.

INDUCED FEEDING

I've said it myself more than once: 'If the fish are not feeding there's not a lot you can do about it.' Which was more of an off-the-cuff remark rather than one that deserved a lot more thought. It was also a remark that should have been accompanied by several qualifications.

There are, without doubt, many times when the fish are not feeding when there most certainly is nothing, or very little, you can do about it. One instance is when the water temperature is so low the fish are in a state of semi-coma; a kind of suspended animation, bearing in mind that the body of a cold-bloodied creature, such as a fish, changes temperature along with the water. Hence it is a foregone conclusion that fish that don't move, don't feed.

Extremely warm water can have the same effect, as in fact can any extreme of any of the conditions that affect water. But it is on those days when the conditions are not particularly extreme, when there is no obvious reason for the fish not to feed, when there is something we can

Induce feeding with flavours loaded with appetite stimulants.

do about the fish's jaded appetites. There are many ways in which we can induce fish to feed, providing the conditions are not so bad they are unwilling to move.

Any kind of feeding inducement relies on offering the fish something that triggers a response. The most well known trigger being a bait that has one or more special ingredients that appeals to the fish's sense of smell and taste. Boilies, pellets and bait flavours, are the most likely baits to carry the message as they contain ingredients that are 'appetite stimulants' or 'feeding triggers'. Some of these appetite incentives have been scientifically derived or discovered and have scientific-sounding names, or a string of almost meaningless initials. Which, of course, makes them sound very important. Others are simple, such as worm extract and hemp oil. Many anglers think that these flavour triggers and stimulants are the only kind of feeding inducement there is. But there are many others, some of which we use every time we go fishing without even thinking about it.

The size of the bait we use has a great bearing on its success. I'm not referring to size of individual hookbaits here (although this has to be taken into consideration) but to the size of the free feed. A couple of dozen cubes of meat, say, may be the same volume of food as several hundred grains of corn, which in turn may be similar in volume to several thousand seeds of hemp, but which bait will hold the fish in the swim for longer? Incidentally, I ask the above question for reasons of clarification only, for it deliberately assumes that the fish will want meat, corn and hemp with equal enthusiasm.

The answer, of course, is obvious, for it will take much longer, and a great deal more effort, for the fish to clear up the hemp than it will the corn, which in turn will take longer to clear up than the meat. Which is why the ploy of feeding lots of small particles - even though the hookbait may be entirely different in size and type - is a successful one. If we could consistently land big fish on small hooks (size 14 and smaller) few of us would use a bigger hookbait amongst the particle feed bait, for there is no doubt that for much of the time the fish are more willing to accept the particles. If they are not, then the particle feed is not doing the job it was meant to do.

One of the best techniques to induce fish to feed relies equally as much on how you feed the swim as much as what you feed into the swim. It is based on the little and often principle and is especially effective on rivers where the flow is constantly carrying bait into and away from the swim. Get the amount and the timing right and you can give fish such an overpowering desire to feed they do so with a confidence that overcomes their normal sense of self-preservation. Match anglers know this better than anybody, and most will tell you that getting the feeding right makes more difference to success, most of the time, than any other factor.

The method appeals to the fish's visual sense as well as the usual senses of smell and taste. When a constant flow of food is passing through the swim, with a little of it settling in the nooks and crannies along the bottom, it must be extremely difficult for the fish to ignore it. Even a fish that has recently fed will be tempted to indulge on such a readily available food that is continually passing before it while flowing through the swim. How irresistible must that be to a creature that probably has days when it finds it difficult to find sufficient food to satisfy its hunger?

Although we refer to a well known feeding technique as 'little and often' it can quite easily be 'lots and often', for the amount that is fed in each time you feed is dependent on a number of factors. These are: size of fish, numbers of fish, speed of current (if any) and how well the fish are feeding at the time. I prefer to call the technique 'rhythm feeding' (I'm tempted to refer to it as the Rhythm Method but I can't think how I can slip it in and still keep things on a serious level) for if the method is to be successful it relies on establishing a feeding rhythm that is exactly right for the four factors I refer to above. The 'rhythm' is established following an hour or so of fishing, which is an hour of suck-it-and-see for both fish and angler. You alter the amount of food you throw in each time according to the frequency of bites. What you do not do is change the frequency of feeding. This should be every cast, or every other cast, or every so many minutes – whatever timing suits you and the situation. Every cast, or 'x' casts, is usually best for then you can send your hookbait through the swim along with the feed.

One of my favourite tricks to make a fish notice my bait is to appeal to the fish's visual sense by twitching the bait along the bottom, or rolling the bait through the swim when legering a river. If I'm fishing over a clean bottom on a stillwater with a not-too-heavy leger weight or feeder I simply take hold of the loop of line on which my bobbin or swinger-type indicator is clipped and pull gently until the bait skips along the bottom an inch or two. A light grip on the line is recommended, for it is not unknown for a fish to grab the bait immediately they see it move.

What happens, particularly with predatory fish such as pike and perch, and, to some extent, chub, is that they hover just away from the bait, watching it intently. Not really bothered, it seems, if they have it or not. But if it moves, that's a different story. There are times when they just can't resist a bait that moves suddenly. Of the so-called non-predatory species, bream are real suckers for the twitched bait method. I've caught hundreds of them from bites that came within seconds of twitching the bait. It is especially effective when using a quivertip. You tighten the line until the bait moves and the tip falls slack, and then move the rod back another notch or two on a proper feeder rest that has several notches, or a slider, to put a bend back in the tip. When fishing heavier leads and feeders it is better to twitch the bait by lifting the rod and then re-setting the indicator.

How often you twitch the bait during one cast is according to what you're fishing for and what is happening at the time. Obviously, if you're fishing for big fish where two bites in a session is as much as you can hope for, it would be madness to keep twitching the bait every few minutes. In such an instance I would only practise the technique when there was evidence (line bites or rolling) that fish were in the swim. I twitch the bait as often as every two or three minutes when fishing for bream over a suitable bottom, when I know the bream are in the swim.

Twitching is a great technique when fishing for pike with a deadbait. I wish I had a pound for every time I've had a take when I've lifted the rod to reel in for another cast. There are many days when a static bait will be ignored, but when a bait twitched along the bottom every few minutes will be taken regularly.

On rivers the equivalent of 'twitching' is rolling the bait along the bottom through the swim. But on rivers it is much more natural, for fish expect to see baits moving in a current. You use a very simple leger set-up that can be altered quickly if need be. The simplest of the lot is a freeline rig (no weight on the line at all) or by pinching shot directly on the line. For dense baits like meat, lobworm and paste, in swims where weight is necessary, the shot is pinched on anything from a foot to 3ft or more from the hook. Buoyant baits like crust and air-injected lobworm are better with the shot just two or three inches from the hook. Sufficient shot should be used so that when the rod is rested the bait will just about hold bottom. As soon as the rod tip is flicked the bait should roll with the flow until you drop the tip again.

My favourite way of fishing a rolling bait is to cast upstream and keep in touch with the bait as it rolls towards me by reeling in the slack line, giving the rod tip the occasional flick to keep it moving when a strand of weed or other obstruction puts the brakes on. When the bait reaches my fishing position I take my hand from the reel and grip the line above the reel between thumb and middle finger. As the bait progresses from here to the full downstream position I'm feeling for bites as well as watching the rod tip, for it is not always possible to read the full picture of what's happening from the rod tip alone.

The rolling leger, as the method is popularly known, can be a devastating technique on those days when conventional sit-and-wait tactics are slow, to say the least. The sight of a bait rolling through the swim, a bait that is likely to get away if it isn't grabbed at once, is often enough to induce a fish into feeding. It may not want the bait; indeed, there is every chance it could spit it out once it has grabbed it, but by then it is often too late, for a good touch-leger angler will have set the hook.

Stirring them up is a little used but deadly method when used at the right time. Raking the bottom when tench fishing is probably the best known of the 'stirring' methods. Not only does this remove any weed that could interfere with good bait presentation, it stirs the bottom, releasing food particles and clouding the water. I'm certain that the clouding of the water has as much to do with attracting the tench as has the release of food, for tench are nosy so-an-so's and can't resist investigating this type of disturbance.

On rivers, following a slow period of conventional quiet and subtle fishing, I often walk into the water and shuffle my feet round to get a good cloud of mud and silt going down with the current. This is especially effective on cattle drinks where the fish are used to seeing and hearing disturbance. Barbel are particularly prone to cattle drink stirring; I've actually seen a group of barbel follow a silt cloud upstream almost to the source of the disturbance. Not me at the time but a herd of drinking cows, which I emulated (with my feet, not my mouth!) three days later and caught barbel.

Following a long period of inactivity when pike fishing from a boat I always try stirring them up before giving up. The theory is that there are some days when the pike just lie in the marginal weeds and can't be bothered to come out and look for food. So I take the boat into the vegetation, usually lily beds, and row through them, making as much disturbance as possible. Very often I'll get a run or two fishing the open water not far from the edge of the lilies. It works too often for it not to be a viable method.

Finally, what about the Spanish Buschello or Clonk, as it is more popularly known? This is the strange piece of tackle used mainly by anglers on the other side of the English Channel to induce feeding in catfish. It is used to smack the surface of the water when boat fishing for cats. Apparently, the noise and vibrations the Clonk sends through the water attracts them. I can't personally vouch for its effectiveness, for I've never seen a Clonk, let alone used one, but too many respected catfish anglers swear by it for it not to be a viable method. Would it work for our other whiskered friend, the barbel? Who is brave enough to try it?

BIG FISH BEHAVIOUR

Do big fish behave differently than lesser, but not necessarily less mature, fish? Do the biggest fish get that way because they behave differently, or is their size in spite of, rather than as a result of, how they behave? Some humans are big because

Is this big carp of 52lb more able to avoid capture than a small carp due to being cleverer?

it is in their genes; they are the product of one, or both, large parents. Others are big because they over-indulge; they eat more than their body needs to survive. Yet other, less fortunate people, are bigger than average through some defect in their bodily functions. But we have to consider that the greatest difference in human feeding habits and ultimate size and wild fish feeding habits and ultimate size, is that humans get it handed to them on a plate, both figuratively and literally, whereas a wild creature has to work for it. Nevertheless, it is still a fact that big fish have got that way to a great extent because they had, and probably still have, rich and freely available fodder. They have more than enough to satisfy their needs, and have to make little effort to indulge. But what I'm interested in is, not how they got to be big, so much as why they got to be big.

I don't know how much the hereditary factor has to do with fish growing big. I do know it has some bearing, for there are certain strains of carp, for example, that are known to grow bigger than other strains. But that side of the topic needs to be left to someone who knows more about it than I do, for I must point out that I write this strictly from an angler's point of view, for I am not an expert on fish biology. But for now, allow me to speculate on big fish behaviour strictly as an angler.

For the sake of argument let us assume that all the fish of a species in a certain water are of the same parentage; that there are no super-strains that have been introduced from elsewhere. So why are some fish bigger, sometimes a lot bigger, than others of the same species, and of the same generation, in the same water? They can only have had more and richer feeding than the other, lesser fish. I can't see any other reason. But the interesting part is why? Have they had more food than the others because they are 'cleverer' at finding the food? Or are they getting more food because they are natural bullies who make sure they sit at the table first and get the richest pickings?

The latter question is disputed, if indirectly, by certain anglers who reckon that big fish 'hang back' from food while the smaller, 'tasters', move in and sample it first. If there appears to be no danger then the bigger fish move in and take their share. I have never been convinced by this theory, for I have doubts that big fish have got big by being last at the table. The law of the jungle applies just as much in the aquatic jungle, which is survival of the fittest, biggest and most aggressive. If it is a true scenario, then there must be some hierarchical structure in the fish world whereby the lesser fish make sure they don't eat the prime food before the bigger fish get to it. I don't subscribe to that theory either.

The anglers who propound the theory that big fish hold back from a newly discovered food source, while the smaller ones sample it first, actually bait and fish swims to take advantage of it. They bait a swim, or swims, then leave them for a while to get the smaller 'tasters' out of way and to make sure the big fish have moved in. But I wonder of this is really what is happening, or is it more a case of the big fish have had more time to find the bait and muscle the lesser fish out of the way?

We also have the notion that big fish are cleverer than smaller fish. They are so clever they are better at detecting food, and better at detecting richer food, than their smaller kin. Or so we are led to believe by some bait manufacturers who produce bait especially designed to catch big fish (mainly big carp). How else can that bait differentiate between big and small fish unless the big fish have the ability to detect the bait before any smaller fish do, or have the ability to sense that the bait contains ingredients that are meant for only big fish? What a load of nonsense!

Nevertheless, let's not dismiss the notion completely out of hand, for although 'clever' has no place in a discussion about fish abilities, there is no doubt that big fish are more difficult to catch than smaller fish, otherwise there would be no challenge to catching them. So what is it that makes them different? What makes big fish more difficult to catch than smaller fish? The easy answer is to say that there are a hell of a lot more small fish in a water than there are big fish, so it is only natural that the bigger fish are going to be harder to catch. There is some truth in that in the majority of waters, but it is by no means the definitive answer. After all, there are a number of waters that hold more big fish than small fish, and those big fish are still not easy to catch.

So the fact that most waters have only a handful of big fish compared to the number of smaller fish is part of the equation, but let's look at the rest of it.

In spite of lacking intellect fish do have the ability to learn, in that they become wary of certain baits, and baits that behave in a certain manner, due to being caught on those bait and the rigs on which they were presented in the past. So it is logical to assume that the biggest fish have had the longest time to learn the most and are therefore more adept at avoiding capture. Yes? No, not entirely, because not all big fish are old fish, therefore a big, relatively young fish has not had any more time to learn about danger from anglers than a smaller, young fish. Yet the big, young fish, is just as hard to catch as the big, old fish.

Opportunity to learn has to come into the equation too, for there are waters where the fish come under lots of angling pressure and waters where they come under comparatively little angling pressure. Surprisingly, perhaps, the fish under least pressure are often the most difficult to catch. Anyone who has fished old, very well matured, estate lakes, especially those that have not been fished for many, many years, will know that the fish in them are usually amongst the most difficult of fish to catch.

Now, I don't believe for one second that estate lake fish are more adept at avoiding capture than fish from any other water. I believe they are more difficult to catch because they are usually more preoccupied with natural food than fish from other types of waters. Perhaps it is more true to say that estate lake fish are more prone to becoming preoccupied with certain types of food, such as bloodworm, which are more prolific in silty estate lakes than in, for instance, gravel pits. Such waters may produce big fish due to a rich cache of freshwater shrimp, for instance, on which fish are not as prone to preoccupation as they are when faced with a profusion of bloodworm, which are much smaller and more numerous.

Can it be that bigger fish are harder to catch simply because they have bigger brains? Is the sheer size of an individual fish's brain an indication of its learning power? Amongst the 'cleverest' species are carp, and they have bigger brains than most other species. As a fish gets bigger, its brain grows bigger too (doesn't it?) so is this physical increase in the brain in direct proportion to the learning ability of the fish; and an indication as to the extent of its education, proportional to the amount of pressure it has come under from anglers?

Big fish most certainly have something going for them that enables them to avoid capture more often than smaller fish, especially considering that some well-known big fish are subject to massive angling pressure. It can't just be a case of them having learned more because they have been caught more, for they are not caught as often as the lesser fish. So what is it then? Is the actual physical size of a fish in direct proportion to its mental power? It certainly looks like it to me.

DOMINANT SPECIES

Whilst corresponding with Mikael Johansson, an angling friend from Sweden, who at the time was fishing for bream and tench, I was reminded about how, at times, some fish can dominate a swim. This happens not simply because an individual fish may be bigger than the other fish in the shoal, but because there may be sheer numbers of one species dominating fewer of another species, even though the 'other' species may be stronger individually.

It is a facet of fish behaviour that we become aware of at an early stage in our fishing careers, and something that we are reminded of quite regularly. How many times do we sit at the edge of the river bank and make a cast into our favourite chub or barbel swim only to be pestered with minnows or dace for a half hour or more? Or for as long as it takes for the bigger, more dominant species to move in and force the smaller species to move out.

Many times I hear an angler say something to the effect that he was pestered with minnows or dace (or whatever) so he stepped up the feed rate and 'fed them off.' Meaning that he fed more free feed into the swim until the nuisance fish were full and so moved out of the swim to allow the bigger species he was targeting to move in. Which of course is a nonsense because minnows and other small species will not prevent a shoal, or group, of bigger chub and/or barbel from entering a swim they want to enter. The sheer numbers of minnows are not a factor in this instance because even in great numbers they are not big enough to cause a fish the size of a chub or barbel of a pound or more in weight a problem. Anyhow, minnows are good feed for chub and barbel if any are stupid enough to hang around when they're not wanted.

When an angler thinks he has 'fed them off' what has really happened is that as the feed is stepped up so more and more nuisance fish are attracted to the swim. This increase in activity in this restricted area attracts the attentions of the target fish. Then, as the target fish investigate the activity, they discover the feed and decide it is too good to share with the nuisance fish, and so, therefore, the nuisance fish are not 'fed off' they're f****d off!

What sparked off these thoughts of domination in fish in Mikael's e-mails was the following story he told me. He wrote:

'Dear Graham

I was fishing last night in the 'bream lake' for tench. For six days I have prebaited a new swim between the shore and the bigger island. The area is covered with lilies and I thought it would be a good spot to catch tench and avoid the bream. Was I wrong or what? I caught over 20 bream and one tench. The tench refuse to be in the lilies!

During my first attempts to fish for tench I chose a couple of swims with interesting lily beds. The lake has not too many of them. Well, I haven't caught any tench close to the lilies yet! All of my tench in that lake are caught in open water far away from the lilies.

I have fished for tench since I was a young boy and at least in my other home lakes there is not any chance to catch them in open water. Okay, maybe 20 metres away from a lily bed or some weed but in the 'bream lake' in the swim where I have caught them there is no weed or anything that they can seek shelter in. The depth in the particular swim is very shallow and it just ruins my thoughts about tench. I have caught them in shallow water in other lakes, nothing strange about that, but there it has been close to some shelter. I am very puzzled.'

I replied:

'Dear Mikael

It appears that the bream are the dominant species in the lake, and that they, for whatever reason, prefer to feed in the spots that we normally associate with tench. Being as bream feed in large shoals, and that tench feed in small groups, could it be that the dominant bream are keeping the tench away from the swims with nearby lily beds?

I do know for a fact that bream can be a very dominant species. I once visited a lake in the south-east of England (this was some 35 years ago) where I was told by the locals that I should only use stewed wheat for bait, for if I used maggots, worms, or casters I would be pestered too much with eels. Remembering that bream are dominant I decided that I would tackle the lake another way, so I fed a swim very heavily with bread groundbait and maggots, some live and some dipped in boiling water to kill them and therefore prevent them from burrowing into the silt on the bottom. I then used maggot as hookbait, and yes, I did catch eels to begin with, and then the bream moved onto the baited area and forced everything else, including the eels, out of the swim. I then went on to catch well over 150lbs of bream, which at that time was a record catch for the water.'

In our angling careers we come across many instances of domination amongst fish. One fond memory I have of tench dominating perch was on a Cheshire mere I fished regularly at the time. The perch grew to just over a pound or so, but the average fish was about 8oz. Most of the anglers who fished the water fished at night, when the odd tench was caught but the bulk of them came out at first light. As soon as that first decent catch of tench was made (on those days when they fed of course) you could guarantee that within an hour you would be pulling perch in like shelling peas. This got so bad that everyone went home then, considering it a waste of time to carry on tench fishing.

At that time, due to a family illness, I couldn't go night fishing, so I was stuck with starting fishing at first light and consequently catching perch following that first tench onslaught before sunrise. But I had a plan! I took twice as many maggots and casters than I normally take and fed very heavily as soon as the perch began to steal my baits. Of course, for a time I caught more perch than ever, and then, just like throwing a switch, the perch turned off and I didn't get a bite at all for several minutes or more. Then the next bite produced a tench, and then another, and I caught tench, off and on, all morning. Only an odd perch was caught in between the tench feeding spells. That became a regular pattern. I would feed heavily as soon as the perch made an appearance, they would come to the net almost every cast, and then switch off in an instant. Several minutes later I would be playing my first tench.

Tough tench soon rousted the perch out of the swim.

It was obvious the tench were revisiting the swim following their early morning breakfast and totally dominating it, forcing the perch to exit very quickly indeed.

Another time I actually saw an instance of bream dominating a group of tench. Not so much dominating but putting the fear of God up them! I was lay across the branch of a tree trying to spot the bream rolling in a distant bay. I couldn't see any but as I was quietly lying there a group of tench swam into view right under the branch about 10ft below me. They began to prod the bottom in the 2 ½ft to 3ft deep swim and were obviously feeding on some creature that lived there. Tiny wisps of mud clouded up and within five minutes the tench were really getting their heads down and feeding ravenously. There were five of them, all looking between 5lb and 7lb. Just as I was having thoughts of shinning down the tree to fetch a rod and a box of worms I saw a dark hump clear surface about 20yds away. Then another, and another. A shoal of bream was heading straight for the swim. It was a big shoal for they were rolling steadily, and as they came closer I could see they were the usual stamp of fish for the water, from about 7lb to just in double figures.

The tench were so busy feeding, and the water was now so cloudy where they routed, they mustn't have seen the bream until they hit the swim. And by now the bulk of the bream shoal had moved in. It was quite comical really, for the next thing I saw was five big bow-waves shoot out of the area as five tench took to their fins and got out of there fast!

I don't think for one minute that a single bream, of whatever weight, could dominate a single tench of more than 3lb in weight. Tench are a much stronger fish. But when a big shoal of big bream moves in on a group of tench then it looks like it's a different story.

I've read the odd piece about how the best way to catch a big chub or barbel that lies with a few of its smaller kind is to tempt the smaller fish away from the big one with judicious feeding. The reason for doing this is to prevent the smaller fish from grabbing the bait before the bigger one has the chance. The consequence of this is that the smaller chub disturb the swim when they're hooked and played and the result is that the bigger fish gets the hump and either sulks or departs.

Now, at first glance, this suggests that the smaller fish are dominant and the big fish being put in its place. But this is not so, it is a case of the big chub being cautious and allowing the smaller chub to explore this new food source before it ventures into the larder itself. But I reckon this only lasts until the big chub is sure that there is no imminent danger, whereupon it will muscle in on the action in no uncertain terms and dominate the prime morsels of food that drift into the swim. Which is why I have several times recommended that one of the best ways to catch a big chub (and often any big fish) is to spend some time trickling bait into the swim before you even wet a line. It's all about promoting confidence, so if you feed a swim (let's say with soaked bread) for 20 minutes or so before casting you are allowing sufficient time for the tasting and accepting process to take place completely undisturbed. By the time you introduce a hookbait the fish should be feeding confidently enough to accept it without any fear. Not only that, if you have the patience to feed the swim for at least 20 minutes there is a good chance that when you put a nice chunk of hooked bread flake through the swim it will be taken by the biggest, most dominant fish.

I have never been an advocate of the theory that big fish always allow smaller fish to get to the table first. They don't get big by always being last in the queue. The old saying in hard times of 'first up best dressed' also applies to 'first at table best fed'. They only get at the end of the queue when they are suspicious of what's on offer. A natural bait like a big lobworm or slug, presented so that it lies in, or passes through, the swim the same way an unfettered lobworm or slug would pass through has a good chance of being accepted by the biggest fish in the swim on your first cast.

Fish domination is an aspect of fish behaviour that should be considered along with all the other aspects of fish behaviour. We can make knowledge of domination work for us by attracting target fish to a swim and forcing nuisance fish out, and by prebaiting (several days prior to fishing, and on the same day prior to fishing) to instil confidence in bigger fish. Providing we are aware of it, any understanding of fish behaviour is another arrow in the quiver and therefore another step to greater catches.

Chapter 2

Preparation and Prebaiting

Time spent in preparation is always worth it

PREBAITING

Does anyone still doubt the value of prebaiting? Apparently they do, for a season never goes by without an angler saying to me something like, "Prebaiting? Never bother myself. I always catch a few fish when they're feeding, so there doesn't seem much point."

Provided the anglers who make such comments are perfectly happy with the number and/or size of the fish they're catching and have no wish to improve their results, then there is no point in prebaiting. But I haven't met an angler yet who could honestly say he wouldn't like to catch more or bigger fish than he already does, regardless of the standards he is currently setting. Even the man who has caught one or more 30lb carp would still like to catch a 40-pounder. And the man who catches a vast number of doubles each season would no doubt like to increase his catch rate. Though it must be said that the anglers who enjoy that kind of success are probably well aware, and are already taking full advantage of, the profits that prebaiting can reap. Yet there are many anglers who are either unaware of the value of prebaiting, or just cannot be bothered to go to the trouble. Then, of course, there are the unfortunate anglers who would be only too glad to take advantage of a prebaiting exercise if only their favourite waters were within a reasonable distance of home.

For the benefit of newcomers to the sport, and for those anglers who have not yet delved into the whys and wherefores of prebaiting, the following may help you to make up your own mind as to whether prebaiting is worth the effort and expense involved. Cost and effort is relative to the type of bait being used and the regularity of the baiting of course. For a lengthy prebaiting campaign white and brown bread groundbait, Vitalin dog food and particle baits like hempseed take some beating.

Prebaiting means introducing groundbait and/or hookbait samples to the water over an indefinite period before starting to fish. There are many variations of how long a period, and the regularity of the baiting, according to what is best for the water and swim in question, and the species of fish being sought. The type of bait being used also has to be considered, in that a bait which is completely new to the water may need to be introduced over a much longer period than one on which the fish are already known to feed. And there are some baits, notably the ones classed as particles, which are used mainly for carp, that are better fed in almost all feeding areas for a period, rather than in one specific swim.

The concept of prebaiting is, in some instances, partly to attract fish to a specific swim, partly to give fish a taste for a new bait, but mainly to wean fish away from their natural food and preoccupy them with a food which is readily obtainable and easily used as hookbait. The fact that prebait does not involve hooks, leads and lines also offers the fish a safe food for a period which they learn can be taken with complete confidence; a confidence which we anglers exploit to the full when the time comes to sneak a hook among all those free offerings.

Before I describe the mechanics of prebaiting it will be as well to give you a couple of instances where prebaiting is not worth the time, expense and effort. The first example that comes to mind is when you intend fishing a river with maggots and casters, and where such bait is thrown in almost daily by the majority of anglers. In this instance prebaiting would be akin to teaching grandma how to suck eggs. The fish already know all about maggots and casters and prebaiting is accomplishing nothing more than giving them a free feed.

Another case for not prebaiting arises when you want to catch specimen eels from a water that holds eels of all sizes. All that prebaiting does is attract all the little eels to your swim, ensuring that your chances of catching a big eel are far less than if you had not prebaited at all. If there is one thing worse than blanking when fishing for big eels it is catching lots of little eels. If you've been lucky enough to find a water that holds only big eels (and they do exist) then fill your boots and prebait for them.

The same thing applies to any instance where there are lots of small fish which are likely to take the hookbait intended for a big one. Far better to be especially careful in your choice of swim, or to stalk the big fish where it is feasible. After all, part of the art of catching big fish is avoiding the small ones, so there is no point in making this part of your task more difficult by filling your swim with them. Fortunately, however, most specimen-fish waters have a deficit of small fish.

Rather than describe in detail how to prebait for each species I'll generalise, but point out where necessary where a certain aspect is especially applicable to a particular species. Anyhow, it's the principle of prebaiting that matters, and once you have learned the basic idea of prebaiting it is easy to make the more subtle adjustments to suit the feeding habits of the species that interests you.

This brings me to the first and most important aspect you should consider before even attempting to prebait a water: do you have a good working knowledge of the feeding habits, and the type of swim they frequent, of the fish you want to catch? If you haven't, then at best you may be lucky and succeed, or catch a different species or, at worst, blank and waste a lot of effort and money, and swear ever after that Marsden and his ilk are talking through their hats when they say prebaiting can be very successful.

Knowing the feeding habits of a species, which means having a good idea of where, when, and how they feed, is essential for consistent success, whether you choose to prebait for them or not. But when you do choose to embark on a prebaiting campaign it is a decided advantage if you also have some idea as to the number and size of fish that are likely to frequent the baited area, for then you can regulate the amount of bait you introduce. By that I don't mean you know if there are going to be 6 or 16 fish visiting the area, but, in broader terms, that you should know if a big shoal of smaller fish, or a little shoal of bigger fish are to be the visitors. For instance, is the water, and swim, more likely to produce big catches of 2lb to 3lb tench, or few tench of 5lb or more? For the same reason, it helps to know if more than one species visits the swim for it would be useless to prebait for tench if a shoal of bream mopped up all the bait before the tench moved in.

If that is likely to be the case, then the correct timing of the baiting is essential, ie, bait should be introduced as close as possible to the time when the species you seek are due to arrive. I do realise, of course, that you won't possess this knowledge unless you have already fished the water for some considerable time. In that case you have no alternative but to prebait on a trial-and-error basis.

There are two ways of doing this. The first, and most accurate, is to begin with the assumption that you need to feed very few fish and therefore introduce only a small amount of bait. After two or three days, if you cannot see the bottom, throw in a drag (barbed-wire wrapped around a stake is eminently suitable) and see what comes up. If there are any particles of bait on the drag lay off the baiting for a couple of days and then drag the swim again. If there is still evidence of bait then it may be a good idea to try another swim. You can always return to the first swim at a later date and go through the whole process from the beginning, for it is almost certain that the original bait will have disappeared by then anyway, through natural decomposition.

If there are no signs of bait after the first dragging operation, step up the amount you throw in. You can continue to increase the amount until such time as the drag produces evidence of un-eaten bait. Within reason that is, for the amount you finally decide is right really comes down to your own judgement. What I usually do is go back to the amount that was thrown in two drags prior to the drag that brought back bait. In any event, it is always safer to err on the conservative side rather than put in too much.

The other way of prebaiting an unknown water is used when it is impossible to see, or take samples from, the bottom, such as when you intend fishing a distant swim that is too far away to drag and a boat isn't available. In this instance it is essential that you get some idea of how many mouths require feeding, if not from other anglers who know the water, then from observation over a prolonged period.

Again, you can form only a general idea, but it is even more important in this instance to bait on the mean side, and to keep your eye on the swim as much as possible over the first few days. If the bait is being taken you will almost certainly see some kind of activity in the swim - surface rolling, bubbles, or mud clouds. Depending on the extent of this activity you either increase or reduce the amount of feed you throw in.

In an unknown swim on an unknown water it is better really to prebait during the season, which means you can fish the swim and gain a good idea of what effect the bait is having, and be in a much better position to be able to judge if the amount is right. I cannot stress too strongly how important it is not to overdo it. Too much prebait will give you even less chance of catching fish than no prebait at all.

Bread groundbait is probably the most popular medium used for prebaiting, with Vitalin coming a close second, if not in their own right, then as a carrying agent for other baits less easily thrown. Unfortunately, bread and Vitalin are also the worst things to have in the swim when it remains uneaten. It is wise, therefore, to be particularly careful how much you put in when prebaiting with bread and Vitalin.

When a water is very rich in animal life, and the main object of prebaiting is to wean the fish off natural food, the best baits are usually worms, maggots and casters. Casters are the best of all because they remain wherever you put them and can last for several days in the water waiting to be eaten. Worms are good, but you need one hell of a lot to do the job properly, and not every-one has a wormery, or at least one big enough, to supply enough worms to prebait for two or three weeks or more.

I have never had much success with particle baits (seeds) for bream, though I do know that stewed wheat in particular has caught a lot of bream in some waters (but not in my locale of Cheshire to my knowledge). I've never found it necessary to look any further than bread, maggots, casters and worms to catch bream on any water, but in these days of most big bream waters also being big carp waters, sweetcorn, pellets and boilies may well be the best baits.

Particle baits are excellent for prebaiting for carp.

Particles are well-proven baits for carp fishing and excellent for prebaiting, being simple to obtain and prepare, and easily used in the quantities necessary. The fact that they are particles, in a size not unlike maggots and casters, makes them an excellent bait for persuading carp, and some other fish to an extent, that they are just as good to eat as natural food.

It is said in some circles that particles are best introduced into a water in all areas, the idea being that carp will much sooner accept them as natural than if they were only fed into one swim. If, so far as you know, you are going to use a particle that has not been used on the water before (and it will have to be a rare particle, or a rare water, to fall into that category), I would go along with the theory and scatter the particles here and there all around the water for a week or so. Then, I would gradually concentrate the particles in my chosen swim, scattering fewer and fewer in other areas until, within a few days of the time I'm due to fish, the bait was going into my swim and nowhere else.

How regularly you prebait is largely a question of suiting your pocket and the time you can spare. This is not so much of a problem if you fish with a group of friends and can share the time and expense. Every day, at a predetermined time, is best of all, or every other day is better than not at all. The less frequently you bait the less effective it is going to be, and if you are unable to bait more than twice a week, it is really a question of whether it's worth it.

There is no fixed length of time for prebaiting, although a week is about the shortest time for it to be worthwhile. Two or three weeks is about right for the bait to have a real effect, but longer periods can only be better. It is not unusual for my friends and I to keep a swim 'topped-up' with bait all through the summer and autumn. And we can safely say that the catches, generally, get better and better as the season wears on.

Where carp are concerned, we usually go through at least three baits in a season, prebaiting with a new one in readiness for the time when the present one loses its edge. This is rarely necessary with any other species.

Prebaiting should be done with care and thought. It is not a matter of heaving unlimited amounts of stodge into a swim and hoping the fish will be numerous and hungry enough to keep shifting it. With proper care, a well-thought-out prebaiting campaign can pay enormous dividends. It can be very enjoyable, too, knowing that you are doing something constructive towards catching fish and reducing the element of chance.

TACKLING A NEW WATER

Every now and then we come across a new water, new in that it may have just been opened to anglers. It could be that it is an estate lake and the estate is feeling the pinch like the rest of us and is, therefore, glad of the extra bob or two that anglers' fees provide. It could be that the lake has changed hands and the new owners have a different attitude. Whatever the reason, occasionally we get the opportunity to fish a new water, a water that has not been fished on a regular basis, where information about the species present, the general size of them, and the whereabouts of the productive swims is hard to come by, to say the least. And when that happens the first thing we ask ourselves is, 'where do we start?'

A big, apparently featureless water, so where do we start?

The bigger the lake, the bigger the problem, and to any angler who has not been faced with this kind of problem before it can be rather daunting. More important, it can also be the source of a hell of a lot of pleasure, for if the task is approached in the right kind of way the rewards can be tremendous, far outweighing any other consideration. The feeling of satisfaction when that first fish slides into the net is difficult to describe.

What makes it all the more exciting is if there is very little known about the water. One thing is certain; rumour will be rife! There will be a few people about somewhere who will have fished it, perhaps by poaching, or maybe they had permission to fish it occasionally. Stories of big fish will be rife, for no matter what the real truth is, human nature will embroider the stories as they are passed from mouth to mouth. It's great! It gets us all excited, for no matter how hard we try to take the stories with a large pinch of salt the optimist that lurks somewhere in even the most pessimistic of us clings to the hope that there is a large grain of truth in what we hear.

Right, where do we start?

The first thing I do, mentally at least, is sort out a list of certainties, possibles and probables. For instance, there are some things we can say pretty definitely, such as the species that are certain to be in the water, for if the water is, say, a Cheshire mere, we can certainly say there will be bream, tench, carp, pike and eels present. There will probably be roach, rudd and perch. And possibly, there will be crucian carp, roach x bream, rudd x bream, and roach x rudd hybrids. How big any of these fish grow to will be the greatest unknown quantity, for it is here where the rumours will have bred and multiplied!

I follow up by doing the most obvious thing: take a slow stroll around the water, soak up the atmosphere, and see what kind of feeling I get about the place. I've found over the years that my first impressions of a water are usually right. Okay, they are only impressions, but as far as I'm concerned they set the scene. Although, if I get negative feelings they don't prevent me from going on to check the place out to establish some hard facts. During the walk I look out for fish at the surface, or in the shallows, or merely signs of fish. I take in the type of bottom around the margins, the vegetation there, where there are overhanging trees, islands, and generally the lie of the land, which is usually a good indicator of depth and overall bottom shape. But mainly, this first, slow walk around the water simply gives me a feel for the place.

The next job is to do a more detailed study; plumb the depths and chart the features on a map of the water, drag a bomb around to find possible snags, and drag a rake through here and there to see what comes out.

A sonar for simplicity

If you haven't got one of your own, try to borrow a sonar device. They provide the easiest, quickest and most accurate method of charting the bottom. The next best alternative is a baitboat fitted with sonar. If neither are allowed you will have to do it the hard way, with a marker float and lead.

The first thing to do though, is make a print of an image of the lake taken from Google Earth in Satellite view. A chart at A4 size is large enough to contain sufficient detail, and small enough to handle in a boat. Note the landmarks; trees, bushes, reedbeds, etc, and then draw lines across the water from one landmark to another. These are the lines you will follow with the boat, marking the depths and features on the chart as you go. Obviously, the more detail you want the more lines you will draw across the chart, joining up a landmark on one bank to several other landmarks on other banks. Distance is the most difficult thing to judge. Estimating the distance from a boat to the bank can be a different proposition than estimating that same distance from bank to boat. Ask anyone who has gone out on a boat to place a marker. It is quite common to place it much further than you intended.

Even with a sonar it still takes quite some time to fully cover a large water, and is best done over a period of several days, spread over as long a period that suits you, sounding one area at a time. Whilst in the process of charting you will be choosing swims based on the information you see, only later studying the chart, revising what you've learned, and making more considered decisions.

So what's next?

A prebaiting campaign is the obvious answer, followed by a period of fish-spotting running alongside the actual fishing. Which means that we prebait the swim(s) we've chosen, based on the information provided by the sonar and observation, every other day for a period of a week or more, then fish the swim(s) whilst watching the water carefully for signs of fish. This way we have an iron in the fire in the shape of at least two rods doing the fishing, and another iron in the shape of observation, both of which will provide information on which to base a judgement about whether to move or stick it out in any of the swims we fish.

Of course, what I'm saying doesn't happen overnight. It may take two or three seasons, or more, to gather sufficient information to get the best out of the water. What we have to bear in mind is the fact that there will be different criteria for different times of the year, and certainly for different species - assuming we intend to fish the water for more than one species. There will be a degree of overlap with some species, such as carp, bream, tench and roach, where at certain times they will share the same swim at the same time, but when it comes to ceasing, say, fishing for bream, and beginning to fish for pike, then it is a different approach altogether, and we have to start collecting, collating, and sifting through information all over again.

But as far as I'm concerned it just means that there is a new challenge to meet head on, a new set of problems to overcome and, very probably, another period of focused fishing from which to draw intense satisfaction and enjoyment.

PREPARING FOR TENCH

Fishing can be a gentle, introspective pastime, where the angler visits a quiet little stream or pool and whiles away his time hoping for a bite whilst counting the daisies and composing poetry. On the other hand it can be a rough, tough, demanding sport, involving trekking over wild country with a full load and then doing battle with a huge fish that, when hooked, tries to dislocate your rod arm.

Then, of course, we have the type of fishing that fits somewhere in between those two extremes, where we take the catching of fish very seriously, no

Good preparation for tench fishing pays dividends.

matter what the species or the type of water, yet still enjoy the whole experience when failing to catch fish. Most of us, however, although well able to enjoy a blank day's fishing, much prefer the taste of success, and those of us who are willing to get off our backsides will do our utmost to ensure a successful result at the end of a day or night by the waterside. Which means that almost every time mine and my friends fishing takes a significant change in direction, ie, switching from, say, chub or pike fishing in winter to carp, tench or barbel fishing in summer, we undertake a plan of action, a battle plan, whose aim is to ensure the capture of as many fish as possible of the heaviest possible weight. It doesn't always work out like that of course, but it's bloody good fun trying!

So while a battle plan; a calculated campaign to catch fish, may not be the most romantic angling concept there is, it is definitely the best way to ensure that many of your visits to the water are successful. And happiness, for most of us, includes being successful.

The planning and the anticipation are almost as much part of the fun as actually fishing. Those first few visits to the water, when a plan is first put into action, are the best times of all. The spine-tingling sense of anticipation, and then the shear joy when the carefully planned campaign begins to bear fruit with the first big fish sliding over the rim of the landing net, make all the work, effort and expense extremely worthwhile.

One year my pals and I had to build a new platform and renovate two others on the Cheshire mere where we planned to catch some big tench. It took many hours work and not a little expense. Before we worked on those platforms we had to be certain of one thing: that they were in the right spot. You don't put all that effort and money into building platforms unless you are sure they are adjacent to swims with either an existing pedigree (which was true of the two renovated platforms) or are one hundred per cent confident that they will be on swims with excellent potential. The same goes for any prebaiting campaign you are likely to undertake, for you don't want to be spending time and money baiting swims unless you are pretty sure it's not going into barren areas. Obviously then, the first job is to do everything you can to ensure you've chosen a good swim.

Incidentally, the easy way of choosing a good swim, on a fairly popular water, is to keep your eye on other anglers who fish the area in which you're interested and note what they catch. It is the most reliable method of all. Trouble is, there isn't a lot of satisfaction in it, for much of the credit for what you may catch belongs to someone else.

While that may be acceptable to some, for me it robs me of much of the enjoyment I get from fishing, which is doing my own thing. Of course, there may not be any choice in the matter. Many waters have already been fished in all areas at some time or other so there is no opportunity to pioneer a swim. In that case you have to accept the situation for what it is.

On our tench water there are areas, as far as we are aware, that have not been fished before. So we had to investigate them to see if they had the features that we normally associate with good tench swims. We did this and found one swim that had a nice drop-off from 2ft deep to 10ft deep within two rod's length. Under the rods tips (or where the rod tips would be) grows a dense bank of weed that would help to keep us hidden from the tench. Right at the side grows the odd clump of lilies, and there is a tree line behind us that will also help to prevent silhouetting. Far more important than any of that is the fact that we had seen tench rolling in the area whilst fishing a different spot. What was especially attractive was that more tench rolled just there than rolled where we were fishing. Choosing swims by depth finding and judgement based on experience is great, and can result in some fine catches, but there is nothing better than choosing a swim based on what has either been caught from it, or seen in it.

The tree line was also the biggest problem, for the branches and odd tree that had fallen into the water over the years prevented access from the bank. So we had to decide whether the swim had sufficient potential to warrant the clearing of these obstructions, and the building of a platform. Or would it be safer, and less strenuous, to opt for a season fishing the swim from a boat, and then make the decision whether or not to clear the bank and build a platform next year based on the results from boat fishing? We took the safer option and boat-fished what was left of the summer months in the 'new' swim and found that it was indeed a good swim, for in just half a dozen visits we took some big tench, including one of 8.14, lost a couple of what could have been bigger ones in the branches, and saw some really big fish rolling over the bait.

Hence the clearing of the fallen trees and branches in the margins and the building of a new platform almost along the edge of the tree line. Now, when we hooked a fish, we could pull it away from the branches each side of the swim, rather than pull the fish towards them. The platform also gave us much more versatility with fishing methods, for although all things are possible from a boat, including legering, they are restricting, if only for the fact that you can't easily go for a walk to stretch your legs. In fact, it isn't advisable to stand in a boat when fishing because of the obvious danger of the fish seeing you. At least on the bank or a platform you can crouch low, move away from the edge and then stand upright for a few minutes. Although float fishing is my first love, especially for tench, there are times when I want to fish leger rods on bite alarms, such as through the night; while I have a meal; and occasionally just to have a snooze or a read for an hour or so. Float fishing demands constant attention, and quite simply there are times when I want to use bite alarms and allow the rods to fish for themselves until the alarms tell me my attention is needed.

We placed a marker in the swim too, which may seem a little strange considering it is just 2 ½ rod's length from the platform. This is half a rod's length farther out than the float swim and it is marked because there are many times when a very clear hot-spot becomes apparent in tench (and bream) swims, to the point where just a foot or so can make a difference. It is very often important to able to place your float in an exact spot and you can only do this with total accuracy if there is some kind of marker in the swim to line up with. There was no danger of losing fish around the marker for we used lengths of 25mm diameter plastic drain pipe that are pushed a couple of feet or so into the soft silt and which bend very easily. When fish go round the tube it simply bends over and the line slips over the top. A marker also ensures that you bait up the same spot every visit. And in our case ensured that we raked the weed out of the same tracks when the major growth began in June.

Raking can be an important part of a tench campaign, not just to clear the swim of weed, but to play on that element of the nature of tench that causes them to investigate disturbances, which they surely do. What I like to do is introduce a few samples of feed and hookbaits into the swim *before* raking, so that the raking actually buries some of this feed. The tench then have to work harder, and therefore remain longer, in the swim. Then I feed the swim again a few minutes later when the disturbance has settled a little.

Prebaiting is undoubtedly a major element of any campaign to catch big fish. Pre-conditioning the fish to finding bait in a certain area; to expect to find bait in a certain area invariably has a positive effect. That the bait should smell and taste good enough to make them want more is another factor. That it should be of a type that causes them to spend as much time as possible in the swim is yet another. Introducing bait frequently and regularly into the same spot will instil in the fish the habit of visiting that spot regularly to look for food, and for this reason the prebaiting should continue right through the whole of the campaign and not just as a prelude to fishing. Baits that smell good and taste good (without overfeeding) will go some way towards making the fish want that bait more than they want the natural food that will obviously be in abundance in a water that grows fish to specimen class. A particle type bait will help to keep them in the swim for as long as possible while they root for the particles, and will also cause pre-occupation on that bait much better than the same volume of fewer, but larger, baits. Particle baits are hemp and other seeds of like size, small pellets, mini boilies, maggot and caster. Large baits are lobworm, bunches of redworm, bread flake and crust, larger lumps of paste, 12mm and larger boilies, large pellets and seeds (don't neglect particles not often associated with tench, such as tares and tiger nuts). In between are sweetcorn, one or two redworm, lob tails, paste to cover a 10's hook, and so on. There are no doubt many others.

Ideally you want to be feeding with an attractant such as a good quality groundbait. I use equal portions of brown and white crumb with a handful or two of Van Den Eynde Expo and crushed hemp. Just enough to attract the fish to the swim, but not enough to give them a good feed. Then a carpet of hemp, followed by a sprinkling of sweetcorn, maggot and/or caster, and a handful or two of mini-boilies if that is one of the baits I intend trying. The exact bait is not as important as the nature of the bait, for the idea is to attract them to the swim, provide them with a particle that will keep them busy, and a not-too-generous helping of hookbaits; sufficient to keep them interested, but scarce enough to keep them prodding around for more.

Tench love to root in a good carpet of hemp.

Usually, at the start of a new campaign, I like to use a proven bait, one that has caught lots of fish in the past, and is a sure banker no matter what the conditions or the temperament of the tench. Of course, if there was such an apparently infallible bait we would have no need to use anything else! But what I mean is that there is always a bait (maggot and caster in this instance for the tench on our water) that is always as likely as anything to be taken at any time or in any conditions. We have complete faith in that bait and know that there is always a chance, to some degree, of getting bites if maggot or caster is on the hook.

The incessant search for a new, 'magic' bait is, of course, part of the fun, and although most of us know that such a bait does not exist it doesn't stop us looking for it. The reality is that such baits as maggot and caster will always be bankers on most waters, and will often be the best bait you can use. Boilies will be the best bait on those waters where carp anglers predominate, and there will be days on any water when a different bait will be better. What I look for is a bait that will work well on those days when the banker baits are struggling for a take, when the fish are tempted by something that is different.

Chapter 3

Weather Conditions

How temperature, wind, air pressure and the moon affect fish.

FACTORS AFFECTING FEEDING FISH

Let me say at the outset that this discourse is mainly about stillwaters. Although what I have to say is generally applicable to river dwelling fish, other factors enter the equation that are not discussed here.

There is no one factor that affects how well fish feed. If there was it would be relatively easy to predict if your imminent day's fishing is going to be easy, hard, or somewhere in between. To a great extent the success or otherwise of a day's fishing can be predicted fairly accurately by an experienced angler, but to do this he will subconsciously be drawing on years of experience. His brain will be diving deep into its data bank and sifting through all those factors that dictate whether or not fish will feed. But it is not easy, for each of those factors has to be weighed against all the other factors – and then applied to each and every individual water - in order to reach a worthwhile conclusion.

The main factors are water temperature, the availability of food, and light (or the lack of it). The temperature of the water is very important. Even the most inexperienced fisherman knows that, generally speaking, most coarse fish do not feed as well in cold water as they do in warm water. It is a critical element due to the fact that fish are cold-blooded and therefore their body temperature fluctuates along with water temperature. If the water gets colder the fish gets colder, not just skin deep, but all through, and the colder their bodies get the more lethargic they become. The exact water temperature, or temperature range, however, is not as critical as it was once thought. In the 1950's and 60's, and to an extent the 70's, there were many articles written by eminent anglers who often quoted feeding temperature ranges for each species. In his classic book, 'Stillwater Angling', Richard Walker says that carp seldom feed below a water temperature of 58 deg F, and rarely when it is more than 68 deg F. A statement that we know now to be no more than a sweeping generalisation, for it is only an unqualified truth; true only when taken on its own and not with any other factor taken into consideration.

Let's look at one example. Take an average carp lake where the fish are mainly double figures, and a few manage to grow to 20lb or so. There is sufficient food to maintain these weights, but no more, and the fishing pressure is not too heavy. Most anglers fish from June till October and then go onto the rivers. In such a water the temperature range quoted by Walker would be about right. It would be right because there are few other factors interfering with the effect of water temperature.

As I've written in more detail in this chapter, and it's worth repeating, the trend of the water temperature is far more important than what the thermometer actually reads. A steady water temperature is usually far more conducive to good fishing than either a falling or rising temperature. But even that has to be qualified, for a rising temperature is best when the water has been decidedly cold, and a falling temperature is best when the water has been too warm. Sudden changes in temperature can be lethal, but a sudden change to a colder water is usually more lethal than an equally sudden change to a warmer water. You see what I mean? There are no hard and fast rules about temperature numbers, it is how the temperature is moving that matters, and where it is moving to and from.

The water temperature is important but it's the trend that is the most important factor.

Let's look at the next factor, the availability of food, and tie that in too.

The most difficult waters from which to catch fish are those that have an abundance of natural food and a small stock of big fish. The two usually go together. Apart from the fact that the fish are more difficult to locate, they are less inclined to feed on angler's baits, and will be much more inclined to feed as the water temperature dictates. They have no pressing need to satisfy hunger, for they can browse for food and feed to excess anytime they feel like it – which is usually when the water temperature is within its most comfortable range for them.

The easiest waters from which to catch fish are those we know as hungry waters, where there is a deficit of natural food and a large head of smaller fish. Again, the two are usually inseparable. In such waters low water temperature has much less effect for the fish are so hungry their need to browse for food takes priority over the torpid effect resulting from low temperatures.

Tied in with these two examples of fisheries, two extreme examples it must be said, is another factor; that bigger fish are more prone to being affected by shifts in water temperature due to its greater effect on their sheer body mass. Also, fully scaled fish are less affected than are fish such as mirror and leather carp. But I don't want to cloud the main topic of this discussion by dwelling on these side issues too much.

Dull, warm, wet days can be best for encouraging fish to feed. But not as wet as this!

The third main factor affecting the appetite of fish is light. Light probably does not affect their urge to feed directly, but, for instance, makes them more vulnerable to predators and therefore less inclined to become preoccupied with feeding. We know that some species can be mainly nocturnal feeders. We also know that, generally speaking, most species feed at their best when the ambient light is subdued, especially when the conditions are dull and cloudy. Of course there are exceptions, perch and pike for instance may feed better during bright conditions when their main mode of hunting at the time is visual. And we know that even the most nocturnally pre-possessed species, such as catfish, big bream, and big carp on some waters, will have periods when they choose to feed during the day, even bright, sunny days. Indeed, there are waters where such fish feed consistently during the day, to the point where it can be a waste of time fishing at night.

Taking the extremes again it would be pretty safe to say that on a bright, frosty winter's day, on a rich water holding very big carp, a water which is seldom fished through the winter period, catching anything will be very improbable. On the other hand, on a mild, dull winter's day, on a well-stocked, very popular water, catching carp will be very likely indeed.

The difficult bit is assessing your chances of catching anything when the conditions are somewhere in between those two extremes, with one or more of the main factors opposing each other (ie, cold water but dull day) on fisheries where the stock level and size of fish is fairly well balanced. Will the cold water be enough to stop the fish feeding? Or will the poor light be enough to swing the situation in our favour? Are there sufficient anglers fishing frequently enough through the winter, and therefore keeping a constant flow of bait going into the water, to keep the carp interested in feeding?

Other issues that have a greater or lesser effect on feeding fish are: wind, atmospheric pressure, and moon phase. And to confuse the issue even further each will have an effect on the other.

Bright, windy days, especially a cold easterly, is a situation where the wind, due to the chill factor, does more harm than good. But, most of the time, the presence of wind is a plus factor, ie, a strong westerly wind, on a warm day, tends to increase the dissolved oxygen in the water and can cause the fish to feed with a vengeance. Most experienced anglers seek out the windward side of a lake and fish directly into it, for very often the fish will be feeding on that side. This is due to more than one reason, and is often a combination of them all. Wind, as I mentioned above, increases the amount of dissolved oxygen in the water. It also breaks up the light as it passes through the surface, allowing the fish better camouflage from predators. Fish prefer to swim against a current rather than with it, so will be swimming against the flow of water along the bottom which will be going in the opposite direction to the wind. Wind also carries food along the surface. Some of the best day's fishing I've ever had have been when the wind has been crashing white horses against the bank I fished from.

Atmospheric pressure has a great bearing on a fish's appetite. Low pressure means feeding fish and high pressure means fasting fish. Usually anyhow. But low pressure usually means dull weather, rain and warm winds, and high pressure can often mean bright weather and no wind. Too hot in summer and too cold in winter. So again we have two elements that have to be weighed with each other rather than separately. Rain too, has an effect, helping to pound dissolved oxygen into the water, where you reap the benefits when the rain eases, for heavy rain tends to put fish off feeding due to the drumming on the surface. The atmospheric pressure alone does, however, make a difference. How often have you made a significant catch when the pressure has dropped to depression level and the storm clouds gather? I wish I had a quid for each time it has happened to me. It can't be anything else but the fact that the air pressure is affecting how the water feels to the fish.

The moon phase is a factor that has to be considered. In fact I almost grouped it in the main three of water temperature, food availability and light. Putting aside folk lore such as werewolves and full moons, and any other claptrap based on superstition, lunar and solar movement not only has an effect on the obvious, ie, the light factor, in that a full sun and full moon make for brighter days and nights, but I'm convinced there are other, perhaps more profound effects too. I do know for a fact that I'm rarely happy to night fish on nights of the full moon, for more often than not they are cold, clear nights with very little fish movement, and certainly little sign of fish feeding. That is, unless there is very heavy cloud cover to retain the heat of the day, and shade the stark brightness. Even then, I feel much better when I know there is little, or no moon behind that cloud.

Yet there are odd nights of the full moon, even on clear, cloudless nights, when the fish feed amazingly well. In fact, some anglers, particularly Americans, have made tables of the best times to fish and you can refer to these tables on the Internet; just do a Google search for 'fishing and lunar tables'. The theory applies to animals as well as fish and is widely referred to by hunters and anglers. I'm not so sure just how much I subscribe to the theory but there is no harm in bearing it in mind.

Lunar tables predicted this 39lb grass carp and other big fish, but was it just coincidence?

In April, for a week, a party of six of us fished Chalet lake near Metz, France. The first day Terry Knight caught a 31lb common and Eddie Bibby a 16lb grass carp. And then we went into a full moon period for the next four nights. There was no cloud and the frosts were amongst the worst I've known for the time of year. Only the odd fish was caught during that time. Then, on the last day, the wind changed direction from a cold easterly to a warmer south westerly, and that night the moon disappeared. Not surprisingly, there was no frost. In the early evening John Charlesworth had netted a 29.10 and 19.12 common. Eddie had banked a 28.8 catfish and another double. And during the night John Wakelyn and Terry caught commons and grass carp to over 39lb. I had three catfish, two doubles and a best fish of 56lb, and Eric Barnes caught a double and lost a biggie. We had more action that evening and night than we'd had all week.

My three cats, Eric's two, including the one he lost, and Terry's and John W's carp were all caught in the two hour period between 9.30pm and 11.30pm. Which coincides exactly with the best time indicated in one of the lunar tables.

More recently, in the latter half of 2010, a few friends and I enjoyed some of the best barbel fishing we've ever had on the river Dove, catching some big barbel to over 16lb from a very hard stretch. One of the very best evenings, and the evening when the 16-pounder was caught, the moon was so bright it was almost like daylight. Even so, given the choice, I would always opt for a dark, moonless night for any species.

Planning fishing trips around weather conditions and how they relate to the probability of fish feeding can be treated like an exacting science, or an instinctive judgement. Either way it can be fun, especially when you predict a good day's or night's fishing and that is exactly what happens. What makes it all the more interesting, as in most aspects of angling, is that when you confidently expect to make either an excellent or a poor catch, it can turn out to be just the opposite. How boring it would be if it was all too easy.

THE TRUTH ABOUT WATER TEMPERATURE

Pick up any old angling book - one that was written more than about 25 years ago - and you will almost certainly find frequent references, if not whole chapters, devoted to water temperature. Very often there were tables showing the temperature ranges at which each species fed, and definitive statements that one should avoid fishing for certain species when the water temperature was not within the specified range for that species.

There were anglers who claimed they wouldn't go fishing if the water temperature was not within a certain tolerance. And they would no more dream of going fishing without their thermometers than they would without their rods. Water temperature readings had to be taken at the depth you intended to fish, no matter what the depth of the water, and much time was spent earnestly lowering, or throwing, thermometers as close as possible to where it was intended the hookbait should lie. The thermometer was retrieved as quickly as possible so as to retain the exact reading, and if that reading was not within the range you believed it should be to make a good catch, you then fished with very little confidence, and as a result caught nothing, and inevitably blamed it on the water temperature being wrong!

I must confess that I have written my fair share of articles that made an issue of water temperature. Although I drew the line at not going fishing at all if the temperature was not what I thought it should be, I sincerely believed at the time that successful fishing was a lot more dependent on having the right water temperature than I believe to be so today. Contemporary anglers attach rather less significance to water temperature and its effects, except in a broad, rather off-hand, way. Does this mean that we now ignore the significance of water temperature? Or do we think it no longer has any significance? Or, have we come to the conclusion that it never did have the significance anglers once claimed it had? I reckon there is more than one answer.

Where carp are concerned I think it is anglers who have brought about the changes, for make no mistake, carp are, without a shadow of a doubt, much more easily caught in winter today than they were 25 years ago, which does not indicate that carp are more tolerant of cold water than they were then, but that they now have an incentive to stay active. That incentive, is, of course, the food that anglers are providing through the winter. It is now an accepted fact that the easiest carp waters to fish in winter, relatively speaking, are those that are still receiving a generous supply of bait on a regular basis.

Conversely, those waters fished mainly by warm-weather anglers, who pack away their rods from late autumn to the following season, become difficult, if not almost impossible. The carp evidently 'decide' (instinctively) that the rewards for remaining active are not worth it. Or, it could be more a case of the carp slowly sinking into a torpid state as their search for boilies (no doubt part of their staple diet) becomes more futile as winter deepens.

When you think about it, there is a case for claiming that all species benefit from anglers continuing to fish through winter. Think about the waters in your area, are not the most popular ones the ones that consistently produce reasonable catches through the winter? The other side of this argument is that such waters are popular *because* they produce good catches through the winter. But I know of waters; great waters in the summer, that for some reason don't receive the attention in winter that others in the same area do, that are extremely difficult for those few anglers that occasionally give them a go.

Fisheries that used to fit in this category at one time, but have now become popular, fish very well indeed through the winter. I accept that what I've said could be very difficult to prove, and in some instances may indeed have a different explanation. But generally speaking I stick by what I've said. So that is one answer to the change in attitude towards water temperature, at least as far as carp anglers are concerned.

For some considerable time now I have firmly believed that fish know long before we do that a change in conditions is pending. Many times I've fished in what I thought were perfect conditions and felt extremely confident of making a good catch, only to finish with a blank, or next to nothing. Almost inevitably, the conditions have taken a nose-dive overnight. Other than listening to the weather forecasts, unreliable as many are, you wouldn't have had a clue that a change had been pending. The change in weather brings conditions that you expect will produce poor catches. It is then you realise that the fish were feeling the effect of this change in conditions long before that change was evident to us mere mortals. Several thousand years ago it is likely we would have detected the change ourselves, at a time when our instincts were more highly tuned. What the fish detect is a change in barometric pressure (it can't be anything else) and sometimes when we look up at the sky and feel, rather than see, that a storm is brewing (an extreme condition) it is our long buried instincts emerging for a brief moment.

It works the other way round of course; equally as often we make a good catch at a time when we least expect it, when the conditions are dead set against fish feeding. Invariably we find that a change of conditions for the better is soon upon us. Very often, this phenomenon is blamed on water temperature, either a rise in temperature, or a fall, depending on the result of the fishing session. I've heard it many times: 'The temperature must have fallen, that's why I've caught nothing,' or, 'The water temperature must have risen, that's why the fish are feeding as well as they are.' I'm becoming more convinced as each day passes that changes in water temperature are nowhere near as responsible as we have always thought them to be, for how well, or how poorly, fish feed. I know of too many waters where fish feed at predictable times, in a variety of conditions, for the water temperature to be of great significance.

For instance, there is a carp water within evening session distance of my home, where the carp, in winter, always feed between 5pm and 11pm, with most of the activity happening between 6pm and 9.30pm, with 6pm and 8pm being the 'red hot' times. It is more a question of 'how many' rather than 'if any'. I hesitated to say 'always' because there are rare occasions when there are no signs of fish feeding whatsoever. But the truth is that even when fishing in the most atrocious conditions - line freezing in rod rings, and the surface tinkling as it begins to ice over - there is usually some indication that the carp are feeding, and most sessions produce at least one fish, with half a dozen being caught on many occasions. There is no way you can safely say that you would be wasting your time fishing for them at the times I've mentioned, no matter what the water temperature is, providing you can get a bait in the water.

Long before I became convinced that water temperature is of less importance than I once thought, I believed the most important element was to have settled conditions. Fish can tolerate almost any extreme, whether it be very high, or very low, temperatures; floodwater or low water levels, etc, once they have acclimatised to them. A water temperature of, say, 38 deg. F is more conducive to feeding fish, than a water temperature of 42 deg. F if the 38 degree temperature had been fairly constant for several days and the 42 degree temperature had been the result of a sudden drop. Water temperature is like most things; it is important, but only when taken into consideration with other things that could affect the issue. It should not stand alone as the standard by which we judge whether the fish are going to feed or not.

The temperature trend is the important factor.

HOW WIND AFFECTS FISH

Most experienced anglers know that the best bank from which to fish on a stillwater is usually the one where the wind is blowing into your face. It may not be the most comfortable place to fish, but there is no doubt that the fish are inclined to feed along that bank. But why? What is it that causes the fish to favour that bank? Let's look at what effect wind has on water.

First of all, wind lowers water temperature through a process known as the chill factor. As the surface water is cooled and blown towards the far bank it sinks and turns over to flow back towards the windward side. On fairly shallow waters, this process mixes the water so that the temperature is fairly constant throughout its depth. Another effect of wind is to impart dissolved oxygen into the water, and this, along with temperature, has a great bearing on whether or not fish feed.

Beyond a certain depth (about 6 metres) the water stratifies into three layers of different temperatures. These layers vary in depth and temperature according to the time of year. In summer the top layer, known as the epilimnion, is warmest, and will extend to the depth the sun's rays will penetrate. The bottom layer, known as the hypolimnion, is coldest, and between the two is a narrow layer of water, known as the thermocline, where the temperature changes rapidly for a small change in depth.

In summer, when the wind has blown with some considerable force over a fairly long period, all the layers of water tilt, the warm layer reaching the bottom at the leeward side, and the cold water reaching the surface at the windward side. Being as most species prefer warmer water they will therefore be more inclined to feed off the leeward side.

In some very deep lakes the temperature of the thermocline and the lower layer hardly alter by more than a degree or two all year round, and it is always wise to carry a thermometer when fishing very deep lakes to be able to check the temperature. There will be lots of areas that can be eliminated immediately due to the water there being too cold, compared to the temperature of the water in other areas.

Now what about relatively shallow lakes, where the water is too shallow for stratification? For isn't it still a fact that the leeward side is still best on most days? Now we are into an area where we can only speculate, for the temperature of the whole lake, when the wind has blown for a prolonged period, will be uniform from top to bottom. What is it now that causes the fish to prefer the leeward side? I have heard it said that the fish follow the food (dead and dying insects, etc) that are being carried along on the surface to the leeward side. Yet that mainly applies to surface feeding fish like carp and rudd, and not all fish are surface feeders by habit.

What we have to remember though, is that when the surface water reaches the leeward side it overturns and flows back towards the windward bank. We usually call this undertow, and the result is that we have to put more shot down the line when float fishing, or use heavier indicators when legering. The overturn of water will no doubt carry some of the more minute surface food with it, and the bottom feeding fish could be there, on the leeward side, to mop up these tiny particles of food that the undertow carries along.

Perhaps more significant is the fact that fish prefer to swim against a current rather than with it. River fish hold station, or swim, facing the current, and only swim downstream a short distance in one swift movement before turning to face the current once again. I believe that this happens when a strong undertow has been set up in a stillwater, that the fish swim against it until they reach the leeward side, whereupon they hold station along that bank (at varying distances from the bank) just as they do in a river.

There are exceptions to every rule of course, such as there being times when it is best to fish with your back to the wind. There will be occasions when the colder water is preferable to the fish, for instance, in high summer when the water has been very hot for a long time; so hot the water has become deoxygenated and the cooler water is more comfortable. Remember too, that when the wind has been blowing with considerable force and then suddenly becomes less fierce, the water layers will tilt back to give the opposite effect. This tilting to and fro can continue for some time until the water settles, presenting the warmer water at one end of the lake and then at the other. The larger the water the greater the effect is of this tilting, and the longer this swinging of the layers lasts until it settles.

In spite of anything I've written previously about carrying a thermometer, the strength of the wind and its direction can so much influence water temperature and dissolved oxygen content you can never be absolutely certain what is happening beneath the water's surface without taking a reading with a thermometer.

FISHING IN WINTER

Cold, frosty mornings are not everyone's cup of tea, but I actually look forward to them, especially when there is fresh snow on the ground and big flakes are falling from a heavy sky. I'm not unique; I know quite a few anglers who actually prefer to fish in winter. That isn't quite the case as far as I'm concerned, for, although I love my winter fishing, I love my summer fishing equally as well. The truth of the matter is that by the time either the summer or winter period is almost over, the following period looks particularly inviting. In other words, I'm ready for a change.

About 20 years and more ago we had some really interesting snowfalls through winter, then we went through a period of wet and mild winters, and now, from 2009, we're back to icy and snowy winters again. I used to risk life and limb to drive the 100 miles and more to and from the upper Severn to fish for chub. It was always best when the snow was freshly fallen and lay new and soft on the ground. Not simply for the reason that everywhere looked and felt good, but because the water had not been subjected to too severe a drop in temperature. In fact a good snowfall usually follows a slight rise in temperature. The next best time is following a freeze-up after it has snowed for several days, when the temperature is climbing and the snow is beginning to melt - but before too much melting snow water has ran into the river. I used to set off in the afternoon so that I would arrive at least an hour before darkness fell. I've fished in some really savage, awesome blizzards, caught chub, and thoroughly enjoyed myself. I used to go home feeling invigorated and that I had conquered my own little Everest. Daft, I know, but what the hell!

I love winter fishing in proper frosty weather so much I have great difficulty trying to understand why any keen angler packs away his rods as soon as the first frosts begin to bite. But there are lots of keen anglers who do just that, who, I'm sure, would look back on all those fishless winters with a lot of regret if they knew what they were missing. The secret is in going prepared for the weather, and dressing accordingly. You most certainly will not enjoy it if you're cold and uncomfortable.

The first and obvious consideration before you even attempt to set foot on the river bank in winter is clothing. Get yourself kitted out with clothing that not only keeps the cold out of your bones, but is comfortable and easy to move around in. There is nothing worse than being wrapped up so tightly it becomes hard work just to cast, let alone move from one peg to another. This means that clothing should be loose and not restrict walking, bending and arm movements. Loose clothing is also the warmest clothing, so whatever type of garment you wear, make sure it is at least one size too large. This applies to jacket, overtrousers, bib and brace, one-piece suit, and footwear. But let's start from the skin and work our way to the outer garments.

You can't beat a good quality thermal tee-shirt and long johns next to your skin, then a pair of baggy trousers (jogging pants are excellent, and definitely not tight jeans) and a loose-fitting sweatshirt or pullover. That can often be enough. In exceptionally cold weather, when the wind is cold enough to cut you in two, I wear a fleece jacket as well.

The best outer garment for overall warmth is the one-piece suit, for it is the next best thing to a sleeping bag, containing your body in a pocket of warm air from neck to ankles. Jacket and bib and brace, or overtrousers, are second best and my personal preference, for it means I can remove one or the other if I get too warm. There is no middle ground with the one-piece suit.

Cat-ice in the margins of the Ribble.

Whatever you wear it's got to be waterproof, but don't think that all you have to do is throw on an old oilskin, or some other kind of plastic garment, over the top of your warm clothing when it rains or snows. If you do that you'll get almost as wet from the inside due to condensation. It costs more, a lot more for the best, but in my view it is essential to invest in outer garments that are made from a breathable fabric, which allow your body to breathe without permitting water to penetrate from the outside. Choose a jacket or one-piece suit that has a hood with a draw-string that, when tightened, almost encloses your face. I wear a baseball-type hat under the hood with the peak sticking out so that my eyes (spectacles) have some protection, especially when it's raining. Seal the neck-hole off with a nice, soft, woollen scarf and enclose your face with a balaclava when the conditions are arctic.

The warmest footwear is the so-called moonboot, which has a thick, thermal-lined sole, and a thermal lining up the legs, though not the best of footwear for walking in. Next best are a stout pair of good quality walking boots, a size too big to allow for two pairs of socks, with one pair being thermal. Ordinary wellingtons and waders are probably the worst thing you can wear, but if you have to, make sure they are at least one size too big, and wear two or three pairs of socks. There are one or two thermal-type waders made from neoprene on the market, so check these out too.

Finally, at least as far as outer garments are concerned, are gloves. When the conditions are not wet I much prefer a pair of fingerless woollen gloves. Wet weather means a pair of fingerless neoprene gloves, neoprene being the material used for wetsuits, that does absorb water, but maintains body temperature. The secret with neoprene is to put it on a warm body, not a cold one. Mittens are better for warmth, but more restricting. Though there are mittens available where the finger section folds over and velcros to the back of your hand leaving your fingers free, if that is what you prefer.

You don't need a brolly, and won't want one if you intend to roam around somewhat, especially when river fishing. A brolly is a comfort though, when you intend fishing from the one peg for the length of a session. It's nice to watch the rain or snow from under cover, and to be behind a windbreak. Otherwise, for all-day sessions when you're playing a waiting game, as in some aspects of pike and carp fishing, there are some nice little pop-up bivvies you can use that weigh no more than a 50in brolly and can be set up almost as quickly.

Okay, now you're ready for anything the weather can throw at you. We've got you covered from head to toe in waterproof, warm clothing that you can actually fish in without feeling you've been slapped in a strait jacket. Now it's time to look after the inner man.

When on the move, or pursuing an intense form of fishing, such as float fishing on the river, where you are continually on the go, it has to be drinks from a flask. Unless, of course, you are prepared to stop fishing for a spell and make a fresh brew on a stove. Which, of course, is fine if the fish are not feeding too well and you welcome the break. Not so fine if the fish are feeding well, following some smart, prolonged feeding by you, and you have them crawling up the rod. Me, I'm loathe to take the time to pour a drink from a flask when I'm faced with that kind of situation. But there is always a lull in the proceedings at some time, and you can enjoy your drink from the flask while continuing to feed the swim. The best flasks are the stainless steel ones, not because they are almost unbreakable (which is a plus factor anyhow) but due to the fact that a good quality stainless steel flask will keep drinks hotter, for longer, than a cheap, plastic flask, although plastic flasks are fast becoming extinct.

The only thing that goes in my flask is boiling water. I reckon there's nothing worse than flasked tea and coffee. I carry tea bags, coffee, sugar and milk separately. This gives me several advantages. The flask stays untainted and therefore so do my drinks. The drink is hotter to begin with, but can be cooled to my liking with milk. I enjoy both coffee and tea, and the odd cup of chocolate-type drink. I like more milk in coffee than I do in tea, and I take sugar in coffee but not in tea. My way, I can enjoy whatever drink I fancy, in the way I fancy it. It takes a little more trouble, but is well worth the effort. Pretty often I also carry a smaller flask just big enough to hold a can of hot soup. That goes down well with sandwiches, or just dry bread for dipping in the soup.

When under the brolly, or in a bivvy for a longer session, you can't beat a stove and all the materials you need to make a fresh brew and hot food. And I don't know of any food, gourmet type food included, that smells and tastes better than bacon when it is being fried outdoors, especially in cold conditions. Two or three, or even four, doorstep-size bacon butties dripping with brown sauce sets you up for the day, and you will have a job to find anything that tastes better.

All the comforts of home – well, almost!

Alcohol. I like a drop now and then, but it is a fact that alcohol does not warm you up. In fact it causes heat loss, so be careful how much you have. And don't have any if you're driving. I must confess, however, that when I'm not driving I do enjoy the odd nip from my little pewter flask, and a drop or two in my tea and coffee. I can't say it either warms me up or cools me down, though I can say it gives me the illusion of warming me up. I don't have too much. And I like it.

The best way of keeping warm in winter, however, and for a general feeling of well-being, is to catch fish. No matter how foul are the conditions, and no matter how much you may have been whinging about it, you'll forget all that when you're getting your rod bent regularly. It's amazing how much pain and discomfort your body and mind can ignore when it is preoccupied with something pleasurable. So regardless of all the advice I've given you on how to keep warm and comfortable, it is still most important to do everything you can to ensure you catch fish. Catching fish regularly, summer or winter, is the best way of enjoying yourself, no matter what the weather throws at you.

Chapter 4

My Angle on Angling Part 1

Fishing thoughts from inside the box

THE SECRET TO SUCCESSFUL FISHING

With every day that passes it's still abundantly clear that the majority of anglers believe that the very best anglers know something that the rest of us don't. That they have access to some kind of secret method or bait, or both.

Unfortunately this myth if propagated by the weeklies with headlines that scream: 'Catch a shedful with Nob Blood's new secret bait!' Or, 'Empty your local water with Nat May's secret method!' Or even, 'Revealed at last, Gerry Hernia's best kept secrets'.

No wonder too many anglers, the kids especially, think that all they have to do to be a top angler is learn these 'secrets'.

Let's get one thing straight from the off: successful fishing is not complicated and it isn't due to an angler having access to some secret that is hidden away from the majority. Those anglers who are exceptionally successful fully realise that there are no secrets; no secret methods and no secret baits. What they have is very easy to acquire, which is a knowledge of the basic principles of fishing, good tackle handling skills, enthusiasm in abundance, determination and........ the realisation that there is no secret way to the top.

I don't know who the best angler in the world is, mainly because there is no such person, but if there were I'd bet a huge chunk of money that he wouldn't be the most intelligent. That bet wouldn't be based on me thinking that anglers are not blessed with high IQ's, but on the simple fact that you don't need super intelligence to be a super angler. I've always maintained that, generally speaking, the best anglers are those who take to the sport instinctively, people who have a real feeling for it rather than someone who has learnt his craft from reading about it. That's not meant with any disrespect to those who are not instinctive anglers, for they may enjoy fishing just as much as the angler who has fallen from the cradle into the water and come up clutching a fish and gasping for breath.

That said, one of our most successful anglers was the late Professor Barrie Rickards, who was also one of the most intelligent, so it just may be that the very best anglers are those who have a very generous supply of both instinct and intelligence. But I rather think not, for I know plenty of other exceptional anglers who struggle to write a shopping list and still take their shoes and socks off to count more than 10.

Over the years I've either fished with or spoken to many very successful anglers. Not all of them were in the public eye. Many of them you will never have heard of for they never courted publicity. Most of them were not involved with fishing as an occupation, either full time or part time. All of them loved fishing with a passion normally reserved for more carnal pleasures. Fishing was not something they did because they couldn't think of anything better to do. It wasn't something they did to get away from a nagging wife, or something they did to smell the flowers (although that's always a good idea in passing). It was something they did because they wanted, above all, to catch fish. All of them, to a man, felt that fishing was in their blood. It was much more than a way of life. It was a life in itself.

None of the best anglers I've known could explain why they caught more than most other anglers. To watch them briefly you wouldn't be able to detect what it was they did differently from the next merely competent angler. The physical skills are obvious, the accurate casting, the manipulation of a stick float, the slick playing of a fish, and so on. But if that was all there was to being a truly top angler there would be no big names that stood out in the specialist world and match winnings would be shared fairly evenly and come down to the luck of the draw much more than they do.

It's true that some anglers have developed an advantage, or an 'edge' as it's known, temporarily at least. They've devised a modification to a method, or developed a particularly good bait, that, usually on a specific water, gives the angler a better chance of catching fish. But not for long, for the fish will soon wise up, and the process has to start all over again. These 'edges' are rarely ground-breaking, revolutionary advantages, in the same mould as the hair-rig, but simple little innovations that cause a method to be slightly less suspicious or more hook-up effective, or perhaps a bait that is a little more tasty, stays on the hook better or retains its flavour for longer. Whatever it is it is unlikely to be something that needs to be guarded in case it becomes known to the masses and waters subsequently 'emptied'.

The best anglers are never happy to sit on their backsides and watch the world go by; they are usually developing their next 'edge' before the current one has ran its course so that they never have a prolonged break from their usual catch rate. Of course, this continual search for the ultimate edge is part of human nature, futile as it may be, but it is this drive that uncovers the little innovations that do make a difference, at least for a while. Apart from anything else this drive for better methods and baits keeps us on our toes and stops us from wallowing in apathy or becoming nothing better than a time bandit.

Yet, as good as it is to always be trying to improve methods and baits, to be searching for another 'edge', it is something much more simple that separates the men from the boys.

One thing that is very clear is that some anglers will never become anything better than time bandits or pools fodder. It doesn't matter how many times they read something, see it in a DVD, or watch a top angler fishing, they just don't seem to take it in. You can show them a hundred times how to mix a bowl of fluffy groundbait and yet they'll still mix up a bowl of stodge. Illustrate time and time again how important it is to keep the feed going in regularly and they'll still be sat there feeding nothing and just waiting for a bite an hour after they last fed. They can sit next to an angler who is catching fish after fish and still not twig that he's just not killing time and waiting for something to happen but actually making it happen.

On many occasions I've spoken about this topic at some length with Stu Dexter, who I rate as one of the best anglers I've ever had the pleasure to fish with and we are 100% agreed on what makes a top angler. Now, whilst I've fished with lots of top specialist anglers and a few top match anglers,

Stu has fished with a lot of top match anglers and top specialists, and where I've got an affinity with the specialist angler Stu has got the same affinity with match anglers. And believe me, we've studied the top guys just to see if we could identify a magic ingredient, to see just what they had in common that sets them apart.

In a nutshell it's this: simplicity and a total belief in their ability.

They keep things simple. They stick to the basics and follow the well-known and well proven procedure. They get to know a water, or if it's a water that's new to them they do their homework, researching as much as possible before they visit it, walk around it when they get there, speak to the regulars, do some plumbing, and then sift through the information for the parts they consider relevant.

Stu Dexter, one of the best anglers I've fished with.

There's no flash of inspiration, no bolt of lightning that strikes them, revealing a master plan. Just simple research and hard work, and then plotting a course of action that they consider is most likely to lead to success.

But with back-up plans should plan 'A' fail.

Next comes the search for the best methods for given sets of conditions, and once they know what they are they'll tweak them with their own little innovations; nothing much usually, but enough to make them feel the methods are their own. They rarely do anything radical, including with baits, no particularly special flavours or special mixes, just good old proven baits that may have caught thousands of fish over the years, and maybe a little, subtle flavour, again to make it their own, but not a flavour that you or I can't buy from the tackle shop or supermarket.

You watch them fish and the first thing that strikes you is the accuracy of their casting, that float or feeder landing in the same tight spot every time. You note the mesmeric rhythm of casting, feeding, and casting again, never losing that sense of timing, not even when playing fish.

They know what's important and they make the important things their priority every time. Specialist and pleasure anglers know that location is the all important aspect, with method and bait second best. Match anglers, who have no choice in swim selection, realise that good bait and an efficient feeding rhythm are all important.

Being one of the best, consistent anglers isn't magic. There are no spells or secret baits, no rods or other tackle that are reserved for the privileged. It's about a thorough knowledge of the basics, a decent command of tackle handling and keeping it simple.

So, if it's as simple as that, why are so few so much better than so many?

I reckon it's a lot to do with belief in your own ability, believing in yourself. It's more than a confidence thing, it's having that sure-fire belief that given good conditions you'll catch, and given poor conditions you'll probably still catch. If you don't believe in yourself you won't make the simple things work, you'll never fish a bait or a method long enough to give it a fair go, for you'll be swapping and changing and trying to make things happen when you should be waiting and being patient. And you'll be exercising too much patience and waiting for things to happen at those times when you should be trying other methods and baits.

Above all, believe that there are no secrets to successful fishing. Get that ingrained into your mind-set and then you can concentrate on what really matters: learning as much as you can, doing it right, and believing that you are as good as, if not better, than anyone else.

TOO EASY!

Over the years I have caught quite a few double-figure bream and none of them were easy to catch. My local waters, the Cheshire and Shropshire meres are notoriously difficult for any species, but big bream are usually exceptionally difficult from any water. I think I've had just two relatively easy seasons in the 40-odd years I've fished for big bream, one in the 1980's and one in 1995.

That season in the 1980's (I can't remember the exact year) I caught quite a few big bream, including several into double figures. They were much easier than is usual to catch due to the conditions being particularly conducive to bream fishing, and I was able to spend more time fishing than what is normally the case.

The water in question, a Cheshire mere, is not an especially difficult water from which to catch big bream, but like all big bream they have to be caught - they don't give themselves up. Big bream are never easy to catch, they are simply easier to catch on some occasions than they are on others. Easier or not, you had to fish the right swim, at the right time, feed judiciously, cast accurately, offer an acceptable, well presented bait, and play the fish to the net on relatively light tackle. Getting everything right is always the difficult bit.

The really significant aspect of my bream fishing on the Cheshire mere that year was that I was able to pick and choose more or less exactly when I fished, which meant I could go mid-week, rather than the more usual restriction of being able to go sometime at the weekend only. This in turn meant that I could often fish the hottest spot on the mere, which is the only spot worth fishing when the bream are using that area of the route to get their heads down. Of course, everyone else had the same idea, so the hottest hot-spot became even hotter because it was receiving more bait on a regular basis than anywhere else.

Anyhow, that season the bream were hungry for angler's baits, and I was able to take full advantage of the extra time I had available. I enjoyed some multiple catches of bream from over 8lb to well into double figures. Another angler on the water was also doing well, mainly for the reason that, like me, he had more time to spend fishing than most of the others who fished the mere. One morning, following a very fruitful week, when on two separate nights we had both caught several bream to double figures, we sat talking about bream fishing in general, and the bream fishing on that mere in particular. We discussed the validity and otherwise of feeding routes, the significance of wind strength and direction, the effect of a full moon and clear, cloudless nights, and all manner of things pertaining to fishing for big bream.

But there was one particular thing he said at the end of the conversation that lingered in my thoughts for some time afterwards. He said that he was moving onto another, nearby mere, to try for the bream there, for he thought it was too easy just now on this mere where we stood. As I later pondered the significance of his words I wished I had asked him to elaborate on what he'd said, to explain to me exactly what he meant.

My first reaction was one of agreement. It was relatively easy fishing at the moment, and the thought lay content in my gut. So what? what's wrong with a bit of easy fishing when you can get it? My next reaction was to feel guilty, for here I was, perfectly happy to indulge in some easier fishing for big bream for a change, and enjoying it immensely, and there was another angler who was obviously dissatisfied, and intending to move onto a more difficult water. Shouldn't I be here, pulling a few big fish out most nights I fished, instead of hoping for just the one bite off a decent fish in a night, as is usually the case?

Forty years ago it was a success if we got one 8lb bream over a weekend on the meres.

My thoughts drifted back over the years, to almost 40 years ago, when I spent every weekend from Friday night to Sunday afternoon on other Cheshire and Shropshire meres, coming home feeling shattered but happy if I'd netted a single 8-pounder, and ready to shout it from the rooftops if I'd had a 'nine' or bigger. Then I had been young enough and daft enough to manage on two or three hours sleep, to suffer anything the elements could throw at me from behind the plastic sheet that I'd wrapped round the brolly (before commercial bivvies were invented). Indicators were dough bobbins that fell off when it rained hard, lit up with candles in jam-jars. Sleep was snatched while sat up in a garden chair, or lay on the ground on a plastic sheet. But not real sleep, for very few had the old Heron bite alarms to allow you to relax, and those who had never knew if they would work at the right time, and were constantly being woken from false alarms - especially when it rained and the contacts got wet.

They were times when two or three 8lb bream, or a 9-pounder, in a session (a full weekend) made headline news in the weekly angling press, and a 10lb bream made headlines plus a story and more pictures in the inside pages.

Now here I was, feeling guilty because I was often catching more than one 9lb and 10lb-plus bream in a single night session. Bite alarms were as near-as-dammit foolproof, and the butt-indicators lit with super-bright betalights, red on one and green on the other. Between bites I was sprawled on a comfortable bed-chair especially made for the job, from the confines of a bivvy that the residents of Cardboard City would have killed for. If I fancied a drop of Irish whiskey in my tea, following a panful of hot stew, then so be it. Christ Almighty lad, I told myself, it isn't often you can enjoy all this - and big fish too. Enjoy it while it's going!

Maybe I'd read it all wrong though. Perhaps the 'too easy' had been a simple, flippant remark I'd read more in than what had been intended. What's wrong with someone wanting to move on to a greater challenge; wishing to fish a water where the bream are fewer but possibly bigger? Hadn't I made a similar remark and felt the same way about the bream fishing in Ireland........?

......The original intention in Ireland had been to catch a ton of bream. Not 100lbs, but for five of us to catch an imperial ton - 2200lbs of bream in one session. That works out at 440lb each. We failed in that we found it physically and mentally impossible to continue fishing for longer than the eight hours between 6am and 2pm we fished, less an hour for breakfast. So we packed in for the day and began again the next day at the same time, and by mid-day we'd caught a total two-session catch of about 2350lb, almost 500lb each if the catches had been equal.

Part of a ton of bream caught in Ireland.

Incidentally, the catch weight had been calculated by counting all the fish caught, frequently weighing individual fish to work out an approximate average weight (7lb) and then multiplying by the total. What made the catch all the more remarkable was the fact that all the fish came from the same swim. All five anglers fished in a line, each no more than 6ft apart. And that I spent far less time fishing than anyone else, which of course meant that the other four caught well over 500lbs each. (This was on Lough Ree, close to the channel where the river Shannon flowed through. Those days of big bream are now long gone, with far fewer and smaller bream around and with roach to a pound or so and hybrids to 3lb or so having taken over).

After about four hours on the first day I'd had enough, and began to spend more time behind the video camera. My only claim to fame was that I'd had a bream of 9lb 2oz which turned out to be the biggest fish of the catch. I was fishing next to John Charlesworth, and I remember telling him it was doing my head in. We were all pulling bream in, weighing anything from 6lb to over 8lb almost every cast. There were times when all five of us had a bream on. It was ridiculous. This isn't fishing, I remember thinking, it's a bloody farce. Water craft had been exercised when we chose the swim.

Fishing expertise was used when we fed the swim and tackled up, and apart from the basic skill of tackle handling when the floats were trotted through the swim and fish were played, it had very little to do with fishing after that. It was a mindless and mechanical activity of casting, striking, and playing fish to the net which anyone, with the least possible angling knowledge, could have done with similar results. One by one, all the lads were flagging, not just from the physical effort of catching so many fish, but through shear lack of interest. An active mind can only take so much cabbage. Believe me, given that bream would have continued to appear and linger in the swim, and that we had the required physical and mental stamina, well over 3000lb of bream would have been on the cards.

Too easy? Yes, it was, I have no doubt about that. So why do I feel so scornful of the same remark made on the Cheshire mere? After all, the basic meaning behind the remark was exactly the same. I was deriving no satisfaction from those bream in Ireland once I'd hauled in two or three hundred pounds of them, and I felt content to pack it in and enjoy myself more with the video camera. And would have been happy to move on to a more difficult water to try for some bigger, harder to catch, fish. Although, one of the reasons we go to Ireland is for some easy fishing, where bites are expected rather than hoped for. But that old adage that says you can have too much of a good thing has a lot going for it.

The most intriguing part of all this 'easy' fishing and 'hard' fishing is that when someone catches a big fish from what we call a 'hard' water we admire the angler for his skill, when really, we should be admiring the angler more for his staying power and patience.

The angler I was talking to on the Cheshire mere was going to another mere to do exactly the same thing he had done on the mere where we stood. The major difference was that there were fewer, possibly bigger, bream in the 'harder' water, which meant he would have to fish for longer periods without a bite. Yes, I know it's not quite as simple as that, but it's not far off.

I think what got to me, and I should have known better than to allow it to get to me, for I've heard it said so often before, was the tone that suggested the bream on this mere were so easy they were no longer worthy of his attention. The inflection in the voice implied that he had better things to do with his time. Which are interesting sentiments coming from the mouth of someone who probably has more time than most to spend waiting for bites, rather than catching fish.

But was my attitude towards those Irish bream any better?

FOOLED BY FISH

How many times do we hear about the one that got away? The monstrous fish that fought with a frightening power that had to be seen to be believed; the fish that would undoubtedly have been a personal best, or a record for the water, or even a British record had it been landed? How many monster fish have you lost over the years?

I've lost plenty, or so I've thought, following a fight from an unseen force that battled with a power far in excess of what was to be expected at the time. But now I'm a cynical old so and so, and try to find all kinds of acceptable explanations for the apparent size of unseen monsters. Experience has taught me that USO's (Unidentified Swimming Objects) are as much a figment of the imagination as are UFO's.

Which is one of my regrets at growing older, and maybe wiser, for it is much more exciting to believe in monsters than it is to search for plausible explanations. I wish I could believe still, but alas I don't, for when I have hooked a 'monster', and then later discovered the truth, I've realised how easy it is to fool oneself. And how easy it is to want to be fooled, which is probably more to the point.

The one factor that is more responsible than any other for causing us to think we have hooked a monster is foul-hooking, especially when the fish has been hooked in the tail. It happens to all of us at some time or other, particularly when we have a big shoal of fish in the swim feeding greedily. What happens is that we strike at a bite, miss it, and then hook into the body of that same fish or another fish feeding nearby. Such fish can fight like no fish you have ever hooked fairly, for when they are hooked in, or close to the mouth, we have some control over them, and we can steer them to some extent after the first few bursts of acceleration. Whereas when we have hooked a fish anywhere but the mouth, and especially somewhere close to, or in, the tail, we have hardly any control at all. A powerful fish can do almost anything it likes, for there is no way, using tackle of normal strength, we can pull it in a different direction to the way it wishes to go. It can swim faster, for longer, and it feels 'different', to the point where we are left wondering: 'What the hell is this thing I've hooked?'

As the fight continues the line may grow weaker through abrasion, and the hook wears an increasingly bigger hole in the flesh or fin of the fish. And then the inevitable happens: the hook pulls or the line breaks. Inevitable because the fight has lasted much longer than most fights you have with fish, and the fish can pull harder than any fish hooked fairly. You are then left with a slack line and a slack jaw to go with it, and you raise the rod like a spear, ready to throw it into the hedge but pull back at the last second when you realise that the throw could cost you a trip to the tackle shop you can't really afford.

Over the years I've landed quite a few big tench, including a number over 9lb, up to a best fish of 11lb 4oz, so I do know what it feels like to have a big tench on the end of my line. Even so, tench can fool me more than any other fish into thinking I've hooked something really special. I bet you've been fooled more than once too, for every so often we hook into a male tench that fights twice as hard as a female tench of twice the size. It's the big, muscular fins of the male that are responsible for those awesome bursts of power that drive us into thinking we've hooked the biggest tench of our lives. We could have been catching one or two specimen female tench over 6lb, or even 7lb, and then hooked into a 4lb or 5lb male fish that made us sit up and take a lot more notice. It is disappointing, to say the least, to find a smaller than average fish coming to the net following a fight that conjured up thoughts of something extra special.

About a decade ago, while float-fishing a Cheshire mere, a pal of mine hooked a fish at 7am and was still playing it at 8.45am when the 4lb line finally gave up and broke at the bottom shot. Okay, so it wasn't especially heavy line, but heavy enough to deal with the 3lb to 6lb tench that we were fishing for from a boat in open water. But that fish was completely uncontrollable, sometimes going off at great speed, other times just trundling away at a steady pace, and often simply wallowing just below the surface, but out of sight enough to prevent us from identifying it. My pal bent the rod into it as much as he dared on the 4lb line, and continually made it fight for every inch of line it took. Which was a lot of inches in the almost two hours it careered away from the boat every time it was brought anywhere near it. We suspected that this was no ordinary tench, and imagined all kinds of things for the first ten minutes or so. Then it became obvious that even a record tench would not be able to sustain a fight like that.

I suggested that it could be a foul-hooked fish and my pal said he didn't think so. 'It doesn't feel like that.' He said. 'When I'm gaining line on it it feels like it's swimming towards me, but reluctantly.' Then, almost two hours later, when he retrieved a broken line, we had come to the conclusion that he had hooked one of the handful of carp in the water that were rumoured to have grown to 30lb or so. Probably a big, fat mirror that was just too heavy to be hauled to the net on 4lb line even when it was exhausted.

We discussed the event over the next few days, reliving every moment, and the belief that he had hooked a big carp became a reality to both of us. To the point where we talked about it to other friends who fished the water as though we actually knew it was a big carp, and not merely speculated that it was.

Five days later I landed a tench from almost the same spot. It was hooked fairly in the lips and fought like nothing I've ever hooked before or since at the same weight. Looped and knotted around the wrist of the tail was my mate's broken line, still complete with hook and shot. It was a 4lb male fish with huge paddles, the biggest fins I've seen on any tench of any size. We couldn't believe that a 4lb fish could fight such a strong, prolonged fight as it did those five days ago. We put it down to the fact that it had complete freedom of movement due to the line being looped round the wrist. Had it been foul-hooked in the tail then it could have been slowed down to some extent, but with the line being attached to the wrist a force of 4lb, or thereabouts, had little effect.

Had I not caught that fish, or had I caught it without the line still looped around the wrist of the tail, we would still have believed to this day that my mate had hooked a monster fish. A very large carp. Today it would have been a fact.

One of the most awesome displays of shear, aggressive power I've ever witnessed was on the river Vienne in France's Loire Valley. On the particular stretch I was fishing there was hardly any speed to the current, but it was, nevertheless, quite strong. I was fishing for carp with the usual boilie on a bolt-rig set-up, right in the margins. I'd had no action for quite some time, then had a run that caused the wet line on the spool to give off a mist that looked like smoke it was spinning so fast. I struck into the fish, and almost had the rod ripped from my hand. The fish took off – upstream – with a speed that had to be seen to be believed. My line was 15lb, and had I been relying on back-winding I would have had the skin knocked off my knuckles. As it was the spool screamed on the drag like a wailing banshee.

Terry Knight stood alongside me with the landing net, and when the fish had gone over 50yds, against a 3lb test-curve rod that had been hooped over with absolute contempt, with me just literally hanging on to the butt with both hands, he said. 'It's a cat. It's got to be one of the big cats in here!' Which was exactly what I was thinking myself. When another 50yds of line had been taken, against another hard turn to tighten the drag, I had to clamp down on the spool, for some terrible bad snags were looming in the distance. In the end I won that one, and managed to get the fish to the net, although very grudgingly. It was a very long, very slim, common carp of 14lbs. I couldn't believe that a fish of that size could fight with such power, speed and ferocity. I've caught elongated common carp and true wild carp before, but none that have fought like that.

But had I not landed that fish, nor even seen it, both myself and Terry Knight would have been convinced to this day that I had hooked a real monster, probably a catfish of huge proportions.

Another incident that will remain in my memory for as long as I live was the day I hooked and lost a big pike on Loch Lomond. This was not long after the Dick Walker and Fred Buller period, when rumour was rife that Lomond held monstrous pike that would easily smash the British record, which was held by a 47lb 11oz Lomond fish at the time. This pike was eventually removed from the list when the British records were re-examined and new criteria laid down. It had also been insinuated by these two extremely well respected anglers that Lomond held at least one pike that could make a mind-boggling three figures. I was one of many who made the pilgrimage to Loch Lomond hoping to hook a monster that had taken on almost greater proportions than her neighbour, Nessie herself.

Lomond is an awesome place to fish even without rumours of monsters to bolster its atmosphere. It is prone to beautiful, calm, tranquil spells that can very quickly turn into horrifying, raging, lethal periods of savage winds and towering waves. So you can probably imagine the feeling we had when fishing Lomond at that time, when a chance of hooking a monster was well and truly planted in our minds. Every run brought on a minor heart attack, and many of us, including me, risked our lives by fishing in conditions we had no right to fish in. Most of us were inexperienced boat anglers on large waters, and totally unprepared for what this often foreboding water could so easily, so unexpectedly, and so quickly throw at you. I still have nightmares at what could have happened, almost did happen more than once, and took the life of the brother of one angling friend.

The day I hooked my Lomond 'monster' was one of the best days I have ever fished anywhere for pike, both for good conditions and incidents. It was flat calm and I was fishing from a boat along the Endrick Bank off Balmaha, maybe even in the exact spot where Walker and Buller hooked their monster. The day was misty, mild and calm and I was fishing float-legered trout deadbaits in a depth of 12ft and at 8am my float sent out a couple of ripples before it disappeared and line peeled from the spool of the Mitchell 300 at a steady rate. The tightness in my chest was matched only be the tightness in the line as I struck the trebles home with the Hardy Richard Walker Mk IV Palakona Carp Rod. There followed a fight better than any other fight I've ever had from a pike before or since – bar one, which was the fight I had with the next fish that day. That first fish weighed a little over 25lb and was duly photographed and returned.

The bait that led to me hooking my favourite 'monster' on Loch Lomond.

Midday arrived and the sun was out hot and bright and the water remained calm. My float slid under again. No ripples, no warning this time. It just disappeared and the 10lb line (standard test for piking at the time) peeled off the spool very rapidly. I struck into the fish and following a period of me giving and retrieving line, when the fish swam away from and then towards the boat, when it didn't even know it was hooked, it must have realised something was wrong and took off for the northern end of the loch 23 miles away. It should have arrived by now, for the 100yds of line I had on the spool, plus backing (again, standard for the time) was in danger of running out when I had to pull hard enough to stop the fish or to break the line.

Neither happened, for the hooks pulled instead. But I did get the dead trout back, which had a jaw mark across it that was two inches wider than the jaw width of the 25-pounder I had caught earlier. If the body proportions of that fish had been the same as that of the '25' then an extra two inches across the jaw makes it a very big fish indeed. I do know that I couldn't do anything with it on 10lb line. It just kept going in spite of the pressure I put it under. Once it had made up its mind that it was going to put distance between me and the boat it did just that – effortlessly.

That fish remains my favourite 'monster'. I don't want to be told any rational explanations. I want to remain convinced that I once hooked a record fish, maybe even a fish that would have become a legend. The dream of that monster is going to my grave with me. Even the good Lord, or Old Nick himself, whichever the case may be, will not be able to convince me otherwise.

But let's spoil it and be realistic for a moment. Let's be honest and confess that if we analyse all those lost 'monsters' there is always a rational explanation around the corner. What we all suffer from at times (apart from the totally unromantic, seriously sceptical amongst us) is a large overdose of self-deception, mainly due to the fact that we don't want an epic battle belittled, for when we lose one of those battles, boy, are we in a state. The adrenaline is still coursing through our veins like the Severn at full bore. Our whole body is shaking and we can't make our mind up whether to scream or cry.

Is it any wonder we refuse to even consider the possibility that the fish we just lost was nothing special? That it was possibly smaller than the last one we landed? That it only fought the way it did because it was foul-hooked? Not on your life! The only way we are going to come to terms with the loss is if we are convinced we have lost the fish of a lifetime. And that is the story we tell our family back home, and our mates in the pub. And in the end we believe it ourselves. It has become written in stone that on such and such a date we lost a fish that would undoubtedly have broken the British record.

And all the time it was a fish considerably smaller than many of the fish we have landed over the years without even moving our bums off our chairs.

But that's life. Long live the monsters. Long live the legends. We need the magic.

FISHING – IT'S TIME WE LEFT IT ALONE

We all have our favourite species, favourite waters, favourite swims, favourite methods and favourite baits. And we all have different views about the whole concept and philosophy of fishing, and where fishing is heading. This is my view.

Going back to prehistoric times the reason for going fishing was simple: you did it to survive. You hunted and fished for food, and if you didn't catch anything you went hungry, and if you consistently didn't catch anything you died of starvation. You had the best incentive in the world to learn how to be a good catcher of fish. There were advantages and disadvantages to fishing at that time. The disadvantages were that you had to look over your shoulder pretty often to make sure some wild animal wasn't about to sink its claws into you, or a rival fisherman about to swing a club at your head. The tackle you had at your disposal was crude, and you didn't have a few million years fishing experience to draw on from the fishermen that had gone before you.

The advantages of fishing all that time ago were that you were fishing totally unpolluted and thriving waters, unspoilt by man. There were no restrictions whatsoever as to what methods and baits you used; not even a minimum mesh size on the net you used if that was your chosen method. You could fish anywhere you liked provided you stuck to your own territory, or even further afield if you were bigger than your neighbours.

So why do we fish today? Commercial netsmen still fish for food, for the whole tribe, so we don't need to fish to survive. Individual fishermen, like myself, are anglers, fishing because we are satisfying that underlying instinct to hunt for food, and by satisfying that instinct we derive pleasure from the act. We use a rod and line to make it all the more interesting. It's that simple, no matter if we specialise in nothing in particular (we call it pleasure fishing) or if we add the extra challenge of specialising in bigger fish or in competitions with fellow anglers. We do it for pleasure.

So forget the whimsical raptures of some of our more poetic angling writers (good as it is at times to read their flowing scriptures). We don't fish because there are wild flowers along the route, or because we love fish with a romantic passion, we fish because we are getting a kick out of satisfying a basic instinct. But there is no denying that wild flowers along the way and fish in pristine condition enhance the experience. And it is vitally important that what we do is potentially versatile, for there can never be passion in stagnation.

Over the years fishing has evolved from a mission of survival to a passionate pleasure for the keenest anglers. And along the way it has picked up a rule book that is growing thicker and thicker as each year goes by. Each one of those rules has chipped a little more away from the absolute freedom to catch fish by any

Wonderful fish like this big carp are the reason we go fishing.

means at your disposal. Many of those rules were born of necessity, some to prevent the depletion of stocks, and others simply to make us behave ourselves while we indulged our pleasure in the company of others.

We should be very careful how far we go with the rule book, for the farther we go the sooner we reach that time when there is nowhere else to go except to ban fishing altogether. If anglers continue to accept (even fight for in some instances) these continual erosions of fishing freedoms (the latest bandwagons being a ban on livebaits and keepnets) fishing will soon reach the point where the angler is so restricted in the baits and methods at his disposal there is nothing really interesting left to do. When that happens fishing will be banning itself, for there will be so few of us there will be no resistance whatsoever to a total ban.

Take a deeper, longer look at what is happening in fishing right now. Where stillwaters are concerned carp have become the dominant species, to the point where other species are diminishing in number. Anglers who are not drawn to the carp scene, as the majority are these days, are increasingly taking to the rivers, with the result that barbel (the river 'carp') are now under great pressure.

I have nothing whatsoever against commercial fisheries, they fill a need for many anglers and I fish them myself. It is those commercials that are no more than a square hole that become a blot on the landscape instead of an enhancement that I object to. More of these fisheries are being cultivated to become nothing more than small carp competition waters, full of F1 carp of more or less the same size. Anglers are sitting around these soporific squares with no more on their minds than to catch more cloned carp than anyone else so that they can pick up the winnings for that day; it is hardly more than a contest that is won by the angler who can hook and net F1's with the greatest speed. There is no passion for the water here; no love for the fish; no feeling for fishing, other than how it can make you feel good if you beat your fellow fisherman and get your hands on the money. At the opposite end of the carp fishing spectrum we have the specialist angler, the angler who wants to catch the biggest carp possible. Generally, this angler is more passionate about his sport than most.

It is the middleman who is disappearing, the angler who neither wants particularly big carp, nor a netful of overstocked clones. It is those waters where you can catch a few carp to double figures, and perhaps the odd 20-pounder, which are becoming fewer as each year passes. At a club meeting recently the cry was for the club's waters to be netted and the carp thinned, so that at least some of the remaining stock would have a better chance of reaching the 'magic' 30lb figure. The fact that any fish that made 30lb will have been caught dozens of times before within a pound or two of that figure seems of little importance. It is the figure itself that has become important, rather than the fish.

So what are we left with? A majority of anglers with no real feeling for the sport, who fish for big catches of predictable fish, and a minority of passionate anglers who fish for equally predictable specimens. So we have one group that doesn't care enough, and another group that are so small in number it doesn't matter how much they care if it came to a fight with the anti-angling faction.

The 'pleasure' angler, as we know him, is fast disappearing, and although the match and specialist anglers are maintaining their numbers, even slightly increasing them, from within pleasure and specialist angler ranks, it is not happening in sufficient numbers. Like instant food and instant everything else, fishing is fast joining the 'microwave' era where sport is packaged with simple instructions and served up on a plate in no time at all.

DECEIT IN THE DIGITAL AGE

The digital age has breathed new life into photography, at least as far as convenience is concerned, but there are still photographers who take pictures and people who take snaps. That will never alter no matter how much the equipment progresses. The big change, apart from the technology itself, is that the digital era has put photography into the hands of the masses; now almost everyone has a digital camera even if it is no more than a camera phone.

Digital photography with a top of the range, multi megapixel SLR camera is now also very close to the quality of 35mm transparency film. You would be hard pressed to tell the difference between a shot taken with the different media even at poster size and the bulk of the photographs you see in magazines will have been taken with a digital camera. We're awash with pictures, and they can be sent around the world via email almost as fast as you can say 'smile please'.

With just a little knowledge of how to take a decent picture it's difficult to take a poor one, and when you check the results in the monitor you simply delete those that are not up to scratch and just take them again. No wasted film, no processing costs. And as if that wasn't enough we have a glut of inexpensive image editing software around these days that can change a poor shot into a work of art. The latest Windows and Apple Mac operating systems have it all built in, so the ability to edit images is more convenient and easier than ever.

But that's the rub, for image editing will be even more open to abuse by those who wish to deceive. And believe me, there are more than a few deceivers around, and some have quite a talent for it. In some cases you would never know the difference between a manufactured picture and the genuine article unless you had access to the original and knew exactly what to look for.

One of the easiest things to do, but the easiest to spot, if you're looking for it, is to just stretch the fish to make it look bigger. Look at the 'before' and 'after' pictures of the chub I'm holding (See Colour Plate 8, page 216). That kind of simple photo editing took about 10 minutes and will fool some people into believing the moderately sized chub I really caught is a massive specimen. The stretched scales give it away of course but with no original shot to compare it with it would fool many people.

The anglers who are determined to deceive will use a different, more elaborate and more time-consuming method. They will take an element from one image and drop it into another image. Where fishing pictures are concerned this usually means cutting a fish from one picture and dropping it into the hands of an angler in another picture. Get the sizing right and the fish of course looks much bigger than it really is. Another trick used by the cheats is the 'angler' who cuts an image of himself holding a fish from one shot and pastes it into an image of a lake or riverside scene, thereby making it look like the fish was caught from quite a different location to where it really was caught. Quite recently one 'angler' openly suggested in print that to do so was a good way of disguising where you were catching your fish.

Obviously oblivious to, or caring not, that to do such a thing would put pressure on someone else's water.

It's prudent to ask why. Why do some anglers wish to behave in that way? The out and out crooks are obviously doing it for the money and the prizes that some angling publications offer. That, in a perverted kind of way, is possibly more understandable than the anglers who do it for the glory and for no other reason than they're just by nature deceitful and dishonest. Why can't it be enough to just take the photograph with an unrecognisable background, or with a brolly or a bivvy in the background? And it's easy enough to take the picture from a high angle so that all that is visible, apart from the angler and fish, is grass. The only conclusion you can come to is that there are some people who actually enjoy the dishonest and deceitful subterfuge.

Worse are those anglers who are total hypocrites. One in particular I've been unfortunate enough to run into on more than one occasion has criticised more people than I care to remember about publishing photos of fish they've caught where he's been able to recognise a blade of grass or two. He's caused more trouble for his fellow anglers and the club he belonged to than anyone else I know. I'll never forget the day we had a toe to toe argument on the Dove when he accused me of publishing a picture of the stretch that showed a club sign (which was a lie) and telling me I wasn't being fair to the others who fished there. Now he's no longer a member of that particular club he's publishing pictures on a regular basis that show swims in detail.

So what can we do about this dishonest image manipulation? One thing I would suggest is that editors really scrutinise the images they're sent. It's not too difficult to spot editing that goes beyond simple image enhancement. A few years ago I took a copy of one of our weeklies to a fish-in and indicated a few points in a barbel picture sent in by our 'friend'. Within a few seconds the dozen or so lads (and lassie) could see where the fish had been pasted and blended none too skilfully into another shot.

Of course, someone who is more adept at image editing would be able to produce an image that would pass scrutiny, so what the answer is then I don't really know. I suppose in many ways it doesn't matter, for any system that relies solely on photographic evidence has to accept that it is wide open to the sharks who will take advantage. And yet the organisation that should be as foolproof as is practicably possible, the British Record Fish Committee, does accept photographic evidence!

I'm not particularly cynical by nature, but some of the images I see in some of our publications cause me to smile wryly at the very least, and others to roar with derisive laughter. Not always due to dishonest manipulation but for the claims made for the fish in the photograph. Apart from those sad people who do this to make a profit, and the even more sad people who do it for some kind of recognition, or to help sell a product, I do wonder what kind of life they've led that has brought them to such a low ebb they need to fabricate fish catches, either through direct lying or photo editing. A few anglers are so paranoid about being second best on the waters they fish they'll stoop to any level to appear to be on top.

They're fish for God's sake, and many of the fish we catch most of the time are largely the result of good luck rather than good judgement. The cheats should get a life, grow up and stop being so bloody pathetic.

CENTREPIN REELS – MAINLY FASHION STATEMENTS?

What's so good about centrepin reels? Two things: they're great for controlling a float when trotting and feel pretty good due to the direct control when playing fish up to a certain weight. After that they're neither use nor ornament. Well, ornament maybe, as I guess that's part of their appeal, looking so quaint and antique-like, and giving their owner an air of superiority. Not all centrepin users of course, just the nerds who want one because they're either fashion statements or the only thing that will go with their tweed outfits.

The centrepin reel.

I'm being facetious of course: I own a centrepin myself and enjoy using it – but only when it's appropriate. Appropriate as far as I'm concerned is when fishing a float in a current, and only when I'm chasing fish that don't need a heavier line than 6lb. Centrepins can't hold a candle to fixed spool reels for legering, and especially when free-spooling. And as for playing fish, centrepins are great where you can let the fish run a bit and total control with thumb pressure is not an issue. There are a growing number of anglers who are using 'pins with heavy lines for bigger fish, but no matter how skilful the 'pin angler he can't control the spool of a 'pin with anywhere near the same efficiency as the drag on a decent fixed spool reel when there is a big, fast-running fish on the end.

Casting further than a couple of rod's length with a centrepin requires either a spool that flips round so that the line comes off the rim (known as cheating to dedicated 'pin anglers), or special skills in Wallis casting or similar to get the float out even a reasonable distance. Fine, if you fancy learning special skills.

But why bother? Why not grasp the latest technology of the fixed spool reel (patented in 1905!) rather than struggling with the antiquated 'pin? Using a centrepin is a bit like fly fishing; designed to make it harder to catch the fish and to make it necessary to learn special casting skills so you can show off to your mates if you're good at it.

The fixed-spool reel.

For trotting in a current that's strong enough to revolve the spool the 'pin beats the fixed spool hands down, but for fish up to about 4lb I reckon the closed face reel is better. If some enterprising manufacturer could beat the line digging in problem of the closed face reel then there would be no contest.

If you think I'm writing a load of rubbish then ask yourself this: if the centrepin is so great why don't matchmen use them? You very rarely, if ever, see today's match angler using a 'pin even when trotting a river for roach, dace and small chub, the 'ideal' species for 'pin fishing. Surely the match lads would use them if they offered any advantage, for when it comes to winning trophies and the pools pot match anglers will use the best method there is for putting fish in the net.

Centrepin anglers seem to fit into one of two brackets:

Centrepin reels are seen as fashion statements, the tweed/Barbour – deerstalker/floppy hat brigade's designer reel, to be used at all costs no matter how inefficient for the type of fishing being followed. Or....
Centrepin reels are seen for what they are, an excellent tool for trotting with lines up to about 6lb at distances up to about two rod's length. Anything heavier or for legering they'll use a fixed spool.

I don't have a problem with those anglers who use a 'pin at every turn, providing they enjoy it and they don't tell me it's the best reel to use for just about everything.

INTROSPECTIVE OR INTENSE? WHAT'S YOUR APPROACH?

There was one time I became involved in a particularly interesting and heated discussion between those who fish purely for the love of 'being there', and those whose only motive is to catch fish. Here we were, we gentle brothers of the angle, with each faction saying they couldn't understand what the other faction got out of fishing. Anyhow, here's my slant on the matter.

I think many of us have 'moods' regarding fishing, in that there are some days when we enjoy just being there to smell the flowers and watch the birds as we fish with no real determination to succeed. We want to catch fish; of course we do, but it's no more a priority than observing the nature we're sharing the day with. There are other days when all we want to do is wind down and let the world go by; sitting or lying by the waterside and allowing our eyelids to droop. Some days we'd do it without a rod in sight, but if anyone saw us they'd think we were strange, so we take the tackle to justify being there.

Then there are days when we're hell bent on catching. It's the number one priority, the kingfishers can go and distract someone else, and we don't care if we're smelling a wild honeysuckle or a cowpat. Catching is what counts, nothing else. The whole of our concentration and determination is focused on our target fish and we hardly notice anything else that goes on around us. We get lost in a world of our own where we strive to get into the mind of the fish as we hatch plans that will lead to their downfall.

Most of the time my mood is a changeable mixture of the two, where some days I'll be more inclined towards catching fish, but can still appreciate my surroundings, and other days when I'm more interested in what's going on around me than I am in catching fish. Yet I don't think I ever have a day when I don't want to catch, just that my determination to succeed in catching fish often slips down my scale of priorities. The mood that most often befalls me is when, for instance, I'm wandering the river, intent on catching a barbel or chub, but thoroughly enjoying the feeling of being part of nature, mixing with the vegetation, the birds and animals as I hunt my quarry. A romantic notion sure, but isn't that part of the game we play? And I say 'game' quite deliberately, for my hunt for fish isn't a life or death mission that me and my family depend on for food. Angling is a game, a sport, and we use it to conjure up those deep, ever-receding memories, of the time when hunting meat and fish really was a matter of life or death.

Yet, I have to ask myself, am I part of a minority? Is there only a relatively small core of us who feel so deeply about fishing because we are still in touch with those far off days when we hunted and fished for food? Are my thoughts on this topic lost on most anglers because they don't share my deep feelings for our sport? Maybe the majority of anglers really don't fish according to their mood at the time, but simply go fishing when they feel like it and can spare the time; angling just being another means to while away a few hours. They probably go to the same two or three haunts and fish the same swims with the same old methods every time they go. Perhaps they just look at their surroundings without experiencing any of the deep-seated philosophical emotions that some of us enjoy. Perhaps they don't even bother to fish those places where nature has blessed them with its best. Anyhow, if your mood leads to the relaxed approach, where you have a mind to enjoy nature as you fish, or if it heads you in the direction of all out determination to catch your target fish, it doesn't matter, for both are enjoyable in their own way. What I find most irritating is the attitude of some who have chosen to firmly belong in one camp or the other and who look down their noses at those in the opposite camp.

Why do some people find it so difficult to accept that there is a tremendous amount of enjoyment in both approaches to angling? There is nothing at all wrong in chucking the rod up the bank and making a brew while you take in the scenery and survey the wildlife. And there is nothing at all wrong in fishing with an intensity that, at times, blanks out the brew and wildlife, in order to achieve a result. I reckon an angler who is open-minded enough to partake in, and thoroughly enjoy, both attitudes is a very lucky angler. To enjoy both all you have to remember is that it doesn't have to be one or the other. You can either choose, or go with the mood.

LEARNING HOW TO FISH

There seems to be some pride in uttering the words, "I'm a self-taught angler, never had anyone to show me how to do anything, just picked it all up myself."

I don't know why there seems to be some kind of status in being self-taught, for there is nothing particularly noteworthy about it, it just means it's taken you much, much longer to learn the basics than it would had you had someone to show you the ropes. I'm a self-taught angler but I really wish I'd had a family member who was an angler who could have taken me fishing and showed me what to do. I had no dad to take me fishing, and although my granddad occasionally accompanied me when I went fishing at a very early age he was only there to keep an eye on me as he'd never wet a line in his life. Fortunately then, as now, I've never been backwards at coming forwards and asking other anglers for advice when I've thought they could help.

But I learnt how to fish mainly by reading as much as I could in books and magazines, and then by joining a local club and keeping my eye on other anglers as they fished. And a lot by trial and error, making my own mistakes, practising and gaining experience. What's wrong with that you may well ask. There's nothing at all wrong with that, but it's just so much better if you can cut out all the trial and error and many of the mistakes through being shown the right way in the first place. If it is better to be self-taught then we would have no schools, universities and colleges, and be stumbling blindly along largely ignorant of so many things for far too long.

There's another, more serious, disadvantage to being self-taught too. You pick up bad habits which, at the time, you don't know are bad habits. Basic things like positioning the reel on the rod in the wrong place, poor casting actions, not using the rod correctly to play fish; all kinds of things that become so ingrained in you that it becomes terribly difficult to break the habit in later years and do things the right way.

I've been a fly fisherman for years, with a break for a few years and then coming back to it about 10 years ago. In my first period of fly fishing I learnt how to cast by practising, never having even an informal lesson off a friend. I got by but that was it, I 'managed' at best, but with more 'wind' knots and heaped casts than you could shake a stick at, and if I got 20yds out with the wind behind me it was a good cast. Then when I took it up again more recently and found that my casting was still lagging behind many others, I decided I was going to have one or two casting lessons and find out what I was doing wrong. What annoyed me was that the best casters made it look so easy; a beautiful fluid motion that put the line well out without any effort. I was straining and trying really hard and getting half the distance. When I had casting lessons I soon realised that it was the effort that was largely to blame for my poor casting, and once I'd learnt the right way it became clear that the right casting technique, from rod grip to action, was the answer. I dropped all my bad casting habits and have now reached a stage when I can cast a reasonable distance with a line that lands straight and true.

Coaching is the norm in fly fishing.

The strange thing is, fly casting lessons, and other lessons in fly fishing, have become the norm. They're not only acceptable, it is, to a great extent, expected that a fly fishing beginner will have at least one or two formal lessons from a professional coach. In coarse fishing it is only just becoming an accepted practice, in spite of the fact that we have the Professional Anglers Association (PAA) to promote the coaches and coaching. And a damn good thing it is too, for everyone who has been on a coaching day with an angling guide swear that it was the best thing they ever did to further their angling skills. The best days of course are the one to one days where there is just you and the coach, when he can devote all his attention to you and your particular needs. But of course exclusivity costs more and sharing with a small group, although not quite as good, cuts the costs.

I once ran a teach-in on Method feeder fishing for 16 anglers, with myself and top match angler Stu Dexter providing the informal coaching. It was the first of its kind for me as I think it was for Stu, but the feedback was so positive I have no doubt I'll be running similar teach-ins on other techniques in the future. Apart from the satisfaction of providing free tuition to a number of anglers who were ready and willing to listen, I saw for myself how valuable the day was to those who had read about fishing the method but had obviously not really fully absorbed what they were reading. That is meant as no disrespect to them, but more an observation about how much more valuable it is to see things demonstrated.

Most of the coaching I did that day was to pass on as many tips as I could to as many as I could as I walked the banks, but it was Stu who gave a formal and, I must say, very enlightening and professional demonstration of mixing groundbait for the method. He explained the tackle to use and the importance of accurate casting and then answered questions. I videoed all this and put the video on YouTube which, if you wish, you can watch by going to http://www.youtube.com/user/GrahamMarsden1.

Incidentally, one comment I heard was that there was no way Stu was going to disclose everything he knew about method fishing, that he would keep some kind of 'edge' to use in a match. Which just isn't true; I've fished with Stu often enough, in matches and pleasure fishing, to know how he fishes and what he uses and in that demo of method fishing he held nothing back. He has no need to for he does what he does so well the only person that will beat him on a match day is someone who can fish as well as he can who draws a peg with more fish in it.

Stu Dexter gave a very informative talk on 'mixing bait for, and fishing The Method'.

I also noticed how many had preconceptions of how something should be done. For instance, some were under the impression that you always mixed groundbait by adding water to it gradually until you got the consistency right. Which of course is quite true for many forms of fishing, but not for some groundbaits made for method fishing, particularly those made from crushed pellet. The correct way, as Stu ably demonstrated, is to add, all in one go, the right amount of water, which is approximately 450ml of water to 900g of groundbait, and then mix thoroughly. It looks like a big, sloppy bowl of thick custard for several minutes and then changes to something like a useable mix, but is only perfect when left for an hour or so or, as Stu does, overnight.

Another thing he did, which some had previously thought was unnecessary when they'd read about it, was to sieve the groundbait, pushing all the groundbait through a fine riddle. But this wasn't just to get the lumps out, as some thought, but to get plenty of air in the mix, which is what made it feel just right after it had stood.

There were lots of anglers who went home that day feeling like they'd really learned something practical and useful, something that would put more fish in the net for them. They went home confident and looking forward to trying things for themselves, which some have and have reported back with tales of success. Not only had they seen a practical demonstration of mixing groundbait for the method, they'd seen it in use and catching fish after the demo.

That's the real value of coaching; you see the advice in action, you see fish being caught with the tackle, tactics and bait that have been recommended. Coaching forms a more positive picture in your mind and inspires the confidence you need to put it all into practice. There is just nothing better than seeing the advice demonstrated and unfold before your eyes, and then trying it for yourself under the watchful eye of the coach.

If you can get your coaching for free, then great, but if not then believe me, it is never a waste of time and money. In the long run it will save you plenty of both time and money.

ASHAMED TO TARGET FISH WITH NAMES?

I have some sympathy with those who have issues with coarse anglers who continually set out to catch well known fish that have been given a pet name. The practice is rife in carp fishing and becoming a lot more common with barbel. But I do emphasise 'some' sympathy for, as always, there is a wider view.

Those who object to, or find it repulsive, to continually fish for known and named fish, can only see one side of the coin; that the angler is desecrating a sport that should be about hunting wild, hitherto unseen, creatures in wild habitats.

If only.

Real life for the UK angler isn't like that. For one thing, we have no wild places left. OK, some places, particularly some stretches of river, will be far removed from the local commercial fishery, but even the wildest river stretch will have been fished pretty often over the years. The conception by some that a 'wild', uncaught fish is harder to catch is a false one, for, apart from the starving and desperate for food fish in overstocked commercials, oft-caught fish are well educated fish and not naive like an uncaught one. We continually rearrange tackle and change methods and baits for the benefit of those fish that have seen it all before, not for the fish that has never seen any of it.

So there are no extra bragging rights to catching a previously uncaught fish. Although, listen to some, and you would think there should be extra points for the longest distance walked from the car park, for sitting in the most uncomfortable swim you could imagine, getting wet through and nettled, and generally suffering in your quest for pleasure.

Unlike most of the rest of the world, where coarse fish are concerned, we operate a strict catch and release system. Not only do most clubs and commercial fisheries make it a rule to return every fish caught, it is now ingrained in our psyche that the only right and honourable way to treat the coarse fish we've caught is to return them. This means of course that nigh on every fish we catch will have been caught some time previously. Which leads us to the conclusion that we are all catching fish that we or someone else has caught before and that the point where that becomes 'unacceptable' is a matter of degree.

There will be some who will be denying that they are catching previously caught fish, but most of the time we don't know if we are or not. When we do know we are making repeat captures is when we catch carp with distinctive scale patterns or another species with a recognisable mark, and/or an especially big fish that we've paid particular attention to and probably photographed, and taken time to study yet again.

The river Dove barbel at 16lb 12oz known as 'Split Fin'. No matter how many times it's caught it's still a wonderful fish to catch.

We've probably caught smaller fish a lot more often, but we don't realise that as we don't pay them as much attention.

Bigger fish often appear to be mug fish because they're the ones you hear about, the ones that make the headlines and the ones that get photographed and passed around in the photo album. The smaller, probably even dafter fish, are caught most often but it goes unnoticed as we rarely pay them much attention, let alone photograph them. All fish, bar maybe a very limited number, are caught over and over again on the popular waters and even the majority of those on the less popular waters are caught several times during their lifespan. There's no getting away from it, it's a fact, and if all fish carried an ID number we would probably be very surprised at just how often they are caught.

However, I think it does become tedious when you read about the same angler, or the same group of anglers, catching the same fish over and over again, particular when it's a record or near record and the only variation is a few ounces in weight. It seems almost comical to see Tom one week holding 'Big Bertha' at XXlb 4oz, Dick with it another week at XXlb 6oz (and possibly claiming the record and all the accolades), and Harry a week or two later holding it at XXlb 2oz (and probably expressing regret that Big Bertha had been on a diet). Of course, we're all expected to forget that the weight variations could be a simple case of scale inaccuracy and/or poor weighing technique. But that's by the by. Tell it any way you like, but it's the same fish and the same group of anglers queuing to have their go at catching it at its best weight. Strange isn't it, that we give the most credit to the angler who catches that fish when it weighs a few ounces more than it did when it was caught previously.

That's just how I feel about it though; if someone wants to pursue the same fish over and over again then who am I to say he's wrong for doing so - it's his business, not mine. He isn't doing me any harm and if he didn't catch the fish someone else would, so he isn't doing the fish any harm either by catching it too often.

As for naming fish - so what? If you catch a fish, or see a fish caught that you recognise then it's only human nature to give it a label (we name everything, including hurricanes) so a pet name is as good as anything. The only objection I have to naming fish is that it humanises them and causes the conservation police to go into hyper mode. Or the peTa prats to launch yet another attack on anglers - a la Nemo.

It's simple, if you fish a particular swim on a lake, a particular stretch of river or canal regularly, you are going to get repeat captures, whether you want to or not and whether you like it or not. But unless the fish you catch are distinctively marked or of a particularly notable size, then you won't know it. Those that you do recognise you are going to label, ie, "the one with a split fin," (thereafter known, if only in your own mind, as 'Splitfin').

And there you go, you've named it. And if you continue to visit that bit of water you'll probably catch it all over again. The big question is, does it matter? Only you can answer that.

Chapter 5

My Angle on Angling Part 2

Fishing thoughts from outside the box

SIXTH SENSE - OR COMMON SENSE?

I had my first book published in 1980, 'Advanced Coarse Fishing' (A & C Black) from which I'll quote the following passage:

'There has been a lot of debate over the years as to whether some anglers possess a sixth sense; a kind of extra-sensory perception (ESP) that consistently successful anglers use to full advantage when it comes to choosing a swim. It is supposed that these fortunate anglers can look at a piece of water, which can be devoid of all character, and say exactly where the fish can be found. I do not know if ESP has anything to do with it, but I do know that I sometimes have a very strong urge to fish a certain swim that to all intents and purposes has no special feature that would normally attract me to it.'

Some 32 years on from the time I actually penned those words I believe even more strongly that we do have a built-in perception that provides us with information that we cannot hear, smell, see, feel, or taste, which are the five accepted senses. I'm not talking about spooks and spirits, or any other unworldly visitor that comes in the night with a message that 'under the willow behind the park pavilion is the place to fish tomorrow,' or anything like that. What I'm referring to is something much more fundamental; I'm talking about an ability I believe we have that stems back to prehistoric days when our lives literally depended on our successful hunt for food.

It was an ability, or sense, that warned us of impending danger, or told us that meat or fish were nearby; food that was out of sight, not making a sound, and that we couldn't smell.

I know of other anglers, as well as myself, who have walked around a stillwater, a large, featureless piece of water, that they have never fished, and know next to nothing about, who have said they fancied a certain swim. From there they have, like all thorough anglers, done what they could to gain as much information as possible about the water. Where they could they scanned the water with sonar from a boat, or failing that, plumbed it quite extensively with float and plummet, or a timed leger drop. They have watched the water in the early morning or late evening, hoping to see fish, or signs of fish. And having done all that they have then fished an area where all the evidence has said they should fish. Sometimes they've failed, but most times they've been successful. But sooner or later they've been drawn back to that first swim they said they 'fancied', only to fish it with more success than they've had in any other swim on that water.

It would be easy to claim it was simply a case of the angler fishing with more confidence in the swim he fancied, or that it was no more than coincidence. But I've seen it happen too often for coincidence to be a factor, and the anglers I know who go along with this 'feeling' fish very confidently anyhow.

And does it end there? If there is an iota of truth in what I believe, could it be possible that this sixth sense can detect not only the location of fish, but also if the fish are feeding or not?

There have been too many occasions when I, and other anglers I know, have spotted fish feeding off a certain bank, and yet chosen to fish the opposite bank where there have been no signs of fish, only to record a good catch, while those who fished the bank where the fish could be seen have caught very little. It is difficult to explain why such a decision is made, in the face of overwhelming evidence against it. It isn't a conscious thought that says: 'don't fish here, where the fish are showing. Go to the other bank, you'll do better there.' It's not like that at all, but more like a nagging doubt about the obvious bank, and a strange sensation that seems to draw you towards the bank where there is no tangible evidence of fish. I've resisted this 'magnetic' pull many times, but I've never been happy until I've given in to it and moved, and, it must be said, generally finished up with a fair catch.

Most anglers who fish at night will know only too well those times when they've been sat or lay motionless in their bedchairs, when there have been no signs of fish, and the indicator has stood limp and lifeless, and they've been nodding off, when all of a sudden they've woke up, sat up, fully alert, and expecting - knowing - that something was going to happen. And not being the slightest bit surprised when, maybe a few seconds; maybe a minute or two, later, the bite alarm beeped as line was drawn through it.

Later, perhaps after you landed, weighed and sacked the fish, you sat back and thought about it. What was it that alerted you to that bite? There was no movement to be seen, or sound to be heard, to warn you what was impending. Yet there was no mistaking the feeling. You didn't sit up and lean over the rod, your hand hovering like a hungry kestrel, for no reason at all. You knew - *knew* - that something was going to happen.

It probably happens to night anglers more than anyone else, for at night your sense of sight is diminished, which means you have to rely on your other senses all the more.

I'm convinced that we still have this sixth sense, but so deeply buried, and largely redundant, it is therefore lying useless like an appendix or a tonsil. But unlike the appendix and the tonsil, which are tangible organs, our sixth sense can be invoked - although not consciously - by some of those who still hunt and fish. Not the casual hunter or angler, who does it between watching football or playing golf, but by those who are totally dedicated to their sport; those who love it passionately and have the ability - the perception - to feel what cannot be seen, heard, touched, tasted or smelled.

If this kind of thing has happened to you many times, as it has to me, you no longer question the feeling. You still marvel at it, yes, but you accept it for what it is: a strange phenomenon that you cannot explain, but one that you're very glad to experience.

A FEW THOUGHTS ABOUT NOISE

Some years ago it was unthinkable that a specialist angler should try to catch big fish with float tackle from a boat. Those that thought they knew what big fish are about claimed that such specimens were far too timid to tolerate the presence of a boat, no matter how stealthy and quiet the approach by the angler. And as for float fishing for them, you simply didn't do such a thing. Specimens were caught with leger tackle only, and the approach was invariably at night, from behind a battery of bite alarms lined up on a rod-pod.

To give you an idea how paranoid many specialist anglers are, I can give you a couple of examples that, although a little extreme, were fairly typical of the latter day breed. One angler I knew painted his rods with kaki and green paint. He made an excellent job of camouflaging them. To the point where one morning he couldn't find them when he decided to pack for home. Truly, he had left two rods on rod rests in the rushes (not cast in, mind) while he wandered round to the far bank with a third rod and his other bits and pieces in a bag, to try and stalk a fish he'd seen. When he got back he thought his rods had been stolen, and it took him all of five minutes walking the area where he'd been fishing before he stumbled across them.

These big tench were caught within one rod's length of the boat.

Another angler who used to fish with a good pal of mine many years ago packed up in disgust one night when my pal opened his basket and caused the lid to creak rather loudly. He stormed off in disgust, muttering that all the bream in the mere would now be spooked and it was a waste of time carrying on. The fact that they were legering at 40yds range was neither here nor there. The point was that you just did not make any noise at all when specimen hunting. No way! It is true that noise should be kept to a minimum when fishing for specimens. It is a fact too, that excessive noise does not marry well with fishing of any description, but to take umbrage to that extent because of a creaking basket lid simply means that you're well on your way to becoming a basket case.

Nowadays, a number of my friends and I think nothing of boat fishing for big fish, float fishing for them as close as one rod's length away in darkness, and hardly any greater distance in daylight. When we consider it necessary we will leave a bivvy encampment where the leger rods are set up, to slip out in the boat and float fish the already baited swim. The decision will be made to abandon the legering approach and float fish if we think it is essential to present a bait on the more versatile and sensitive float tackle. Such tactics were unthinkable not too many years ago, and still are with some die-hards of the specialist world. To approach a swim, where the fish are already feeding, with a boat, no matter how quiet and stealthy the approach, is tantamount to angling suicide, so they think.

I'm glad I took the chance a long time ago and decided that the boat and float fishing approach was worth it, for since then I have taken tench to over 9lb, eels to 5lb 10oz, carp to 27lb, and lots of bream well into double figures from a boat. And I can honestly say that the great majority of those fish were caught because of the boat and float, and not in spite of them.

It can be amazing just what fish will tolerate at times, for quite often when you are thinking that an accidental noise (or some other kind of disturbance) you've made has put paid to your fishing for a while they surprise you by continuing to feed as though nothing has happened. Or by ignoring your obvious presence in, or close to, their territory. More than once I've drifted across the surface in a boat right over one or two, or a shoal, of big fish, only for them to completely ignore the boat, and me peering over the edge of it. At most they have casually drifted away, and many times simply carried on doing whatever they were doing at the time. I do believe, though, that on many occasions when this happens it is because the fish are sleeping, or at least their version of sleeping, and really are unaware of our presence.

One time I will never forget was when I had anchored the boat in a swim 40yds from the bank and had thrown in a bucket of groundbait, followed by a scattering of maggot and caster. Before I hauled up the mud weights I lay across the boat and peered into the shadow it cast on the bottom to see if I'd managed a good spread of bait over the swim. I couldn't believe what I was seeing when I spotted this big, black shape obviously hoovering up the caster and maggot. It was a bream of at least 9lb. What made it more incredible was that I hadn't tried to be particularly quiet about anchoring the boat and baiting the swim, for this was 5pm on a sunny day, and at least six hours away from the time you could expect a bite on this notoriously difficult bream water. I still haven't figured that one out, and have never had a bream from that water, before or since that incident, fishing at the time it happened. And that incident really inspired me to try, I can tell you!

I've caught pike and tench actually fishing in the shadow of the boat I've sat in, fishing so close the bait was lowered into the swim from the rod tip. And the number of times fish that have been hooked away from the boat have made a beeline for it happens too often to be coincidence. It is my guess they looked on the boat, or at least the shadow it cast into the water, as some kind of safe refuge, rather than the danger it really represented. It is a well-known fact that divers are rarely feared by fish, obviously because they are accepted as part of their own environment. Perhaps boats are accepted, although to a lesser extent, in a similar manner. These experiences have convinced me that boats are not anywhere near as intimidating to fish as we may imagine. It is what the fish perceive things to be, not what they really are, that matters.

Isn't it true that some species are far more tolerant of disturbance than others? The best example of this is where tench are concerned. Many, many times I have hooked and played a tench that fought so well it almost churned the swim to foam; mud and debris swirling around as a result of the tench boring along the bottom in the swim. Then, a mere minute or two later, as fast as it took to unhook the fish and present a new bait in the swim, another tench is hooked. There is often a good explanation for such behaviour, the most likely being that the disturbance caused by a hooked tench is akin to the turmoil created when they are spawning. But this has happened to me many times when spawning has been long finished, or well before it is due to begin.

No, there is no doubt that tench are not a fearful fish, and they support that view very clearly when they begin to feed in a swim almost immediately following it being terrorised by a big rake dropped in from a boat, or thrown from the bank, and hauled out several times screaming with weed. If there is ever a time I am hovering over my rod like a hawk over a dove it is following my first cast into a raked swim. The tench are drawn to the swim like a magnet, either because of the disturbance, or in spite of it, in their haste to feed on the food the raking dislodges. Splashing can be as much an attraction to fish as a deterrent, so perhaps it is the splashing of the rake going in that causes the tench to home in on the swim immediately the splashing is finished. I reckon tench are like cats, with an insatiable degree of curiosity that often gets them into trouble, the trouble in this instance being a baited hook.

More than once my pals and I have broken a hole in the ice to fish through, and been catching fish within a minute or two of casting in. There is a theory that says it is the higher oxygen content in the area where the hole is that attracts them. But I don't fully subscribe to that theory, although I dare say that is part of it, I think it is the noise and disturbance that arouses their curiosity, to the point where, once they have recovered from the initial shock, they have to come and investigate what it is and then find the bait we've laid for them.

It is well known that barbel can be attracted to the splash of a big swimfeeder crashing through the water's surface. They have become accustomed to the noise and have learned to associate it with a free offering of food. They know that if they lie downstream of the disturbance it will not be too long before a steady stream of tasty titbits comes their way. On heavily fished rivers, where barbel are subjected to a frequent bombardment of feeder-fed food it is not uncommon for them to actually attack the feeder once they are well on feed. Invariably, though, this is only the case on the major rivers, like the Severn, and particularly the middle reaches, that have a large head of hungry barbel almost continually on the look-out for food.

Throwing a 3oz feeder, filled with several ounces of feed, into the upper Severn, or into any small river, is not the thing to do. It is more likely to scare the barbel into the next stretch than it is to attract them to your hookbait.

Continental match anglers have never been afraid to bombard their swims with huge balls of groundbait. We used to think that they caught fish in spite of this gross violation of the surface, but now we have come to realise that the disturbance is part of the attraction. Once the initial shock is over the fish home in on the bait.

Noise and disturbance can also be used to attract pike, or to cause them to waken from a dour mood and change to attack mode. When all conventional tactics have been tried it is often worthwhile taking the boat right into where you expect the pike to be lying and whacking the surface with an oar. Bizarre tactics I know, but many times we have shocked the pike into leaving the confines of a weedbed and into open water, where they have vented their anger onto anything that moved, particularly our lures and/or live and deadbaits. But I must say it again, such tactics are a last resort, the last thing you try, not the first, or even the second.

The spatter of bait landing on the surface can attract fish.

There are many cases where minor moments of noise and disturbance attract fish. The slap of a brace of Chum Mixer landing on the surface from a great height can do the trick when the same bait, cast gently and almost unnoticed, lies ignored by the carp. The same species can also be attracted to the multiple plopping of boilies hitting the surface when the swim is fed from a catapult or throwing stick. Bream often rise to a groundbait feeder that has smacked onto the surface and begun to spray its load of goodies through the water as it sinks. There are many more instances that you can no doubt recall from your own experiences.

It should always be remembered, however, that like all matters to do with fishing, noise and disturbance, and the effect it has on fish, is all relative to the situation at the time. Where a good slapping of the surface one day will make pike come out fighting, another day it could cheese them off to the point where they withdraw even further. A heavy feeder cast into a shoal of barbel that are already well fed may have the effect of scaring them out of the swim altogether, whereas a small bait on a light leger may have tempted one or two.

The answer, of course, is to always try the conventional before delving into the realms of the unconventional. Yes, use noise to your advantage when you think it is what is needed on the day, but do everything you can to make sure it is what is needed before going ahead. And remember that no matter what a good friend noise can be some days, there are many other days, even with the same species on the same water, when it can be your worst enemy.

My policy is, and always has been, to be as quiet as possible when fishing, not simply because it could scare the fish, but because peace and quiet are usually good partners of fishing.

THAT BITCH - THE GODDESS FORTUNE

My dictionary defines luck as: 'The chance happening of fortunate or adverse events.' But it was William Blake (1757 - 1827) an English poet, who described luck better than anyone I know. He said: 'The Goddess Fortune is the devil's servant, ready to kiss or kick anyone's arse.'

An old mate, John Charlesworth, and I certainly experienced our fair share of luck during one period some years ago. Both good and bad. My brush with 'The Goddess Fortune' began one early December when I caught a 29lb pike in Ireland within a couple of hours of packing for home. That fish was a personal best, won me £25 and, best of all, made Terry Knight choke on humble pie. It was January before the next spell of luck chanced upon us, but this time it was the kind you can do without.

The bad luck began with a tale we had heard on the infamous grapevine that a 24lb pike had been caught from one of our favourite stretches of the upper Severn.

The story had it that there was a lot of pike activity along there, to the extent where anglers fishing for roach and chub were packing up in disgust due to being seen off too often. Still, while the pike are the cloud over the chub and roach anglers, they are the silver lining to the pikers. And what made the prospect better is that we hadn't been out for a while, what with Christmas and bad weather, so we were raring to go, all keyed up and ready to jump five-barred gates. So we arranged to meet Terry and a pal of his half-way there.

John and I took it in turns with our vehicles, travelling in my camper van one trip and then in John's car the next. This time it was John's turn, and he picked me up at 6.30am on a cold and frosty morning. It was the steady procession of overnight frosts that were keeping plenty of snow on the fields and minor roads. Luckily (there goes that word again) the main roads had been gritted and were clear. It had been snowing on and off for weeks, and freezing frequently enough to keep the snow around for longer than usual, so what snow remained was as hard as a rock. Some of the side roads where the gritting wagon hadn't been were like skating rinks, the snow being continually compacted and frozen.

It was one of those side roads, a short cut a little before our journey's half-way mark, that John turned into, probably on automatic pilot because we make the journey so often. It is only a gentle curve, and our speed was subdued, but the road was like glass. We slid off it like a manic bob-sleigh, took a couple of fence posts with us, and finished up in a hedge. I saw it all happening as though in slow-motion, the fence posts coming at us, the hedge looming nearer. And then the muffled crunch. Everywhere was quiet except for John's cursing and the tick of the engine as the metal contracted. No physical pain though, we weren't hurt, that was the main thing. Shook up yes, but we got over that pretty quickly. Worse though, the car was stuck solid, and a day's fishing was in jeopardy.

Steam clouded up from the heat of the Sierra's skidding wheels as John tried to reverse out, but we both knew it was futile. So we set to with a broken fence post apiece, digging away at the frozen turf behind the wheels. But the problem was that the back end of the car was perched on a mound that had to be dug away. John borrowed a spade from a farm up the road and ten minutes later the car was back on the road. Yes! A day's fishing loomed on the horizon again. The car was an insurance job with broken lights and gouges across the wings and bonnet from barbed wire but - we could go fishing! Or so we thought, until we spotted the steam coming from under the bonnet and found the radiator was caved in and burst at the bottom. We went home on the back of a breakdown truck.

The next weekend we decided to fish another stretch of the upper Severn for chub, but changed our minds at the last minute and elected instead to fish a lower stretch where the water was a little deeper. We thought the deeper water would be favourable considering the severity of the conditions. The stretch held a few decent pike we could have a go for too. Another pal of ours, however, Eric Barnes, decided to fish our first choice with an elderly friend who had been fishing the Severn two or three times every week for over 50 years.

John and I fished hard but didn't have a run from the pike nor a bite off the chub. Two match anglers, without a contest to fish, stood in the river 200yds away and they too fished hard for no returns. John and I were having a rough time, but at least we were not suffering on our own. Or so I thought, right up until Eric phoned the following day and told me they'd had four or five big chub apiece, and that one of the chub was a personal best for his elderly friend who in his time has caught scores of 5lb-plus chub from the upper Severn. How big - only 6lb 2oz! A big fish for anywhere, but a massive fish for the upper Severn. A personal best after trying to catch one for over 50 years. Pleased as I was that such a fish had been caught from one of the stretches we fished I couldn't but wonder if John and I had unwittingly killed a robin.

Two days later we planned to fish the upper Severn again, three miles higher than where the 6-pounder had been caught. That piece of river could wait until the fish had settled again. Two days after so many of them had been caught is too early. That catch of big chub, and especially the 6-pounder, had fired us up though, and we looked forward to the trip like kids on Christmas eve. The night before, as I emptied the dishwasher, I stabbed my hand with a pointed knife. It went into the ball of my thumb about half an inch and hurt like hell. It wasn't my right hand, my rod hand, but it was going to cause me some problems all the same. My wife Anne, who worked in a care home at the time, is a dab hand at tending the elderly and infirm (she has to be, she's married to me) dressed and bound the wound sufficiently to enable me to go fishing still.

The next day, the fishing day, my hand was a little better, and I picked up John in my van. John told me he was having trouble with his insurance company. Apparently they were dragging their feet sending him a claims form. So on the way to the river we passed the time by moaning about our bad luck, and John said at the rate he was going he would never catch a 5lb chub. I hadn't realised it but his biggest chub to date at the time weighed only a little over 4lb. That wasn't a bad fish considering it came from Cheshire's river Dane, but nothing to shout home about from the Severn. But you had to take into account that John had only been fishing the Severn for a few years, while I, who had been fishing it for over 30 years, had caught a number of chub over 5lb, but never a 'six'. So I said to John. "You'll get a 'five' today, you'll see. We're due for a spell of good luck for a change."

Although there was still plenty of rock-hard snow around it was a little better on the roads. Nevertheless, I drove carefully and we arrived safely at our destination. We were travelling light, just one rod apiece. I had my rod, landing net pole and a couple of banksticks in my quiver holdall, while John had bundled his together with elastic bands. "Put your bundle in my holdall and you carry it to the water and I'll carry it back." I suggested. Which was exactly what we did. Trouble was, after a quarter mile hike over the hard slippery snow, we got to a slope that runs down to the river. No, neither of us slip and slide into the river. Nothing that bad. What did happen was that John slipped and fell on the rods, breaking both of them clean in two just above the butt.

The worst part was the deadly silence right after it happened, when we sat there on the hard snow, each with a broken rod butt in our hands, and just said nothing. Then the spell was broken and we turned the cold air blue with some heavy cursing. Two broken rods and another day's fishing sacrificed to The Goddess of Fortune. What a bitch! I tried to bring a little humour into the situation by saying, "It could have been worse, we could have been carrying a spare rod apiece, and how our luck is at the moment all four would have been broken."

My rod had suffered a clean break, snapped fully in two about a foot from the cork handle. John's was slightly better in that it was shattered but was still joined at the break, though just as useless. As the agonising gloom began to lift from us and clear thought slowly crept back I began to wonder how we could salvage the day's fishing. Could we do a temporary repair to the rods? John had some insulation tape in his ruckbag so that was a start. I searched my holdall for a bankstick that would slide inside the broken ends of my rod, but the outer tube of my banksticks were too big in diameter, and I had nothing to cut off the threaded ends of the sliding inners. There was only one thing I could try, and that was to cut a thin branch from a tree, spigot the broken rod with that, and hope for the best. Either that or go home, and I was too desperate to fish not to try something - anything in fact. So that is what I did, and John 'repaired' his rod by taping a wooden splint up each side of the break in his rod.

One of the 'repaired' rods.

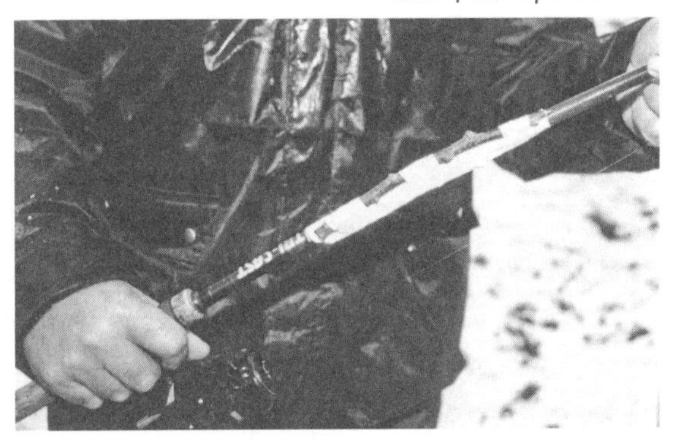

They were the most useless repairs you've ever seen. There was no way they were going to hold a decent chub, especially one that is diving for a snag. So that ruled out quite a number of swims to begin with. The only way we would be able to cope with a good chub was to use our reel hand to support the rod above the break. If we could do that when a chub was still lively, and then hold the rod above the break with our rod hand when line needed to be recovered, we could maybe, just maybe, get away with it.

It wasn't much of a plan, but it was the best we could come up with. We were not going home just yet!

Have you ever cast a light leger tackle with a piece of stiffish rope? Well, that's what it felt like. I fished the straight, 250yds below the bend where John had set up, and made my first cast. It landed within a yard of where it should, but more by luck than judgement. The rod felt terrible, and as I placed it in the rest to treat myself to a nice brew while I relaxed and wound down I couldn't believe it when the tip kicked. I had enough presence of mind to grab the rod above the break and, following a pretty dogged fight (why is it that chub fight when you don't want them to, and give up when it doesn't matter?) got the fish close enough to net. A good fish too, certainly over 5lb. But what happened? That Goddess Fortune took charge again. My landing net was frozen to the snow and I can't pull it free because of the pain in my stabbed hand. And as I transferred the rod from my good hand to my bad hand, so I could free the landing net with my good hand, the fish slipped the hook. I was not pleased.

There was only one thing I could do and that was to fish closer to John. That way we could net each other's fish. Assuming we got the chance and the rods stood up to it. I got my tackle together again and was half way along the high bank when John yelled, "Got one, and it's a big ****er!" By the time I got to him the fish lay in the landing net at the edge of the water. He had unhooked it and was rummaging in his ruckbag for a weigh-sling. I couldn't see the fish for there was a fold of net over it to prevent it from escaping. To put it mildly, John was excited. "It's over five," he said. "I've got my five. I thought it was a small common carp when it surfaced!"

John's 'magic' six-pounder, 6lb 4oz.

I got the weigh-sling ready and zeroed the scales. He fetched the fish and when I got my first look at it I just gaped. It was massive. It was the biggest chub I'd ever seen. At that time, in more than 30 years of fishing the upper Severn, it was the first six-pounder I've laid eyes on, as surely it was a magic 'six'. I'd had them to 5.14 from the upper but this one was definitely bigger. My hands trembled as I held up the scales and it seemed an age before I could hold them steady enough to record an exact weight of 6lb 4oz. The only way I could have been more pleased was if I had caught the fish myself.

He'd done it again. And by that I mean John had pushed a mediocre personal best fish to a breathtaking PB. The first time he did it with pike. His best fish was 17lb, then he caught a '32', skipping the 'twenties'. Now it was chub, his best fish a little over 4lb, now a 6.4, skipping the 'fives'. And what was I saying about chub fighting? This one had come in like a lamb, as though respecting he had a wounded rod. The Goddess had kissed arse this time, rather than kicked.

We had a brew and calmed down, then cast in again, me in the neighbouring swim 25yds away. I got a bite almost immediately following the cast. It was a good fish and headed straight for the tree roots to the side of the swim. I fumbled the rod and held it in the wrong place. The stick spigot snapped and the curved rod became a one-piece rod with a hinge in the middle. I lost the fish, another good chub, but how good I shall never know. I retrieved the tackle, hook and all, and poured another brew. My thoughts were scrambled; elated with the capture of the six-pounder, but despondent that I could no longer fish.

John said, "Let's go home." And walked towards his rod. As he reached for it, it arched over, and before he could think what he was doing he struck, as you normally would, from the butt. Another rod bit the dust, the fish slipped the hook. And we went home.

Do you think the story ended there? No way. A week later we fished a different stretch. A stretch we had never fished before. I had a 5.8 and John had a 6.3.

That's luck for you. The two extremes. I can't complain, for I've had my fair share of good luck over the years. Actually, I'm not a big believer in fortune, for I think that to a great extent we make our own luck and get what we deserve in the end.

WE KNOW NOWT!

Three basic things in the coarse fishing world have changed that clearly demonstrate that when it comes to understanding fish we know next to nothing. Either that, or we're experts at kidding ourselves that we do know something, and then think that we can 'prove' it by catching fish, which may or may not have anything to do with it. Of course, there are many more things that have changed in fishing, but the three I'm going to write about illustrate my point exceptionally well.

Resistance in Rigs

Take a simple leger rig, for instance, and go back a number of years, to the days when we used bite indicators as simple as a fold of flake on a loop of line between butt ring and reel and to freeline, when you could manage without any weight at all, was the ultimate presentation. Otherwise it was a time when you used a lead that was just, and only just, heavy enough to reach the swim. Everyone always struggled for maximum sensitivity, to the point where it was against your instincts and frustrating having to fish with a heavier lead in order to cast to a distant swim in windy conditions, and the butt indicator (of whatever type) was constantly crawling to the butt ring as a result of undertow. So reluctant were we to increase the weight of the lead or the indicator we drove ourselves mad trying to decide what was a bite and what was a pull from wind or water. We had become completely convinced that the lightest and most sensitive presentation was always best.

Then it swung the other way, with most anglers, particularly specialist anglers, using a form of heavy resistance rig for most of their fishing, including fishing for the smaller and weaker species like roach and bream. It was the birth of the bolt-rig. Swinging took on a new meaning as we swung from resistance-free rigs to resistance creating rigs. And now there is a trend to running rigs in carp fishing rather than bolt rigs, and the heavy indicators are giving way to light ones. Exponents of the running rig and light indicator are swearing that their method is best.

A modern bolt-rig that offers resistance.

A long time ago, long before the days of bolt-rigs, I remember experimenting with heavier indicators - stiff rubber connectors on swingtips, etc - when it began to dawn on us that resistance rather than sensitivity was often the best option. Many times such realisations come about almost entirely by accident. Bream anglers who night fished and fell asleep, with the result that they were late getting to the rod to strike at a bite, so late the reel handle was revolving backwards by the time they got to it, realised that they were hooking a far greater percentage of bites than when they were quick off the mark. This was in the days before Baitrunner reels. It eventually became standard practice to wait for the reel to backwind before striking, with the angler sitting on his hands to help him resist striking too soon! What we didn't know at the time was that experienced big bream anglers up and down the country were all discovering this at around the same time.

Bait Colours

Just what colours can a fish actually see? Well, without getting too deep into that particular topic, if you accept scientific findings, fish do see colours, but not in the same way that we do. Nevertheless, whatever you believe, anglers have always experimented with bait colours, some swearing by one colour and others in different ones.

Not too long ago we had a preponderance of bright red, yellow and orange boilies. Sweetcorn caught (and still catches) a lot of fish, which we know is bright yellow. Red and bronze maggots were the only ones worth buying, etc, etc. Then the next thing I heard was that someone had decided that the reason he wasn't catching as many fish (barbel in this instance) was due to the bright yellow corn he'd been using had blown and the barbel were spooking away from it. So he'd dyed some black and that had revived his catches. Black corn and bright red corn is now commercially available.

Carp anglers reverted to dull brown and, in some cases, black boilies for the same reasons. Bright colours were spooking the carp and it was better to use boilies that matched the colour of the bottom, so we were told. Now what do I hear, that some of the best known carp anglers are using fluorescent boilies; day-glo bright pink, yellow, red, orange and even white.

Bait Flavours

Some very successful carp anglers tell us that most of us over-flavour baits, to the point where we're making them a deterrent rather than an attraction. That we should at least stick to the recommended dosage when making boilies. Other, equally successful anglers, actually recommend over-flavouring baits, especially single hookbaits, to make them more attractive. Some say the hookbait is better soaked in a dip so that the flavour is even stronger.

I could quote many more instances where one school of successful anglers actually contradicts another school of successful anglers. Each of them are quite rigid in their opinions, swearing that what they believe is responsible for their success.

To flavour or not to flavour?

So who is right about all this? Is it better to offer resistance in a rig, or better to avoid it? Are fish spooked or attracted by bright colours? Are strong flavours or weak flavours best? Now don't tell me the answer is according to the water, the conditions and what the fish are used to – this diverse approach to fishing happens on the same lake at the same time, with fish being caught all round!

It must be absolutely mind-boggling to anyone who is just beginning in this great sport of ours, keenly reading such contradictory opinion from equally successful anglers. Especially if they get hold of some of the stuff written years ago by anglers who were successful in their own era (and perhaps successful even today if they're still fishing). Some of the old stuff is so at odds with modern views it makes you wonder how they ever caught anything.

But doesn't it all come down to the fact that when it comes to fish we know nowt! We think we do, and we go out and catch fish and say to the world, "look, this is how you do it. I use this rig, and that bait, and this colour, and that flavour, and I bag up regularly by doing that." And then someone else goes fishing and does just the opposite, in every department, and catches just as well.

Who really knows best? Us, or the fish?

OUR FRED

I miss my old mate Fred Tunnicliffe. He was one of the nicest men you could wish to meet. Not 'nice' in that he was a goody two-shoes who never did anything wrong; oh no, our Fred had a devilish streak in him all right, no two ways about that. But he was without doubt your genuine nice bloke who had few harsh words for anyone, even for those who had treated him like dirt. 'Was' is the word that hurts, for Fred died of a heart attack 20-odd years ago at the youngish age of 58. Yes, he really was a nice bloke and one of life's great characters.

Fred was famous amongst his friends for having absolutely no sense of smell and one day we'd made the long journey to fish the famous weirpool at Throop on the Dorset Stour. Fred had a great liking for belly pork steaks and

Our Fred, one of a kind.

that's what he was frying on the camping stove on the banks of the river on that sunny summer morning. I'd just returned from a visit to a bush toilet and was tackling up a few yards away, and normally my nose would be twitching as it savoured the mouth-watering aroma of frying food in the fresh air. But not that day, my nose was twitching with the smell of something else entirely; dead body, the unmistakeable aroma of fetid meat. Fred had put one of his belly pork steaks between two thick slices of bread and was just about to chomp down on it when I shouted, "Fred! Hang on!"

The doorstep stopped an inch from his mouth, "What's up kid?" He asked, a puzzled look on his face. I was always 'kid' or Gra'.

I picked up the remaining uncooked slices of belly pork that were destined to end up in my belly and grimaced with the stench that was coming off them. They were covered with fly blows and I don't know how Fred had missed that when he unwrapped them.

He looked up at me, with that familiar expression of innocence on his face, and said, "It'll be all right when it's fried well done, crispy, won't it Gra'? I'm fair clemmed (hungry)."

Fred was married to a wife he thought the world of, but he was a real ladies' man. With his swarthy Italian looks and thick, black wavy hair, and all the smooth charm to go with it, he had every woman he spoke to looking at him with unbridled longing. Living not far from the theatre in Stoke he'd bedded a bevy of showgirls, including, he said, Yana, a famous ballad singer from the 1950's. He had two regular mistresses and kept as many other casual girlfriends happy along the way. The campervan he invariably used for fishing was also his passion wagon.

Most of our clan who fished the meres for big bream had our moments with the ladies and on one occasion when I was making some good progress with one of the local village girls, right on the point of making a date with her, Fred whispered to me, "Don't go there kid, she's pregnant." This was in the days when if you got a girl pregnant you were expected to marry her.

Later, when the girl had rode off on her bike, I said to Fred, "How do you know she was pregnant....you haven't....?"

"No, no, kid, she's too young for me." And she was, she was only a teenager and Fred always preferred women at least his own age, and usually a little older. I knew it couldn't have been Fred anyway, as the girl had only that week returned from staying with relatives somewhere down south. "So how do you know then?" I persisted.

"I had a good look at her hands on the handlebars of her bike. I can always tell by their hands. Don't ask me how I can tell 'cos I don't know, but I can. She's only just pregnant and she might not even know herself."

Just over eight months later the girl gave birth, named one of the locals as the father, and had the baby adopted, which was another thing that was fairly common then.

He could charm the animals and birds too, often sitting there with some bread or maggots, feeding field mice and birds that would come much closer to him than anyone else, regardless of what food they offered. But there was one animal who spurned Fred while me, Eddie Bibby and the late Roger Harker, looked on. He was a stallion he'd christened Gyp (short for Gypsy we guessed) who lived in the meadow that rolled down to the mere. Fred boasted to us that the horse had become his great friend. "He loves me that horse does," he said to us as we trudged along the lane to the stile that gave us access to the meadow that led to the mere. "I've always got a few sugar cubes in my pocket for him, and as soon as I get over that stile and he spots me he'll be over for a stroke of his muzzle and a few sugar lumps. You watch this." He said, with a smug grin.

We got to the stile and Fred said, "Let me go first, you lot might frighten him off. He'll come straight to me."

Fred clambered over the stile and we passed his gear over to him. Gyp was grazing over to the left, about 80yds away. Loaded up again, Fred slowly strolled along, looking over at Gyp, who raised his head and looked back but didn't budge.

"Gyp." Fred called. "Gyp!"

Another few yards. "Gyp........ Gyp!" Louder this time. But Gyp stayed put.

"Gyp! Gyyyyyyyyyyyyyp!" A few seconds passed.

"GYYYYYYYYYYYYYYYYYYYYYYYYYYYYYYP!"

Gyp dipped his head again, turned his back on Fred and chewed more grass. That was bad enough, but to make matters worse (for Fred anyway, for we were doubled up with painful giggling) Gyp's tail lifted and he propelled a loud fart, followed by a heap of manure.

Fred turned to us, a pained and embarrassed expression on his face, and said, very solemnly, "did I tell you he's almost deaf. He can't hear me."

"Yer didn't tell us he was blind as well Fred," somebody remarked.

Gyp, by the way, was responsible for coining a phrase that Eddie and I still use to this day. You see, Gyp was well hung and very often displayed his huge schlong, so anyone or anything that was well hung was forever after that described as being 'Gyp-rigged'.

At the bottom of that meadow, not far from the water's edge, was a huge oak tree. After we'd tackled up and before we nipped off to the local for a couple of pints before dusk, we used to sit under the tree and swap yarns. Or rather, we sat and listened to Fred tell us about his adventures. Fred had christened the big oak tree, 'The Singing Tree', for when you sat quietly with your head resting against the trunk you could hear all sorts of whirring and buzzing noises. We knew those noises were caused by the various beetles that lived in the bark, but that was too simple for Fred, "It sounds just like somebody's singing from deep inside the trunk," he used to say, "I wonder if somebody's trapped in there and singing to pass the time?" In a strange kind of way I think he meant it.

Fred was forever concocting strange baits, and every single one was heralded with the words, "this is the one kid, totally irresistible." He believed it too. He caught most of his fish off the back of the massive confidence boost his latest 'irresistible' bait gave him. One bait he came up with for bream was sultanas soaked in a flask of hot water. Of course, sultanas being dried grapes, they swelled back up to grape size. He fished with those for two or three sessions, and caught a couple of big bream on them before moving on to his next 'irresistible' concoction.

Boilies hadn't been invented at the time we were carp fishing with Fred, but it was in that era when pastes made from cat meat, etc, were in vogue. One bait he 'invented' later became a well-known and very successful carp catcher. It was cat meat flavoured with a generous dollop of curry powder or Tikka Masala, and spices of that nature. We were catching well on Fred's curry powder recipes long before the flavouring caught on with the rest of the carp world.

Another time we were fishing the river Vyrnwy in Wales. It was winter, with two or three inches of snow on the ground and the river was swollen a little with snow melt. Today I wouldn't have bothered fishing, but then I'd fish anywhere, anytime, just to be fishing. Fred was sat on his basket, on a little promontory that jutted into the river. It didn't look safe and I remember saying to him, "that nib's nearly ready to break off Fred, come back from the edge a bit."

I was fishing about 30yds downstream and twenty minutes later Fred goes sailing slowly past on the nib, still sat on his basket, rod in hand. Luckily there was shallow water just below where we fished so he wasn't in any great danger. "Hey up kid," he said, deadpan, "catch these bacon butties before they get wet." And tossed me his pack of sandwiches. Never mind the rod and the basket that held his other gear, saving the sarnies was his priority.

There was a small mere of two or three acres close to one of those we fished regularly, and no one bothered with it as it was claimed it was bereft of fish. Which was probably quite true as some of the local sewage trickled into it (something that wouldn't be allowed to go on today) and none of us had ever seen so much as a dimple on the surface to suggest anything but bugs were alive in it. But Fred insisted that he'd seen a monster bream rolling out in the middle. Monster bream that rolled in the middle were something that Fred saw on every mere he fished. We could be sat with him, all looking across the water and Fred would spot a monster bream that no one else saw. He had a favourite monster in one mere that he christened 'Greyback'.

Anyhow, he insisted he'd seen this monster bream in the little mere, and even when a local told him the mere was more silt than water he'd made his mind up he was going to fish it. So one evening I stood on the banks while he rowed out a little boat and spread some groundbait over the spot where he'd seen the monster. Back at the bank, almost, he threw the boat's rope to me but had forgotten to tie the other end to the boat. Before I could stop him he had slipped out of the boat (in waders), sunk down rapidly about 2ft and then slowly continued to sink right up to his armpits. He hung onto the side of the boat, which was the only thing that stopped him from disappearing. Huge clouds of thick black oily silt boiled at the surface and the stench was overpowering.

I threw the rope to him and somehow managed to pull him out. He was covered with that black silt and stinking like a heap of dead and decaying bodies. He lay there on his back, still on the verge of losing consciousness from the lake bed gas. He fumbled in his pocket and said, "gis a fag kid, mine are wet."

Back at the campervan he stripped his clothes off and threw them in a bag, draped a small towel over his nether regions and drove home, which was some 20-odd miles away, changed clothes, and returned for the night to fish his baited spot. Only to blank, as we all, except Fred, expected.

"Never had a bite kid, but saw that big bream roll again as it broke light."

That was Fred, there will never be another one like him.

Chapter 6

Barbel

Want a bend in your rod? Then barbel fit the bill

BARBEL FROM BIG RIVERS

The title begs the question, 'what is a big river?' Well, I think a big river is one where you can't see the bottom on the far bank, no matter how clear the water is.

But a big river can mean different things to different anglers, so let's say that the big rivers I'm writing about are the bigger spate rivers that turn chocolate brown at times of floodwater.

Many big rivers are obvious, such as the Severn, Trent, Wye and Ribble. Lesser rivers, but not exactly small, are the Dove, Dane and Teme. There are others, of course, and far too numerous to mention. This year I've been having a good run on a few of them, catching smaller ones and some big ones to well in double figures, with several 8's and 9's for good measure. So how do we tackle big rivers to catch barbel? What do we look for when choosing a swim? What methods and baits are best? Well, this is how I approach big rivers, and it works for me.

Fish-spotting is not easy on big spate rivers. Even in clear water conditions the water is never anywhere near as clear as it is on the chalk streams. So what we have to do on spate rivers is read the water's surface.

Barbel will visit all types of swims, from fast rapids to slow, almost still pools. In fact, they will seek food anywhere they think they can find it when it suits them to do so. Never rule out anywhere is the answer then, but it is wise to start with the most likely swims in a given set of conditions, working your way down to the least likely. A rule of thumb is to choose fast, oxygenated water in early season when the conditions are warm and there has been little rain for several weeks. Fast water will most often be shallow, which means it will also be weedy, and that too is a good place to fish for barbel. In near-bank swims you can try to spot the fish, which is a lot easier if you have a decent pair of polarised glasses, and I mean a decent pair. There is a lot of rubbish around; cheap, coated lenses instead of the proper job where the polarising is built into the lens itself. I have a pair of polarising glasses made to my prescription. They're not cheap, but if you want the best then you have to pay for it.

In large rivers, though, as I said earlier, it is usually a case of reading the surface water, and finding the weed in shallow water, and laying traps with bait. Let me describe what my ideal barbel swim looks like, bearing in mind that it is not necessarily the best swim to catch big barbel, but probably the best swim to catch a lot of barbel, which may or may not have one or two big barbel amongst them.

I look for a steady flow of fairly deep water, say 4ft to 8ft deep, that breaks up quite quickly as it hits a rapid rise in the river bed. If there are weedbeds with channels 3ft or more wide between them then so much the better. And if this feature happens to be on a bend as well, forming a pool of fairly slack water, then that is the cream on the cake. The exact spot to fish, or it usually is but, don't forget, there is always room to experiment, is just before the water breaks up, along the crease that will be formed between the flow and the pool. If there is no pool then fish in the clear channels between the weed, again just before the water breaks up.

Any swim with a steady flow, weedy or otherwise, providing you can get a bait on the bottom, will produce barbel. Where the surface water is part smooth and steady, but with faster water forming a crease, it is usually the crease where the hot-spot lies.

Big barbel like slacker water, apart from that short spell following spawning, before they leave the shallows. Perhaps this is because they grow lazier as they grow bigger. Or maybe they have been lazy all their lives and are big because they chose to live most of their lives in slacker water and have never had to expend the same amount of energy as their smaller cousins. Everywhere I've caught big barbel, and by big I mean big according to the average size of barbel found in a particular river, which could be 7lb in one river and 10lb and more on another, they have consistently come from slower, steadier water, and usually water with a little more depth than average in that particular stretch. The downside is that they are usually the most difficult barbel to catch, not simply because of their size, but because there are fewer of them. You have to wait longer for bites, but when you do get a bite chances are it will be from one of the biggest fish in that stretch.

All barbel love snags in any shape or form, but particularly fallen trees and branches and tree roots where the bank has been eroded from them. Don't fish such areas unless you are prepared to use tackle that can pull them out.

And that applies no matter if you are targeting big barbel or small barbel – they can all fight hard enough to make short work of flimsy tackle. Small barbel make up in speed and aggression for what they lack in weight.

My usual barbel rod is 12ft with a 1.75lb test curve and in these days of low diameter, braided and pre-stretched mono lines, I can't see the point in fishing anything less than 10lb line on the reel when barbel fishing, even for the smaller barbel of some rivers. And 10lb reel line to an 8lb hooklength is as light as you need to go for most barbel in open water, with a step-up of at least 2lb on both reel line and hooklength for snaggy swims. The main line can be a braid if preferred, with either a braid or mono hooklength.

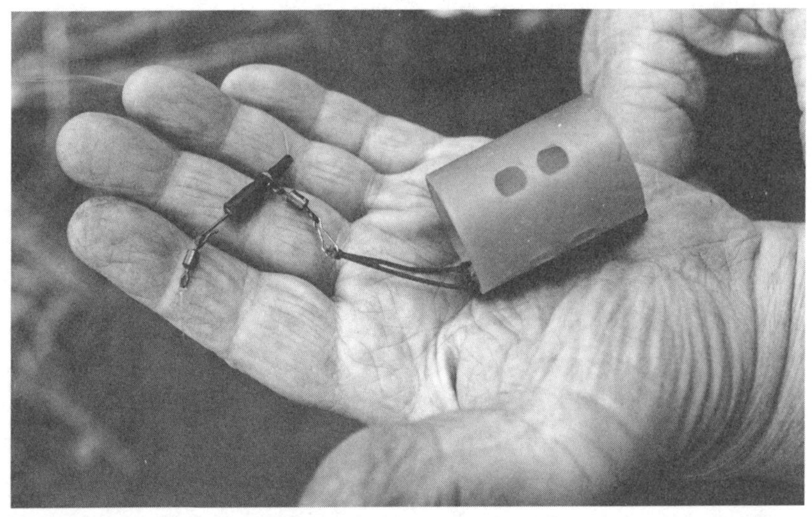

My standard barbel rig for swimfeeder and bomb fishing.

My standard rig for both swimfeeder and bomb fishing is the one that uses a running ring swivel stopped by a swivel with a tapered sleeve jammed onto it, and is perfectly suitable for big rivers.

In the early season, especially when the water is running clear, there is little to beat the hemp and caster combination, fished with a suitable block-end feeder.

Of course, baits like sweetcorn and luncheon meat will catch too, but there is little, if anything, to beat hemp and caster for working up a shoal of barbel into a feeding frenzy on a big river where the fish could be shoaled some way downstream of your fishing position.

In darkness, or when the river is carrying colour, large, smelly baits come into their own. Flavoured luncheon meat, Peperami sausage, boilies, pellets, meatballs and other meaty products all have their day. Large lobworms and small redworms are always worth a try in coloured water too. Plain luncheon meat is still a good bait but I think it has an edge in these days of heavy pressure on some barbel swims with the addition of some strong flavour. Canned meatballs, fished on a hair-rigged bait band, offer a good alternative. I've had great success flavouring them with various powders, such as tikka and garam masala, from the local supermarket.

My approach is to arrive at the river in mid to late afternoon and fish into darkness for an hour or two, how long depending on how well the fish are feeding. I begin the session with a feeder, using hemp and caster in the feeder and caster on the hook, usually beginning with three casters on a 14's Drennan Super-spade. But before that I give the swim a good feed with a couple of pints of hemp and about a half pint of casters. In near-bank swims this lot goes in with a bait-dropper, But in more distant swims I use a small spod, in my case the Gardner Pocket Rocket. I haven't seen many anglers using one on the river before, but believe me a spod beats a catapult hands down. For one thing a catapult has a restricted range, but even at shorter ranges there is too much spread from a catapult. With a spod you can keep the feed in a nice tight path down the river. In the first instance I was wary of the splash and disturbance the spod caused, but on too many occasions I've had a barbel within five minutes of casting in again. Following the initial heavy feed the bait path is maintained with regular casting with the swimfeeder. Although an occasional top-up with the spod is advisable if you drop on a big shoal of barbel that need lots of feeding.

The Gardner Pocket Rocket for feeding river swims.

It's best to take a spare rod for the spod, and then it's always ready for use. The procedure is to cast to the swim with an empty spod and then clip up the line. After that it's easy to cast to exactly the same spot every time. You overcast, not too hard, wait for the pull on the rod and then ease the spod down. It takes a bit of practice but it stops that sudden braking of the spod that causes the bait to spray in a wide area. When the spod drops in, turns over due to the buoyancy built into the nose, and deposits its load, give it a couple of flicks to make sure it empties and repeat until you've fed what you've judged is the right amount to begin with.

Then I settle in to fish the feeder, casting regularly to keep a trickle of feed going through the swim at all times and being prepared to change to a strong, heavy gauge, 16's hook (in open water) if the barbel become finicky. When barbel are being suspicious when feeder fishing with caster and maggot it takes the form of them snatching at the bait, and very often ripping it off the hook without getting hooked. I'm convinced that barbel are rarely line-shy when legering (a different story when float fishing) and changing to a finer line makes little or no difference. Swapping to a smaller hook most certainly does make a difference, however, and those snatchy bites when the bait goes missing become hooked fish again.

When the sun drops and dusk is looming it's time to change to a big, smelly bait on a bigger hook, preferably banded or hair-rigged. Keep the feeder on and continue to feed the swim with hemp and caster as long as you have bait left. When the hemp and caster runs out then change to a bomb and continue to fish the baited path with the big bait. Barbel will still be rooting along the path for some time, clearing up the hemp and caster, but will be especially partial to that big bait when they home in on it. That big bait will also give you the best chance of picking up a big fish from that swim too.

One of the best aspects of bigger rivers is that they normally (but not necessarily) hold more fish than smaller rivers. Think on this too, when you narrow a big river down to a hot swim that big river disappears, and all you have to do then to catch lots of them is to corral enough of them into one area with judicious feeding and then sort 'em out! Simple, eh?

FLOAT FISHING FOR EARLY SEASON BARBEL

There are some anglers who don't fish for barbel until the new season has been under way for several weeks. Indeed, some don't even bother until autumn, thinking that barbel are not at their best until then. I think much of that opinion, however, is not based on how fit the barbel actually are, but more if they're going to be at their best weight. The heaviest weight a barbel can reach is not necessarily an indication of its condition, but more of an indication of its attraction for those who put the weight of fish at the top of their list of essentials.

It's a different matter if the barbel are not back to their best condition following spawning, but them being a little on the thin side is not a bad thing, but simply a quite natural result of that activity. As soon as they're fully fit, thin or not, that's when they can offer some great sport and, as it happens, when they need our baits the most to help them put the ounces back on. So do yourself a favour, and the fish as well, and get that barbel gear along the riverbank just as soon as the season opens.

Low and Clear Water

There's a reasonable chance (and that's as much as you can say with our climate) that the weather will be warm and dry in mid-June when the season opens, which means the rivers will be low and clear. And that in turn means that stalking fish will be much easier for we will be better able to spot them. But never forget that they can see you much better too, so those camouflage clothes and a quiet, stealthy approach are the way to go. Make good use of the trees, bushes and the vegetation along the banks and give it the full Red Indian crawl up to the water's edge when you have to. On good days it's great fun in its own right to be able to sneak up on fish and watch them feeding. And you learn so much about their feeding behaviour that stands you in good stead when you can't see them.

Most of us will be fishing stretches of river we know well and will often have banker swims where we know barbel reside almost permanently, but I still like to take a stroll before choosing a swim. There are times when you can spot barbel in swims that you don't normally fish, and if it's not one of the usual well-worn swims then you probably have a better chance of making a good catch, for it's less likely the fish will have been caught or well fed with angler's baits.

Of course, if your stretch of river is one of those that is little fished then you don't have such problems to take into consideration, but unfortunately not all stretches of river are like that and previous activity has to be taken into account. On popular stretches I always have a look for signs of bait on the bank and move on if there is any. I'm lucky in that I have a good choice of stretches on several rivers that vary between very little fished to being very popular and quite busy on a daily basis. The popular stretches are, as you would expect, the easiest, so if I have little time to spare and just want to catch a few fish, then the popular stretches are the obvious choice. Other times, at the opposite end of the scale, when I have the time and I relish the challenge, I visit the little fished stretches and enjoy the success of just finding fish, let alone catching them.

Even if you're not into stalking and roving and much prefer to settle in a swim and feed it, taking a walk along the river before deciding on a swim is a wise move anyway. Half an hour spent just strolling and looking is worth an hour or more of fishing 'blind'. And you can always do the old trick of feeding a few likely swims as you come across them and then fish each in turn as you see fit and according to what develops.

Resolve to Float Fish

I've made a promise to myself this year; I'm determined to do more float fishing, not just for barbel but for most of the species I fish for. Like most specialist anglers I tend to arrive at the riverbank an hour or so before dark and then fish into the night for a few hours. And that means there isn't enough daylight time to make float fishing an option.

So this year I'm going to arrive earlier, or just shift my barbel fishing to the morning rather than the evening. Again though, it's not the way to go if the biggest fish are the priority, for legering into darkness usually has the edge when it comes to catching the biggest fish. However, if enjoyment of the method you use to catch the fish scores heavily with you then delivering that float through a swim and seeing it go under to the pull of a barbel, then playing such a fish on a stepped-up float rod, should definitely be top of your list.

Float fishing for barbel can be tremendously exciting.

Stick or Waggler?

Where rivers are concerned I have to confess that my first thought is almost always towards a stickfloat or Avon type; floats that attach at both top and bottom. I seek out swims that lend themselves to such floats, which are swims along my own bank, or no more than a yard or two beyond that. The times I've fished the river with a waggler has been when I have been unable to resist a good looking swim that was just not suitable to being fished with a stick or Avon. But after seeing Stu Dexter fish a swim on the Dove with a waggler, a swim that I would have fished with a stickfloat, in spite of it being a little too far out for comfort, this year I'm going to choose swims on the basis of their fish-holding potential and then choose a float type accordingly, rather than the other way round.

The thing to remember when choosing a method (float or leger) is that there is little point in using a float if you're targeting odd individual fish. Float fishing on rivers is for those swims where a shoal resides. This can be a big shoal of 4-pounders or a small group of half a dozen or so 8-pounders, or larger, but anything less does not fit into the usual concept of float fishing, which is to create an active feeding area where the fish are taking bait 'on the run' rather than seeking out baits that lie on, or trundle along, the bottom. Of course, I know there are times when it is easier to deliver a float-fished bait to a big individual fish than it is to deliver the bait on leger tackle, but for the sake of clarity let's put to one side the exceptions and discuss the general concept of float fishing.

The Advantage of Float Fishing

The big advantage of the float is that it keeps the angler active, and an active angler is a thinking angler. You'd think it would be the other way round, that an angler who is legering with a static bait would have the time to sit and think while he's waiting for a bite. Not so, the float angler is picturing his swim all time he's fishing; every little pull-under, duck and dive of the float is building up that picture. All the time he is assessing the amount of bait he's loose feeding into the swim, not just the amount but the regularity of it, continually adjusting according to the response, or not, he's getting from the fish. The float angler has more options when it comes to both major and minor tackle adjustments and can deliver his bait through the swim in a much wider variety of ways.

The downside of float fishing is that it usually demands lighter tackle: softer rods, finer lines and smaller hooks, which isn't exactly what you want when barbel fishing. However, the reality is that I've caught a lot of barbel on the float, usually using 5lb to 6lb hooklengths and 18's to 14's hooks, and not lost any more fish than I have when legering with heavier tackle. What happens is that when you've got the beef, when legering, you tend to use it, and therefore the fish react accordingly by fighting more tenaciously. When float fishing you have to take a much more softly-softly approach to playing them, measures more akin to subtle persuasion rather than uncompromising heaving.

But what about the snags I hear you ask. What use is a 6lb line when an 8lb or bigger barbel is charging for the sunken branches?

That's just it, they don't seem to charge off when they're not having their heads pulled off. While you don't allow them to have all their own way, you certainly don't try to bully them. What's the point when you don't have the fire power? No, the answer is to keep the line tight and steer them, sometimes with a pull away from the snags, sometimes with a pull towards them. And I can't tell you any more than that for what you have to do is react to what they do, and what that reaction should be can only be judged at the time. Certainly they'll take off at times and all you can do is hang on and hope, but most often they'll behave as though they don't know what's happening to them, and if you don't bend the rod into them unduly it's best to keep them in a state of ignorance.

Baits

The decision to float-fish ties in nicely with the fact that daylight fishing for barbel usually means fishing with particle baits, especially when the water is low and clear. Bigger meat, paste, boilie and pellet baits are fine for legering on bigger hooks when there is colour in the water and when it goes dark, but particle baits, especially maggots, casters and hemp are the ideal float fishing bait, with casters as my first choice, followed by maggots (if the minnows are not too plentiful and suicidal), then sweetcorn and small pellets.

Have a go?

So why not try something different yourself and give float fishing a go for barbel? Do you have to sit and leger every time you fish the river? Or wander the river with a leger rod? Do you have to have the best chance of catching a double to enjoy a session? Do you have to fish into darkness? You don't have to do any of those things. And if you've never had a barbel on float gear you don't know what you're missing. It's barbel fishing with the emphasis on fun!

AUTUMN AND WINTER BARBEL

The Importance of Water Temperature

I've never been one for taking much notice of exact water temperatures. You know the kind of thing I mean: roach feed best at X degrees F, and so on. But when it comes to barbel feeding in winter, 45 degrees F seems to be very significant; the point at which the situation takes a turn for the better or worse. More than 45 degrees and you've definitely got a chance of catching them, less than 45 degrees and your chances diminish rapidly with every falling degree. As I wrote in chapter 3 in more depth, it's the trend that is very important; 44 and rising can be excellent, whereas 46 and falling can be dire, with the speed of the temperature change regulating the enthusiasm, or otherwise, of the barbel's appetite. Due to taking a lot of notice of water temperature when barbel fishing in winter I will often take a couple of readings though the week just to keep an eye on the trend and the rate of change. A digital thermometer is the ideal tool, but any thermometer will do the job.

Of course, you can ignore water temperature if you intend to fish only those perfect days when the river is running coloured and the temperature is unseasonably mild and it's obvious the barbel are going to be on the prod. Great if you always want the odds to be on your side - and nothing at all wrong with that. However, a real challenge is to catch barbel all through winter, even when there is ice and snow around. I've fished all through many a winter and caught barbel regularly right through from November to the end of the season, even fishing when the water temperature was below 40 degrees F. And yes, I did catch the odd fish, but it was through actually trying to catch them, going religiously no matter what the weather was doing, that taught me how very significant that 45 degrees F really is.

It leads to a lot of blanks but believe me, there is no better way of learning about how to catch barbel in winter than fishing all through at least one winter when nothing, absolutely nothing, deters you from having a go. The one thing that helps to keep you going is that you very occasionally get that odd fish when you least expect it, when the conditions are at their very worst. Fish at least one winter all through for barbel and then do what I do these days: watch the weather, and the trend of the weather, keep an eye on the water temperature, and go barbel fishing when you know you have at least a reasonable chance of catching them. And take a chub rod for those days when the temperature dips below the significant 45 F.

Water Levels

Barbel love extra water, especially when that extra water is accompanied by extra warmth. Most winters the level will most often be well above the usual summer level, indeed, river level readings by the relevant authorities refer to 'normal summer level' and 'normal winter level'. So once the barbel have got through the transitional period of late autumn and early winter and settled to 'normal winter level' it no longer becomes significant until that level increases by several feet. That's the time when you have to look at the river through new eyes.

It's often been written that high water levels and the speed of the current should not deter you from fishing the usual barbel swims, that you should increase the weight of your bomb or feeder and get out there. No argument with that, barbel definitely do frequent the same swims that were 3ft in summer that could now be 10ft deep or more during a winter flood. But what you should never forget, and this is equally important when choosing winter barbel swims, is that when that water has risen several feet, new barbel swims are created.

For example, gravel patches that were exposed to the elements throughout most of the summer are now covered with several feet of flowing water. Marginal vegetation, trees and bushes become submerged, pools form where previously no pools existed, back eddies are created in places that were dry just a few weeks ago, and creases form in smooth glides that previously had no crease.

And remember, some of those newly created swims will be untapped areas of food, for previously they were either dry or just too shallow for the barbel to forage them. There is no doubt that when previously dry land is covered with water of sufficient depth (and that need be no more than a couple of feet) it will be exploited by fish, and particularly by barbel who are dab hands at finding newly exposed larders of natural food.

Don't make the mistake that many anglers do, of only looking for big, obvious swims. Those pools and back eddies don't have to be a score of square yards or more to attract barbel. Some of my favourite winter swims are no more than a single square yard of quiet water lying close to the bank with a crease separating them from a raging current. If you walk along the river and look carefully at the margins you'll find several of these tiny pools and back eddies, and one or more of them will be a favourite larder for barbel. The best part is that barbel seem more inclined to frequent these newly formed little swims in winter than in summer, probably because they also offer respite from heavy currents which even barbel must be glad of at times.

A productive barbel swim across to the willows at normal summer level.

And the same swim with a few feet of extra water, but now the hot-spot is under the rod end.

To give you a better idea of just how close to the bank some of my favourite winter floodwater swims are, they are so close I can't fish them unless I'm about 6ft back from the edge. Yes, I know I could go upriver a few yards and drop a bait in from there, but by far the best option is to sit back from the water's edge and just lower the end tackle and bait straight down from the rod tip. I've got this off to a fine art. I set up two rod rests so that the rod is held at an angle of about 45 degrees. The rod is pushed forward on the rests until the tip, with the baited end tackle dangling below, is directly over the exact spot where I want the bait to enter the water. The reel is then back-wound very slowly until the line falls slack as the tackle finds the bottom. The rod is then lifted off the front rod rest and dropped into another front rod rest that has been planted about a yard to the upstream side.

Of course, the positioning of the rod rests has all been worked out on arrival at the water, or previously if fishing a known swim, so that while fishing there is never any need to approach the water's edge and risk spooking any fish that could be feeding right under your feet. Many times you will get a distinct warning of a pending bite, for the rod tip will quiver a little, or nod a few times as the barbel pokes around. Be ready. Even so, in such swims I always use a reel with a baitrunner facility and make sure this is set when waiting for a bite. Bites can come out of the blue and the first thing you'll know about it is when the rod does a sudden nosedive for the river. If there wasn't a free-spool facility involved it could mean a lost rod (or a broken line) for you have only to take your hand off the rod and look away from it for a single second for it to happen when fishing such a short line. The baitrunner allows the fish to take off in safety, and you can then grab the rod, disengage the baitrunner, and walk downstream so that you can play and land the fish well away from the swim, leaving it undisturbed and ready for another bait.

I've had half a dozen big fish in a four or five hour session from such tiny swims in winter, mainly due to the one little spot being so attractive to them; an oasis in a desert. And also, the swim was never corrupted because I walked downstream for 20 yards or so before giving them enough stick to bring them in.

A good idea is to have a really close look at good floodwater swims when the river is well back within its banks. That way you can pick out the detail and able to pinpoint exactly where your bait will do most good and exactly where any snags can be found.

The actual approach to catching winter barbel, as far as rigs and baits are concerned, is not so different to what you would use in summer, except that you have to modify a few things to suit the conditions you're fishing, particularly in the amount of feed you use when that temperature is not moving in a favourable direction. Generally speaking the barbel will be found in the same swims they're found throughout the warmer months, except that heavy winter floodwater will create new swims that the barbel are sure to exploit. Make sure you exploit the situation too.

BACK-END BARBEL

I'm often asked when is my favourite time for catching barbel, and I have no hesitation in answering that it has to be the last two or three weeks of the season. I've probably caught more barbel in that period than at any other time. Obviously, conditions are, as always, the governing factor, and a set of poor conditions over these last few weeks of the season will have the same degenerating effect on the fishing as ever. Given reasonable conditions, however, this run-down to the river season can be a most magical time for catching barbel.

The most difficult choice I have to make is whether to visit a stretch where the fish are above average size for the river and sit it out for a something a bit special, or fish a more prolific stretch and enjoy a few more bites and possibly good sport for most of the day. Fortunately, my lifestyle right now allows me to fish two or three times a week and I can, if the fancy takes me, fairly regularly follow both options. Although what tends to happen is that I become engrossed in one pursuit or the other and usually end concentrating on one option.

Most of my barbel fishing takes place on the upper Trent, the Dane and the Dove, with occasional trips to the Ribble and the Wye. All those rivers are capable of producing doubles, with the Dane least likely. The trouble with most of the northern spate rivers in winter is that they are prone to fluctuating water levels and different degrees of clarity (or more likely, lack of it) and whilst this is a good thing at times it can also be too much of a good thing, with the unsettled conditions putting the barbel off feed as often as it turns them on. I know that this can be a problem on other rivers throughout the country, but when the water rises on chalk streams the difference is mainly confined to extra water.

Feeding barbel and a rising water temperature over several days in winter go together like a dovetail joint, so when the water temperature is rising - from whatever figure is lying on the starting block - there is an excellent chance that barbel will get their bibs on and feed sometime during that session. A steady water temperature, if that temperature has been pretty stable for at least several days, is also favourable to barbel sitting at the dining table. A drop in water temperature obviously has the opposite effect. So, although a rising temperature does not guarantee feeding barbel, nor does a falling temperature guarantee fasting barbel, the movement of water temperature is, nevertheless, a very important factor.

What it comes down to is that you have to plan your barbel fishing through winter and to the end of the season by not having a plan at all. It is a simple opportunist scheme, whereby you go fishing (given that there are no other factors - like work(!) - to prevent this) whenever the trend of the temperature is reasonably good and the river is in good enough condition to offer you a realistic chance of catching fish. Of, course, you don't wait for ideal conditions or you would never fish at all at the back end of some winters. What you do is watch for the trend to be right. If the river level is high and possibly falling, or has been fairly steady for a day or two, and the water temperature is rising, or steady, then that is usually the best time to go.

To make this type of opportunist fishing much easier you need to be prepared to go at almost a moment's notice, for reasonable conditions have to be taken advantage of while they last, which is usually not very long. So it makes sense to have bait at hand, ready prepared, where the only effort you have to make is to lift the freezer lid and transfer what you need to your rucksack, usually the night before you intend to fish so that it has plenty of time to thaw out.

What I do is prepare about 10 pints of hemp. Nothing special here, simply soaking the hemp overnight in cold water and boiling it for about 30 minutes in a pressure cooker. I add a tablespoon of bicarbonate of soda to darken the seeds (which I don't think makes much difference to what the barbel think of it, but it makes me feel better) and 10ml of some spicy flavour. The hemp is then allowed to soak in the juices until it cools and then thoroughly washed off in a sieve under a high pressure cold water tap. It is then split into separate one pint portions in sealed plastic bags, left at room temperature for another 24 hours to allow it to mature a little and bring out the flavour, and then stored in the freezer. When I fish a swim where there are few but bigger barbel I can take one or two pints of hemp, or several pints if I choose to fish a more prolific swim. Any unused hemp can be re-frozen two or three times without any ill-effects; in fact, hempseed that has 'gone off' slightly is preferable to very fresh hemp seed. Although I would exercise more caution about this in summer when higher temperatures can accelerate the deterioration process.

Pre-tied PVA mesh bags of pellets ready to use.

Boilies and pellets are currently the most popular barbel baits for the bigger fish, and possibly the smaller ones too on most rivers except those that host regular matches when maggot and caster will reign supreme. Shelf-life boilies are always ready for use and can be kept in your rucksack, but many anglers prefer frozen boilies and it isn't much more trouble to take a session-size bag from the freezer when needed. Halibut pellets are the most popular pellet, and these, like boilies, can be glugged in a favourite flavour to give them an extra kick. Mesh PVA bags of pellets for feed can be pre-tied and ready to go.

If I'm using luncheon meat, or some other meaty bait, that is pre-prepared too. I cut the meat into cubes and triangles of various sizes, spray it with whatever flavour I fancy (again, a spicy one being a firm favourite) place in a plastic bag, and then in the freezer. Freezing, and then thawing prior to fishing is an excellent way of drawing the flavour deep into the bait. This ensures that there will always be some flavour emanating from the bait even when it has been in the water for an hour or more. This is particularly important in winter when cold water prevents a great deal of flavour from being released.

Luncheon meat can also be made into a paste and flavoured much more effectively than when in semi-solid cubes. I make mine by squashing it up with a potato masher and then adding a few drops, or a few sprays, of whatever flavour I fancy. Daft as it may seem, I've done quite well with strawberry flavour. Perhaps fish are like kids in that they too like weird flavour mixtures of sweet and savoury. Another thing about paste is that the flavour, natural or otherwise, can escape much more readily in cold water.

I like to have lobworms on hand too, for these can be a tremendous bait when the water is coloured, providing the temperature is not too low. I collect these through the summer months in the usual way, ie, at night from low cut, damp grass. I store them in a lidded, plastic dustbin that has a fairly good depth of soil in it. The best soil is two layers of largely unbroken, grassed turf, each layer a spade deep. Keep the bin in a shaded area and don't allow the soil to dry out, although I have never had a problem that way. Also, throw in the occasional helping of kitchen scraps, such as potato peelings, used tea leaves (break open the tea bags!) lettuce and other green leaves, etc.

You can keep lobworms for months in such conditions, providing you change the turf every month or so, or every time the worms have wriggled their way through it often enough to change it into a fine texture. All you have to do when you change the soil is tip the bin over, load the new turf into it, then pick the lobs out of the old stuff and lob them into the new. In no time at all they will have dug their way into their new home. Use the old soil to fill the hole from where you dug the new.

Rods are always made up and ready to go.

My rods are always tackled up and ready to go. Apart from the fact that I can't be bothered to tackle up and strip down my rods every time I go fishing, it is a great help to opportunist fishing if all you have to do is pick one or two ready-tackled-up rods from your tackle store and stuff them in your holdall. A holdall that already has rod-rests, bank-sticks, brolly and landing net in it.

The rods I use are 12ft in length with a 1.75lb test curve. They are fitted with fixed-spool reels loaded with 12lb line to a 15lb Kryston Jackal hooklength. Terminal tackle is a simple link that can be trapped on a tapered rubber, but will pull off easily should a fish break the main line. It is a simple matter to change leger weight sizes, or to change from bomb to swimfeeder as the swim demands or the fancy takes me. Hooklength is usually a foot long but very often I will use a yard or more if I think the barbel will respond to such a long hooklength, or the swim is better suited to one. I prefer the longer hooklength when fishing a swim with a particularly slow current, for in such swims the barbel have more time to 'test' the bait before accepting it. A long hook length generally presents a bait that behaves more naturally.

Barbel swims are not a great deal different in late winter/early spring than they are in summer. The essential difference, really, is that the extra water that the river carries at that time often makes many of our summer swims unfishable. The speed of current and the features we look for, however, remain the same, it is just that we usually find them in different places.

An extra foot or two of water means that my favourite type of barbel swim, where a smooth glide meets more racy water - where the river bed rises - is found a foot or two lower down the river, and obviously a little more lead is needed to hold bottom, for the smooth part is not quite as smooth and the rough bit is even rougher. Given yet another foot or so of water though, and these swims often become unfishable, especially when the extra water is carrying rubbish of some description.

Barbel love smooth glides; anchor your bait along the crease in the current.

My second choice is a nice glide with a depth of 8ft to 12ft, and if that glide meets a slack running along my own bank then so much the better. When the height of the river reaches the point where the glide becomes a torrent then the slack usually moves up the bank and becomes the place to fish. Otherwise the glide and the crease between the glide and the slack are the places to anchor your bait. What is noticeable is that the onset of darkness, regardless of the amount of extra water, often causes the barbel to move out of the glide and into the slack. Not always, but often enough to make it well worthwhile offering your bait there if you fail to get a response in the glide.

Go steady with the loose feed. Where you can almost certainly get away with overloading the swim in summer, you can't in winter, and little and not so often should be the order of the day. One pint of hemp trickled in, along with half a dozen samples of hookbait is enough to kick-start any barbel swim in winter, and may very well be all you will need for the whole session. My inclination is to introduce a little more at the start of the session, and then top up as and when there has been any activity in the swim, or after I've caught a fish.

More often than not the barbel will bite with the same vigour with which they bite in warmer weather, giving big rod-benders that simply cannot be mistaken for leaves fouling the line, or any other activity that is anything but barbel. Anything else and it is usually too late to do anything about it anyhow. The main difference between summer and winter barbel fishing is that usually the barbel bite more consistently in summer. Not necessarily producing bigger and more fish when they do feed, for just the opposite can be true on the really good days in winter, but feeding on a greater number of days, and often for several hours longer.

NIGHT FISHING FOR BARBEL

During the summer months I'm very partial to night fishing for barbel, not all night but at least for several hours into darkness. The river is generally quiet and in good conditions it is a particularly exciting time to fish, the eerie stillness being rapidly converted to heart-stopping action when that rod bends to the power of one of those muscular fish. Although you can catch barbel during the daylight hours in summer you have a much better chance in darkness, especially when the rivers are running low and clear.

If you are contemplating fishing for barbel at night then it must be assumed that you already have some experience of fishing for barbel in daylight. If not, then you should have, for night fishing brings problems you can well do without when you are fishing for a species with which you have no experience, and for which you need all your concentration.

The author with a night-caught barbel.

So, assuming you have already caught barbel in daylight you will already know where the barbel swims are on the stretches of rivers you fish. If, as may be the case, you intend fishing a stretch you have never fished before, then it is essential you at least wander the stretch in daylight as often as possible and try to spot the barbel. Better still, fish for them.

Barbel often haunt the same swims in darkness that they do in daylight, but many times they move to and feed in the shallower water at night. Darkness provides the essential security. So if you have spotted barbel in shallow water, but have only succeeded in scaring them away when you've tried to catch them, try these same swims at night, for the cover of darkness may be all they need to give them the confidence to feed in shallow water.

It is sensible to use strong tackle for barbel at all times, unless of course there is no way you can get them to bite on bigger hooks and heavy line. And even then you should be sensible, for there is no point in using very light tackle to hook barbel successfully, only to lose them in the nearest snag, or even during that first powerful run. At night, there is no good reason at all for using exceptionally light tackle, and the minimum line strength should be 10lb, with 12lb by no means too heavy if bigger fish are the target.

I use a 12ft rod with a 1.75lb test curve. The tip is fitted with a silicon sleeve set at about 30 degrees to accommodate a betalight.

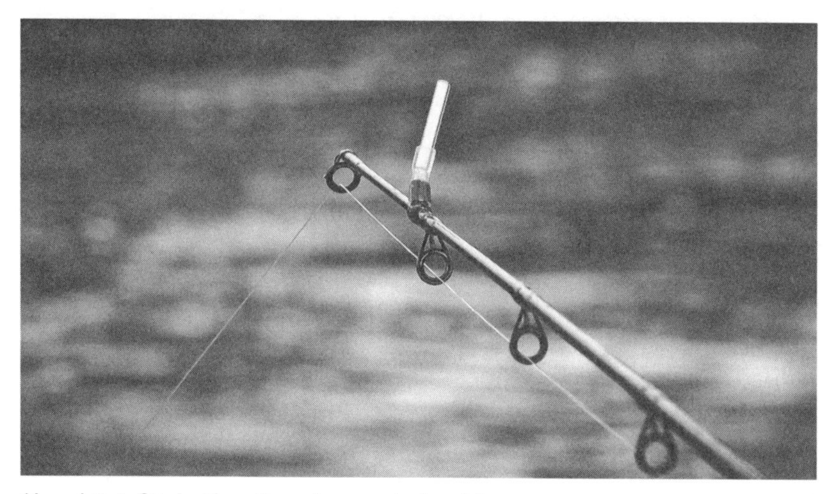

My rod tip is fitted with a silicon sleeve and a betalight.

This type of indicator is very good in short doses, for after a while betalights begin to play tricks on your eyes, and you imagine you're seeing bites when in reality the tip has hardly moved. They are especially prone to this when there is a wind and the tip is moving from the wind action. The answer is to frequently not look directly at the betalight, but to see it through your peripheral vision. Look anywhere, providing you can see the betalight from the corner of your eye. You'll know when you have a bite just as surely as if you were looking directly at it. Using two betalight attachments, spaced about 4 to 6ins apart, is better. It has to be said though that seeing bites with a betalight on the tip is more of a problem with other species than it is with barbel, for barbel invariably give a bite of such magnitude there is no missing it unless you are looking in a different direction altogether. Shining a torch beam onto the rod tip is better still, but the problem is that your night vision is never allowed to develop and once you look away from the rod tip you are almost totally blind for some time after, which is a disadvantage when you come to play and net a fish. I use a headband-mounted torch for baiting up and any tackle changes I may make. Otherwise I can usually manage without a light.

My rig for both swimfeeder and bomb fishing is very simple, purposely so, for there are times when I want to switch quickly from feeder to bomb and vice-versa. My standard rig is a running ring swivel stopped by a swivel with a tapered sleeve jammed onto it. The ring of the running swivel can be jammed onto the tapered sleeve if you want it semi-fixed, but it will come off easily should you break the main line, thus freeing the barbel. The smaller ring of the running swivel has a clip attached for easy changing of bomb to feeder or vice versa, or changing from one size to another. The hooklength is tied to the other eye of the swivel stop. The length of the hooklength is varied but is usually around 15 to 18ins.

For night fishing it's rare I use anything other than boilies or pellets, but I will try the occasional lobworm or meat bait when the boilies and pellets are not getting the results I expect.

At night I normally fish swims I've come to know well through fishing them in daylight. That way you know exactly where to cast so that your bait is lying in that certain area you've learned is the hot-spot. A lot of night fishing is done through feel and instinct, but you can only get that feel and that instinct for a swim by frequently fishing it in daylight and acquiring the necessary feel. Night fishing enhances that feel, for when your vision is impaired your other instincts become more sensitive.

Always arrive at your swim with at least an hour of daylight to spare. That way you can check if any snags have been washed into the swims you intend to fish, and equally important, give yourself time to bait up accurately and settle in before darkness. What I do is choose a swim where I make my base, usually the most favoured swim, and then feed that and two or three others as back-up swims, which I'll wander off to if the main swim is not producing to expectations. Don't go mad with hookbait samples. Throw in just enough to capture their interest, and then top up as and when required, which is according to how well they feed. The only bait I feed heavily at times is hemp, using several pints over several swims in a session of six hours or more.

Finally, try at least one swim that hasn't been baited in any shape or form. Just drop your hookbait in, preferably a really big, strong-smelling bait, maybe a meaty bait that the barbel can detect easily. Many times my biggest barbel of the session have been caught this way.

BARBEL MYTHS

Very often theories about angling are conjured up to match what the theorists want them to match. That happens a lot in fishing, especially with bait and rigs. Take long hooklengths for barbel for instance. Some experienced barbel anglers will say that they aren't bothered if the feeder is yellow with pink spots but that they are bothered about the barbel brushing against the line above it. Now this long hooklength business for barbel has had me thinking about it for some time and I'm still not entirely convinced it makes much, if any, difference. The point made about long hooklengths (when fishing downstream at least) is that it keeps the barbel away from the main line. The theory behind the tactic is shared by many and I don't doubt that it has at least some validity. However, I'm inclined to question just how true the long hooklength theory is, in that the contention is that when the barbel touch the main line it spooks them. Are barbel really so clever they can tell the difference between brushing against weed and brushing against line?

If the main line from the weight on the rig was taut, as it most often is when carp fishing, then I could understand it more, for the fin or barbule that touched the line would be like a finger plucking a guitar string, but when the line is reasonably slack it can't feel much different than a thin strand of weed. Another thing is that I know quite a few anglers who deliberately do not slack line or back lead when fishing for barbel, for they use the pluck-pluck of the barbel touching the line as an early warning system that barbel are in the swim. These anglers probably catch as many, if not more, than those anglers who are ultra-fussy about keeping the main line away from the fish.

It could be said that if you're fishing in or close to weed then the fish expect to feel the fronds as they root around and feeling the line won't cause undue alarm. And that if they're feeding in open water they don't expect to feel anything and that's when you need to keep the line clear of them.

I'm not saying the long hooklength theory is without relevance, what I am saying is that perhaps it's something else that needs to be thought about some more before applying it rigidly. All too often we take up a method, or bait, or some other idea that's worked wonders for someone. It then, sometime or other, apparently, works wonders for us. And so the legend is perpetuated.

Chapter 7

Bream

Big bream can be the easiest and the most difficult species to catch

TARGETING SHOAL BREAM

Fishing for smaller bream, or shoal bream, as we like to call them, is a much different proposition to fishing for those elusive double-figure fish.

Rivers

Location will always be the key factor towards catching any fish, but what can make it difficult is that most bream rivers are not blessed with character, for they are usually slow, featureless waterways, not unlike canals with a little extra flow. Granted, there will be many stretches of many rivers that do have lots of character, such as deep holes, shallow water dropping away to deeper water, ledges, etc, etc. But there will be hundreds of others where the bottom is as flat as the proverbial pancake. The bream can be anywhere where either the mood or the food takes them. They will still have their favourite areas, of course, or hot-spots as we know them, but they will be much more difficult to find.

Seeing the bream roll is, of course, a dead give-away, but we are not always fortunate enough to see this happen, and it could be one of those rivers where rolling bream are a rare occurrence anyhow. We are left with few choices if that is the case. The first, and no doubt easiest option, and usually the best, is to chat with the locals, especially those that you meet along the river bank, although the local bar is as good a place as any providing you take a sharp knife to pare away the exaggeration. In spite of there being too many secretive anglers around these days there are still plenty who will be willing to help. The locals may not tell you where the best swims are, but second best is a good place to start if the alternative is to start completely blind.

The next best option when river fishing, and you are not fishing alone, is to use the fenland pike angler's trick. Pick two or more swims adjacent to each other, and then leap-frog along the river until someone has some action. Then pile the bait in that evening, in that area, and hit it hard the next day.

Prebaiting

When fishing those deep, slow, but strong flows like those found in many stretches of the middle and lower Severn, the Trent, Thames and Ireland's Shannon and Inny, prebaiting groundbait has to be mixed more dense and heavy than usual. You have to make sure it gets down to the bottom and stays there long enough for the bream to find it. Once found the bream will make short work of attacking it and breaking it up to a manageable size. Use stale soaked bread stiffened with coarse white and brown crumb. Lace it with particle such as sweetcorn, wheat and groats. The particle keeps the bream occupied for long periods, for the object is to stop them in the swim during the night when they are on patrol, and then keep them interested long enough to still be there in the morning when you return. Unless the stretch is hammered very regularly, don't worry too much about overfeeding, at least not when prebaiting. Prebaiting should feed the fish, for the idea is to make them so well-fed and satisfied they will want to return for more. Overfeeding need only concern us when we are actually fishing and we want to keep the fish in the swim for the longest possible time.

Float Fishing

Along those stretches where the flow and the depth will allow, and there is no necessity to cast too far, a big stickfloat can be an excellent method, with the shot spread along the line for the really slow swims, and bulked more in the faster ones. Otherwise, an Avon-type float, or a waggler for the mid-river and beyond swims, will do a better job. Then for the deeper swims, too deep for fixed float methods, a slider has to be used.

Usually it is best to start the day with the shot bulked, for the bream usually begin their day by feeding hard on the bottom. Only later, when the groundbait and loose feed is tumbling through the current at all depths, and the bream, with luck, have shoaled in the swim and are feeding competitively by coming up off the bottom to intercept feed, do you need to make the bait sink slowly.

A match rod from 12ft to 14ft is fine for float fishing for bream. A closed-face or fixed-spool reel loaded with 3lb line, 2.5lb hooklength, and a 14's hook for bigger baits, and 16's or 18's for smaller ones, will be a good outfit. Obviously, there is always the option of changing to lighter hooklengths and smaller hooks for those tough days when the bream are in dour mood. And on the other hand there is the option too, of tying a bigger hook direct to the 3lb line to allow you to land fish faster on those days when they can't shovel the bait down fast enough.

Legering

Your favourite quivertip rod for river fishing, providing it has the backbone to handle big feeders, will be right for the job when legering. The fixed-spool reel will hold 4lb line, but 5lb line will not be too heavy. Hooklengths will vary from 2lb to 4lb, and hooks from 18's to 12's, depending on bait. My favourite end rig for legering for bream in deep rivers, where there is a steady but appreciable flow, is a simple running rig. You can, of course, use a bomb instead of a swimfeeder, but there is no doubt that a feeder, especially a groundbait feeder filled with an explosive type of groundbait laced with hookbait samples, is more deadly, more often, than any other method.

Feeding

As is the case with most river fishing, it is best to feed frequently and regularly rather than giving them huge helpings of bait at sporadic intervals. Providing the bream are feeding steadily, then keep feeding them steadily. This means filling, or part filling, the feeder and casting regularly when legering, or hand-feeding more regularly when float fishing. Try to judge at what rate they are consuming the feed and top up accordingly. I know it isn't an easy thing to do, and at the best of times the most you can hope to do is make a fairly accurate guess. It is a case of throwing plenty in until you realise the bites are slowing, and then cutting down on the feed accordingly. And later, when you have revitalised the biting rate, increase the feed to suit. On a good day, when the bream are well on feed, that will be the pattern throughout the day, increasing and decreasing the feed. Note that I am not saying that you should modify the rate at which you feed, for that is not the case. Feed should only be regulated by the amount that is thrown in each time, but the frequency and regularity of feeding should always remain fairly constant. Establishing a feeding pattern is essential.

As with all types of fishing, when you are in the process of establishing the swim make a mental note of where you cast each time. There is always some kind of focal point on the far bank, or along the horizon. Before too long it will become clear exactly where the hot-spot is and you can then home in on that spot every time you cast.

Stillwaters

Locating the feeding areas is, as always, the first thing to do. And as with rivers it can be the easiest thing in the world when the lake, mere, reservoir or smaller pool is popular and every man and his dog knows where the bream are being caught. Even if you are the shy, retiring type, you will have no problem finding those well-worn patches on the bank where anglers have made their mark. But when you are faced with a not-so-popular water, especially a large one of 50 acres or more, it can be a rather daunting prospect to try to find the productive bream fishing areas.

Quivertipping for stillwater bream.

On a large water it isn't always possible to use a boat to plumb the depths and find the obvious features, ledges, deeper holes, etc, where bream are likely to feed. So, failing that, the best thing to do is pick a swim out of the most likely ones, based on that good old gut feeling, get some bait in, and fish. At least then you will doing the thing you love most, fishing, while you keep your eyes open for rolling bream and keep the bait going in. Possibly, too, you may come across someone who can steer you towards a good catch - assuming, of course, that you are not already bagging up in the first peg you fish. On less popular waters most swims have to be well fed for a day or two before the bream shoal there in any number.

How far you cast when fishing an unknown swim depends on the water, whether it drops rapidly right from the edge of the bank into deeper water, or if the lake is relatively shallow with a saucer-shaped contour, ie, shallow margins and deeper in the middle. My rule of thumb, until I know more about the water, is to cast about 20yds to 30yds to begin with, and then adjust from there. Usually deeper waters fish better closer in, and shallow waters fish best at long range. Another restriction is the method you choose, for float fishing will obviously cut down on the range compared to what you can achieve with a legering outfit.

Float fishing

Float fishing needn't be too different to that used for rivers, except that a big waggler is almost always the best float to use on large stillwaters where undertow could be a problem, unless you are fishing very close in, in shallow water. In some deep swims, where I have to use a big sliding waggler, I often use one that takes six or more SSG. This gives me the necessary control as well as distance when this is called for. Or a float/leger outfit that utilises a bomb or swimfeeder. Those self-locking floats can be excellent for deep water bream fishing. A swim deeper than 20ft has to be tackled with a sliding float that the line will slide through pretty rapidly, for if there is a big wind on you can't afford for the tackle to be out of control. If that happens the tackle and bait will be swept out of the swim before they have chance to settle. Bulk the majority of the shot about 5ft above the hook, with one or two smaller shot about 15ins from the hook. When float/legering use a fixed paternoster end rig with a long hook tail.

Legering

Leger tackle for stillwater fishing can be exactly the same as that which you use for the rivers, except that I would favour a fixed paternoster with a long tail rather than a running rig. But this is more of a personal thing rather than something based on what will catch the most fish. I'm happier with a fixed paternoster in stillwaters, no matter if I am swimfeeder or bomb fishing.

The really important aspect now, as it was for rivers, is feeding the swim. If you're using a swimfeeder then it is a case of establishing a casting/feeding rhythm, and only varying the amount going into the swim by filling the feeder with greater or smaller amounts. An open-end feeder is best, filled with a groundbait, laced with hookbait samples, that will explode out of the feeder as soon as it hits the water, thus producing an attractive cloud of feed to fall through the swim. On very windy days, when there is an excessive amount of undertow, it will be necessary to stiffen this feed a little to ensure it doesn't get swept out of the swim in the strong currents. This has to be assessed along with the depth of the swim, for the deeper the water the more chance there is of the undertow causing problems.

Bait and Groundbait

Redworms of some description are essential. Small redworm in bunches, two or three brandlings, or one big dendrobena are all very effective. I can't imagine bream fishing anywhere without any of those. They are the first bait I try, and usually the bait that catches the most fish, no matter how many times other baits are preferred. Red and white maggot, caster, lobworms, sweetcorn, and bread flake are the other baits I wouldn't want to be without.

Groundbait for prebaiting can be on the rough side. As with bream in rivers prebait should feed the fish somewhat. After all, the purpose of prebait is to attract fish to a swim, keep them there for long periods, and make them want to come back for more. To do that you have to give them a good, satisfying feed that they haven't had to work hard for. The concept of attraction without feeding is more important when you are offering a hookbait, and you want that particular item to be the sausage amongst the beans.

Groundbait for the time you are actually fishing can be as plain or fancy as you like, providing it breaks down easily and does not feed the bream too well. My favourite mix is approximately 40% each of fine white and brown crumb, 10% of something like Van den Eynde Expo, and 10% crushed hemp. This is laced with hookbait for hand or catapult feeding. It should be mixed in a wide, shallow bowl, to allow plenty of air to get into the mix, and the water added very gradually, preferably from a spray once you are close to the right consistency. The final mix, after it has been allowed to soak for at least ten minutes, should hold together for throwing or plugging feeders when squeezed with one hand, but be dry enough to explode into a cloud on contact with the surface of the water.

Finally, when legering and the bream are well on feed, a quivertip is the best indicator. With a quivertip you can vary the resistance they feel, which is important at times, and quivertipping is fast. You can cast and be ready to see a bite as soon as the bait hits the water. Bite alarms and bobbins are fine when you want a more relaxed approach and bites are few and far between.

TARGETING BIG BREAM

I have never been hesitant to assert that big bream – those weighing over 10lbs - are the most difficult of all coarse species to catch. I have said as much for many years and in that time have never had cause to change my mind. I've known, however, that there will be many anglers (notably those who have never fished for big bream!) who will scoff at the claim and put it down to the self-deceptive ramblings of a long-time bream fanatic. And who can blame them? We all think our favourite species are the hardest to catch. Yet I may differ from many who make the claim for the simple reason that I am not a single-species man, but an angler who will fish for anything that swims and, indeed, have done just that where most coarse species are concerned.

Today there are two approaches to catching big bream, the traditional way, using lighter specialist tackle, and baits such as maggot, caster, bread, worm, etc, or the 'new' way, comprising the now standard hair rig/bolt rig tackle, along with boilies and pellets. This is the traditional way.

Techniques and Tackle

Specimen fishing for big bream has an atmosphere like no other; it has a special, unique feeling to it, that defies logical description, but culminates into a deep sense of satisfaction when that pot of gold slides over the rim of the net. Perhaps it is the stark contrast between smaller bream and really big bream that provides the answer, for on the one hand we have large shoals of relatively big fish, which are easy enough to catch in decent numbers, and on the other hand we have the bronze giants, usually in small shoals, that can be extremely difficult to catch, and present the ultimate challenge. Many years ago I considered a bream to be a specimen when it reached 8lbs, but today, with the ultimate growth of most species increasing, that figure has to be 10lbs, a 'double'. But this of course, has to be tempered with where you are fishing, for there are certain areas of the country where a 10lb bream is nothing particularly special.

Choosing a Water

Although there are one or two rivers that hold big bream, it is stillwaters - large lakes, meres, reservoirs and gravel pits - that are the typical venues for this fish. You can make it a rule of thumb that any water that has a reputation for producing big nets of bream, made up of individual fish weighing less than 6lb, is very unlikely to hold bream of more than 8lb. It is essential then, that you look for a water where it is said that bream of 8lb plus have been caught. Don't be put off if only an odd one of this weight has been taken, for big bream are rarely caught by accident, and just such a water may be waiting for someone like you to come along and set their stall for these big fish.

A productive swim on a known bream water.

Choosing a Swim

Once you have found a water that holds big bream, the best way of selecting a swim is to visit the water at first light and watch for the bream performing their well known habit of rolling at the surface. Take particular note of each spot the bream are seen and you will soon realise that a pattern is forming; that the surface is being broken along a certain line, or arc, along the surface. This route along the surface is a reflection of the route the bream are taking along the bottom, and anywhere along the route is the swim to fish. There are some waters where the bream are hardly ever seen, where they appear to have forsaken the rolling habit. In such an instance another method of selecting a swim is to plumb the depths, from a boat preferably, or as best you can from the bank, and find where the ledges, bars and basins are. These features are usually very attractive to bream and are the best places to begin fishing. If there is one, choose a feature that lies off the south east bank, so that any north westerly wind will be blowing directly at you. And bear this very much in mind: the vast majority of big bream are caught at least 25yds from the margins.

When to Fish

Through summer and early autumn big bream tend to be nocturnal in nature and feed sometime between dusk and dawn. So night fishing is important, if not essential, to get the best of them. From late autumn onwards, they begin to feed more during the daylight hours, and the early morning to lunchtime period is usually the most productive.

Weather Conditions

The best conditions you can wish for are a warm north westerly wind which has been blowing for at least several hours. Then, if you want icing on the cake, hope that this wind will continue to blow through the night, and that it will be a moonless, muggy night, with maybe a hint of rain.

Baits and Prebaiting

The most successful baits for big bream are maggots, casters, lobworms, redworms, bread and sweetcorn. Not necessarily in that order, for bream in different waters have different preferences. Before you wet a line bait the swim for at least several days with hookbait samples. This is usually done with two baits, a holding bait and the main hookbait. This can be a bed of casters as the holding bait, and a handful or two of maggots as the hookbait. Other combinations are, with the holding bait given first: sweetcorn/lobworm; groundbait/bread; squatts/maggot (or caster) casters/redworm. There are several permutations of these baits, all of which are worth a try. Many anglers will add another holding bait, as well as the main one. Hempseed, rice and stewed wheat are popular.

Redworms are an excellent bream bait, on their own or in combination with another bait.

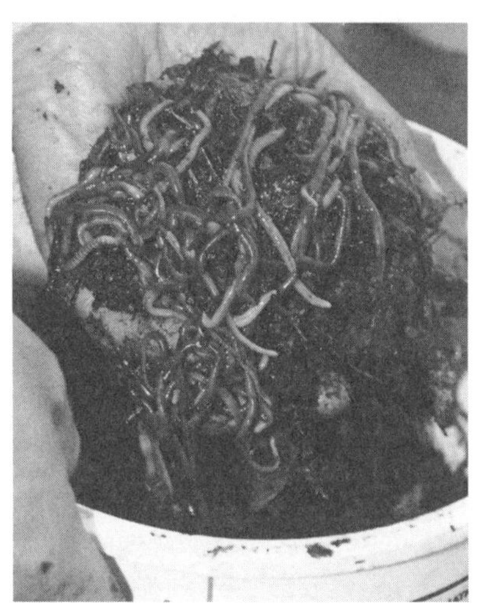

The most difficult thing to recommend is the amount of bait to use when prebaiting, for this will vary from one water to another. A pint of maggots, two tins of corn, 3lb to 4lb of dry weight groundbait, and similar amounts with other baits, should be regarded as about the minimum, with twice as much as the maximum, until you know, from experience, what is the right amount for your water. Try to prebait at the same time each day, preferably at the time you will be introducing bait on the night you intend to fish. And always place it in exactly the same spot each time.

Tackle and Technique

Rods are always a very personal item, with one man's meat being another man's poison. My own preference is for a rod 12ft long, with a 1.5lb to 1.75lb test curve. The action is quite supple for a third of the way from the tip, and the rest fairly stiff. The stiffness gives me the means of casting long and accurately, and the power to pick up a long line on the strike, and the suppleness in the tip is the shock absorber I need to play big fish on light line and to give me a safety margin when striking. I fill the spool of my fixed-spool reel with 5lb line and use hooklengths of 4lb when fishing open water, which is almost always the case when fishing for bream. I use spade-end hooks up to size 12, then eyed hooks in the bigger sizes. A 14's is my favourite size, when using maggot, caster and redworm, but I'm always prepared to go smaller when the bream are being fussy. A size 12 upwards is better for bread. sweetcorn and lobworm. My favourite rig is the fixed paternoster with a long hooklength, which allows a slow-sinking bait for when the bream are taking 'on the drop'. A swimfeeder or a bomb can be used on the short link. I always use two rods and place these on a rod-pod, with bite alarms at the front. A hanger or swinger butt indicator with built-in betalights for visual indication, can be used. Always have the landing net, baits and torch within easy reach. Arrive at the water at least an hour before darkness so that you will have plenty of time to bait up, tackle up, and settle in. Note any tall tree, telegraph pole, or similar on the far bank whose silhouette will be a good guide for accurate casting through the night. Make sure you cast to the swim several times before darkness to give you a feel for the cast. Big bream have a habit of feeding at approximately the same time each night (on the nights they feed at all) so always make a note of the time when you catch one. Eventually you will learn their feeding times and know when to be especially alert. When you catch a bream, get a bait back into the swim as quickly as possible, for bream can enter a swim, feed for a short spell, and move out pretty fast.

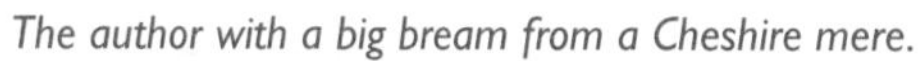

The author with a big bream from a Cheshire mere.

Deliberately setting out to catch specimen bream began in the 1960's on the Cheshire and Shropshire meres. The target weight then was 8lb, with a double figure fish the ultimate goal. This remained so for many years, until the T.C. Pit in Oxfordshire came along and produced a glut of giant bream to over 14lb, and broke the record at the time. The bream record was then broken with a 16lb 6oz fish at Copmere, a private mere in Staffordshire. Then another gravel pit known as Queenford Lagoon came to prominence and also came very close to breaking the record, producing a number of giant bream to over 16lb.

Today bream are topping 20lb. It is only in fairly recent years that bream have grown to such phenomenal proportions (not because anglers and their equipment are getting better) as has happened with tench too. The main cause of this change is the mild winters we've been having; the so-called greenhouse effect, that has provided fish with the right conditions to feed for many more months of the year and, of course, the right conditions for the food on which bream and tench feed, to multiply more often. Now we seem to be back in an era of icy winters it will be interesting to see what happens with average fish growth rates. Will they reduce, or can they be maintained?

Today, and for the past 20 years or so, as the popularity of carp fishing increased to a point nobody expected, and an increasing number of waters stocked with the species, many waters are being well fed with highly nutritious baits in the shape of boilies and pellets. On some waters this is affecting the growth rates and ultimate weights of all the species in that water that take advantage of these rich foods. Consequently the bream record could have reached an almost unbelievable 22lb 9oz, but it was never claimed.

CHOOSING A SWIM ON A KNOWN BIG BREAM WATER

I asked some of my fishing pals this question: 'When selecting a bream swim on a water you know, what factor influences your choice more than any other?'

I wasn't too surprised at most of the answers, but I was surprised at the variety of the answers. Here they are, not in any particular order:

1. I always go by the wind. No matter which way it is blowing I fish into the wind. If there is no wind blowing I fish from the bank where it was last blowing into.

2. I head for the swim that is on form at the time, regardless of what the weather or anything else is doing.

3. I don't care where I fish as long as it's on the known feeding route.

4. I fish a turning point, or the end of a feeding route.

5. I ring my mates who have been fishing the water and fish wherever they've caught, or where they may have seen them rolling if they haven't caught anything.

6. I fish one of the features, a ledge or basin, if there are any.

Answers 2 and 5 are more or less the same, and I can't argue that it is the best formula of all if the prevailing conditions don't change. In any case the swim currently producing most of the fish may very well conform to any of the other answers. And incidentally, all the anglers I asked are good bream catchers, so whatever method they go by it is certainly right for them.

I've debated before the issue of whether or not bream do have an established feeding route, which they are loathe to wander from unless some extraneous influence (such as regular and frequent prebaiting and baiting) persuades them otherwise. I concluded that, yes, bream can be pulled off their normal feeding route, just the same as any creature can be persuaded to change its natural habits, but that there was no point in doing this if we can find the feeding route and feed that. Less work and groundbait, and less effort all round is necessary, with the likely result of more fish being caught anyhow. And, with the knowledge that if the frequent groundbaiting should cease the bream will still be following that route, which is not the case if the bait has been going into a swim that is not on the feeding route. Let's have a closer look at each answer.

Fishing into the wind

Very important, but not quite as simple as that. But first of all, why is fishing into the wind generally considered a good thing? This is another subject that has been hotly debated over the years, with various theories offered, ranging from the fact that the wind pushes oxygen into the water which in turn gives the fish an appetite, to the fact also that it stirs up the natural food, especially along the bank it is blowing towards, which attracts the fish to that area.

As far as those theories are concerned then fishing into the wind is a good thing, but it cannot be a simple black or white exercise that some anglers would have us believe. For instance, there isn't much point to fishing into the wind if that wind is a cold easterly, blowing into a bank where there is only shallow water. There is also little merit fishing into the wind if the known feeding route does not take in part of the bank the wind is pushing towards, unless of course a swim along that bank has been regularly and heavily fed and bream are known to visit the swim. And, there is not much sense to fishing into the wind if that wind is expected to change during the course of the fishing session you intend to put in. Finally - and I reckon this is more important than many anglers seem to realise - it isn't necessary to fish into the wind if the weather is expected to becalm, which it very often does during the course of a night. In fact, it is better to fish the leeward side in such an instance, for the undertow will swing in the opposite direction and give the same effect, for a while at least, as a change in wind direction.

Fishing the swim currently 'on form'

As I said earlier, fishing the 'on form' swim is all very well if the prevailing conditions remain the same, and it must be said that if this favourite swim is receiving bait two or three times or more a week it will take a drastic change in conditions to move the bream. Food is God to creatures that appear to do nothing else but feed at every opportunity, and procreate maybe once a year. A slight change in oxygen content, temperature, and whatever else influences fish to move from one feeding area to another, has got to be pretty influential to convince fish it is worth moving away from a regular food supply.

But the situation on most waters is that more than one swim is baited regularly, including at least one swim on the opposite bank, so that when there is a change in conditions the bream quite happily move to the bank where they are more comfortable, knowing there is another larder there with rich pickings. So the answer in this instance is to stick with the 'form' swim when that is the only swim receiving bait, but move to other swims as conditions dictate when more than one swim along both banks is being baited.

Anywhere along the feeding route

Not a very wise course of action this one, for bream do not always feed along the whole length of the route every time they travel it. In fact, if the route covers opposite banks of the fishery - and it usually does - most often they will feed along only one bank, the bank where the conditions are right.

Turning points and terminal points along the feeding route

The turning point is the point along the route where it changes direction; where the bream are seen rolling one way, then when they are next seen they are rolling in a different direction. The terminal point is where the bream are last seen to roll, or perhaps a few yards beyond that. Most often these will be the favourite swims anyhow, discovered through trial and error, and receiving bait regularly to make them even better swims. You're always in with a chance in one of these swims, whatever the conditions in other areas.

Finding out where they've been seen rolling

Not necessarily a formula for success, for as I said above, the bream do not always feed along the whole length of the route, although they may be seen rolling in the area where they haven't been feeding. Spotting rolling bream and fishing where you see them is a good bet when you don't know where the feeding route is, but otherwise seeing bream roll is only part of the picture and should be considered along with the conditions, regularly baited swims, and so on.

Fishing features, ie, ledges and basins

Again, if the are found along a known feeding route, and the wind, well-baited areas, etc, fit into the equation, then great, you should be on a winner. But to head for a featured area regardless of any other factor is a recipe for a lot of disappointment. It is obvious that no one particular thing is the answer to choosing a swim for big bream, but a combination of all elements. But I would add one very important point to the previous comments. If I arrived at the water and found someone in the swim I fancied myself, my second choice would be a swim that the bream are known to visit before the fancied one. If the fancied swim is the first on the feeding route then I would choose the swim immediately following it.

Why? Because the adage of first up best dressed, is similar to first swim best fed. In other words the fish will feed best in the first baited swim they come to. Every other swim they visit thereafter they will be so much less hungry.

BIG BREAM BITES WHEN LEGERING

How many carp anglers free-line today? How many use a running lead? Hardly any, I'll bet. The strive for sensitivity when carp fishing ended a long time ago. The success of the bolt-rig put an end to that, although it's made a bit of a revival lately with the slack-line method. And like many modern methods innovated by carp anglers the bolt-rig now has a place in fishing for almost all species at some time or other, including bream. The secret of success is knowing when that time is apt, and how far to go with it.

A modern 'hanger' makes an excellent indicator for big bream.

One of the greatest disadvantages of fishing too light and too sensitive for big bream, apart from the fact that you don't hook as many fish, is that most of the time you don't realise you have a bite unless the fish runs directly away from you. Drop-back bites just don't register, for the bobbin, or other light indicator, simply does not have sufficient weight to drop when the line falls slack. Drop-back bites are a particular peculiarity of big bream too, which is not surprising when you consider the shape of a bream and what it has to do to take food off the bottom.

The action of a bream taking food off the bottom is the same as that of any bottom feeding fish, except that the bream's movement is more exaggerated. Also, bream spend more time cleaning a bait than most other fish, sucking and blowing repeatedly until they segregate the morsel they want from the debris it lay amongst. Not surprising when you consider that bream habitually feed where the silt is thickest and the bloodworm and other edible creatures are at their most abundant. They also blow at the bottom to dislodge small food items and so make it easier to pick them off. The sequence of events when bream decide to feed is that the bream grazes along the bottom, sucking and blowing at the bottom to release interesting tit-bits as it goes, cleaning, tasting and probing for something that takes its fancy. It can do this from an almost even keel, for the bream has eyes that look downwards and lips that are angled downwards too. When it comes across something that it really wants to consume, something that will not be sucked in easily, it tilts down to it and sucks from a shorter distance, or actually picks it up with its lips. To tilt back to an even keel it has to move a considerable distance; the bigger the bream the greater that distance is. And that movement is as near as dammit as vertical as you're going to get. A light set-up, especially when using a long hook tail, will cause that movement to transmit through to the indicator, for the line will follow the curve through the water, through and beyond the link, and move the indicator.

Fishing for big bream on a Cheshire mere in recent years.

Striking at that indication will sometimes result in a hooked fish, but there are many other times when it won't, and that will be those instances when the indicator has moved simply because the bream has sucked at the bait, then rejected it by blowing it out, and then repeats this action several times over. Both sucking and blowing at the bait cause the indicator to rise, for any movement of the line will transmit to the indicator as a pull. The fact that bream spend so much time cleaning food with this frequent sucking and blowing gives rise to the fact that many bream bites are missed - they simply do not have the bait in their mouths many times when the indicator is moving. Even when the indicator has travelled a foot or more this can be nothing less than an accumulation of sucks and blows that all cause positive movements of a light indicator, usually all in the same direction.

Resistance, and the lack of free travel between bait and lead, is the key, for when these elements are offered the bream is given a simple choice: take the bait firmly, or reject it totally. A full bolt-rig is often too much for bream, ie, a hefty (2oz plus) fixed lead direct on the line, but what I can only describe as a semi bolt-rig is usually most acceptable. This is offered by fishing a somewhat heavier than normal lead (1oz to 1.5oz even at short range) on a short link (7ins to 10ins), which is the same as the main line and a short hooklength (4ins to 6ins). Everything is connected together via a swivel, and I incorporate a length of 0.5mm rig tube above the swivel as an anti tangle measure and a line protector at that point. This is shrink-tubed to the swivel and stopped with a large rubber float stop at the other end.

There is no point fishing a short hooklength with a very light lead, for the fish will shift the lead too easily once the free travel of the hooklength is taken up. Remember that I am talking about big bream, hefty fish of at least 8lb and usually much bigger, although the same principles apply to smaller bream, only to a lesser degree. Smaller fish will have a correspondingly less powerful vacuuming action and will therefore need lighter leads and longer hooklengths to deal with them.

Right, so at the business end we have a rig that allows the bream a short length of free travel, enough to let the bait be sucked off the bottom and sufficient free travel to give the bait free movement - but only to a point. From that point the bream has to grasp the bait in its lips, or right in its mouth, in order to take it. Once it has done that any further movement has to shift the lead, and if this is a fairly substantial lead, 1oz to 1.5oz is plenty for bream, the hook will have pricked the fish and caused it to bolt. If the line is tightened right up to the lead - as it should be - and a fairly heavy bobbin or swinger type indicator has been hung on the line at the butt end of the rod to maintain that tension, then the indicator should fall immediately the tension on the line is released. In practice, once the fall of the indicator has been initiated, the bream usually continues to travel in that direction and the line carries on falling slack. A strike has to be a matter of winding in the slack as fast as possible, followed by a firm tightening into the fish, to ensure the hook has penetrated past the barb. Micro-barbed, rather than hooks with rank barbs, are essential to ensure good penetration, apart from being kinder to the fish. But I'm not prepared to risk barbless hooks on these fish that are so difficult to get on the hook in the first place.

Line bites then come into the equation. For those who are not sure what these are, they are movements of the indicator caused by fish brushing against the line somewhere between the lead and the rod, and often picking line up on a fin and running with it. Striking at line bites can result in fish being foul-hooked, with the result that you spook the whole shoal and ruin your chances until the next feeding spell. In the case of big bream this can be anything from 24 to 48 hours or more later, depending on how well they fed before they were spooked, and if the water temperature is suitable thereafter. The bottom line (pardon the pun) is that you avoid line bites like the plague. Or, you take a risk finding out as quickly as possible if the indications you are getting are line bites, rather than it being a case of you missing genuine bites. If you make that choice you strike at all movements of the indicator at first, until you realise they're line bites, and hope you don't spook the fish. Or you tackle up in a way that avoids line bites registering at the indicator, thus preventing you from striking at them.

The middle ground, however, is that you can try to establish why you're getting line bites and hopefully do something about it. Contrary to popular opinion, line bites are not always caused by a big shoal of fish that is passing through the swim, or between you and the swim. They can be caused just as easily by a small group of fish that are milling about in the swim, or between you and the swim, rather than passing through. Very often it is a group of fish that are interested in the free feed you have laid down for them, but are not yet hungry enough to feed on it. The first thing to do when you suspect line bites, especially when using a three-rod set-up, is to cast two of the rods at shorter range, one, say, three yards closer, and the other six yards closer, and then leap frog these until the bites either stop, or you connect with fish. Once you have established where the line bites are happening, you can cast different baits into that area and try to tempt a fish or two. Although I must confess that you invariably fail in these circumstances, for persistently 'line-biting' fish are very rarely feeding fish.

Heavy, stainless steel indicators are now in vogue.

Carp anglers, and I include myself in the following when I'm carp fishing, are inclined to use back-leads to avoid their quarry fouling the line between rod and end tackle. Back-leads are slid onto the line following casting and run down the line to the bottom, and thus pin the line to the bottom from that point not far from the rod tip to the end tackle. I've tried back-leads when bream fishing but I don't like them. I don't think bream are a powerful enough fish to 'deal' with them. These days, when the bream I'm fishing for run well into double figures, I am more inclined to use a set-up that does not register line bites, a set-up like the semi bolt-rig I've described earlier. With such a rig the bream can still foul the line, but the difference is that you don't know about it, and are not going to strike 'just in case' it's a genuine bite.

That, in my view, is the most important reason for using the semi bolt-rig when fishing for big bream - only genuine bites will be indicated, preventing one striking at false bites that could spook all the fish in, or near, the swim. That the semi bolt-rig is partly a self-hooking rig is a bonus, and it also follows that a self-hooking rig promotes more relaxed, less intense fishing, particularly through the night when one bite from one big fish is usually all you can hope for, and that is the cream on the cake.

DIFFICULT BREAM

Never make the mistake of thinking that big bream anglers are just the specialist version of any old bream angler, for that is a great mistake. They are a unique breed that smiles with a knowing smile at those anglers who scoff at the idea of catching big bream, for they know full well that only an angler who has never deliberately set out to catch them could scoff.

Big bream are derided for the fact that compared to carp or barbel of equal weight the bream lacks fight. Yet there are many big bream anglers who are eternally grateful for that, for the time and effort required to hook a big bream in the first place is seen as sufficient. Personally, I don't think I could tolerate the trauma of having to fight with a bream too much to get it into the net. Furthermore, when I have lost such a fight (and I have on the very rare occasion the hook has pulled) it has been devastating.

The consistent capture of big bream is usually as a result of a well thought out campaign rather than the opportunist or casual approach. Big bream are rarely caught accidentally, even when anglers are fishing for other species that feed along the same routes that bream use. There are very, very few anglers who have caught a double-figure bream, and even fewer who have caught several, including those who deliberately fish for them on a regular basis. I know quite a number of very good anglers who have tried and failed to catch a double-figure bream, most of whom have given up and gone back to catching something easier like carp and barbel. I know quite a few household names who have tried and failed to catch big bream, names who have enjoyed tremendous success with every other species they have attempted to master.

So don't listen to the words of derision concerning big bream, even from those who are very successful with other species. They can only be coming from those who have never caught them deliberately.

So what do you need to do to catch double-figure bream? Bearing in mind that I can only outline a plan as it would take a whole book to completely cover the subject. The first essential is a burning desire to catch one. It simply isn't enough just to want to catch one. It has to be an all-consuming ambition; something you have to do, not just want to do. The approach that goes along the lines of, 'Oh, I think I'd like to catch a 10lb bream, I've never had one of those,' is not enough. Unless you are very lucky indeed you will not last long enough to realise your ambition.

The second element in a campaign to catch big bream is ensuring you fish a water that without a shadow of a doubt holds them. And that is not as obvious a statement as you may imagine, for you would not be the first angler to assume that because a water has produced a number of 8lb bream, and the odd nine-pounder, it is a certainty it holds one or more doubles. It doesn't work like that. I've fished lots of waters over many years that have produced 8lb and 9lb bream like clockwork, but never a double. Furthermore, beware of judging the size of bream from viewing them either beneath the surface or rolling through it. Even bream in the 6lb to 8lb bracket can look a lot bigger when viewed side-on. In fact, much of the difference in weight between an 8lb bream and a 10lb bream is packed across the shoulders and in the gut, a difference that cannot be seen unless viewed at little more than arm's length.

It is best to forget the wild stories that gravitate along the grapevine, at least for the time being, and concentrate on waters that have already established a history of producing double-figure bream. There is plenty of time to investigate unfounded rumours of monster bream when you have caught a few from known waters.

Make sure there is no doubt that your chosen water holds big bream. This one, Oss Mere, was famous for its big bream.

Anyhow, the honest truth about modern-day specialist angling is that it is highly unlikely you will ever have the opportunity to investigate 'new' waters. The sad fact is that there are few, if any waters left to discover, and very little left to discover about those that are fished. This makes reconnoitring waters, at least in the time-honoured way whereby you walk around them at dawn and dusk in the closed season and watch for rolling fish, a redundant exercise. On most waters we no longer have a closed season on stillwaters, and so it is unlikely we will ever get much opportunity to walk round without one or more anglers being present. Which is not to say that you shouldn't do it, for it can be a pleasurable exercise, and you may just learn a little something you wouldn't have learnt by lying in bed. There is, however, a lot more to be learnt by walking those same waters and watching and talking to those anglers who are willing to be watched and engaged in conversation. But expect to come up against many brick walls. Few are willing to talk openly.

Better still, having established the identity of a big bream water and gained legitimate membership of the controlling club or syndicate, just get down there and start fishing. Establish your right to be there and most often you'll find that most then will be willing to divulge information. After all, you have already staked your claim and there is no longer any point in maintaining an unfriendly attitude. Although there are always a few who like to maintain an air of mystery. They are the same ones who shun publicity, rarely let anyone see their photo albums, and generally promote an aura around themselves of being the strong, silent type. They are the worst kind, the inverted snobs, the parasites who feed off everyone else and give nothing in return. If everyone who ever fished had had the same attitude we would still be fishing with bone hooks.

This kind of attitude, although generally only evident in the minority, can be found throughout the specialist world; it isn't exclusive to any particular species addict. Yet I have to add that during the time I've fished for big bream, since the early 1960's, and in that time fished for big fish of most other coarse species, there is definitely a distinct, more acute rapport amongst the most dedicated big bream anglers. Certainly different and sharper than the rapport I've found amongst anglers of any other species. I think this is due to three main reasons, the first being that big bream anglers know they do not belong to a popular following, and therefore there is a stronger bonding. The second reason is that they have heard and read the derisory comments such as 'snotty' etc, and recognise the ignorance with a knowing smile. And third, no matter if the angler is about as popular as swine 'flu, he deserves respect if he consistently catches double-figure bream.

Anyhow, the next step towards catching big bream is to gather as much information as you can while fishing and observing. After a few visits you'll see where the bream reside when they are not travelling and feeding. It is an area where they can occasionally be seen cruising and basking at the surface, and an area where they are very rarely tempted to take a bait. You will note where the bream roll when they are on the move (if it is one of those waters where the activity takes place, for there are waters where it is a rare event). Note how far from the bank they roll, the direction they take, and the time at which it happens. This rolling does not necessarily take place as a prelude to feeding, but it does indicate when they are on the move, when they may, or may not, feed. Generally, the first and the last positions along the feeding route will be the hot-spots, and if the route shoots off at a tangent anywhere along its course, this will be a hot-spot too. Most often, the bream will follow this route religiously, but from time to time they can be seen to follow it in the opposite direction, or they will cut short their travels, do an about-turn, and will be seen rolling back towards their resting area.

On most waters they will feed at the same time every time they feed, which can be every day/night when they are feeding frequently, or less often (much less at times) when they are not so hungry. They can be extremely punctual with their feeding times, to the point where it is possible to predict to within half an hour when you will get your first bite (if it happens at all) and they often stick to this feeding routine – where and when – for many years. In fact, several big bream waters I've fished for over 30 years are fished exactly the same today as they were 30 years ago; same swims with the bream feeding at the same time. The only thing to have changed is the bait and, to some extent, the tackle. These waters have fell to the lure of the maggot and caster, or boilie or pellets, through familiarity, rather than bread and/or worms. And the tackle is finer for its strength, with sharper, stronger hooks, and the end tackle cast more easily over longer distances due to better rods and reels.

Incidentally, give me a modern carbon rod, a well-engineered modern reel, today's line, indicators (electrical and mechanical) and all the rest of current angling technology, any day of the week. If I'd had the equipment I have today those 30-plus years ago I would have caught a lot more fish, and been a lot more comfortable in doing so. And if anyone tells me I enjoyed it better using a cane or heavy glass-fibre rod while getting wet under a cloth brolly with a sheet of plastic round it, while watching a dough-bobbin in the light thrown from a candle in a jam-jar, I'll have to tell them they're wrong. Nostalgia is a pleasant exercise when you think about it, but a pain in the arse to practise.

Most big bream waters fall into one of three categories as far as bait is concerned. They are either bread waters (usually those waters that have not been put under a great deal of pressure). Or maggot/caster waters, which are usually those that have been fished extensively and which also rarely respond to anything other than maggot or caster, but where, on occasion, redworms will make a killing. Or worm waters, which fall somewhere in between the latter two, where big lobworms, lob tails, and redworms are best, but other baits are always worth a try. Those waters with carp in them – getting to be most waters these days – will respond best to boilie and pellet.

Many big bream anglers, including me, use a swim marker. This, of course, is not the exclusive territory of the bream angler, for such gadgets are useful for many species, including carp. They are especially important, however, where big bream are concerned, for these fish have a habit of developing a hot-spot within the baited area. Let's say, for instance, that we are feeding and fishing an area covering a circle approximately 6yds in diameter, which is by no means a large area when you may be casting in excess of 40yds. More often than not there will be one particular part of that circle that produces the vast majority of bites. Not once or twice, or even most of the time, but all of the time. There will always be one spot in that circle that by far outfishes anywhere else. It is obvious then, that a swim marker will ensure you cast to that specific spot every time. Not an easy thing to do at long range, especially at night, but I don't mind making half a dozen casts until I'm satisfied my bait lies in the right spot. My polystyrene block swim markers are often fitted with a large starlight when I'm night fishing.

It is a fact too, that on those fisheries where you are allowed to leave your swim marker in situ for several weeks at a time, you are certain you are feeding and fishing the same spot every visit, including those times you pre-bait between fishing. You may be only a yard or two out if you have to place the marker each visit, but I believe that can be a disadvantage.

For the majority of my big bream fishing I use a simple paternoster rig that entails a 2ft to 4ft hooklength and a 9in bomb/swimfeeder length, the main line, hooklength and bomb length joined via a tiny swivel which I have more faith in than any line to line joins. Perhaps unnecessary, but that's one of my idiosyncrasies that I'm sticking to. Otherwise, if the bream are behaving in a manner to warrant it (difficulty in hitting apparently good bites) I'll use some type of bolt rig, or a semi-bolt rig that is a simple reversal of the hook and bomb lengths, ie, the hooklength becomes the short one, and the bomb length the long one, and with an extra heavy lead and weighted indicator to boot. My other choice, especially on a water which is carp fished is to use small, 10mm boilies with a Method feeder.

I use a weighted bobbin for mechanical indication coupled with an electronic bite alarm. Whichever bite indicator you use it should indicate drop-back bites as well as the usual pulls. There is no other species that can give as many drop-back bites as a big bream.

No matter how many years you fish for big bream you will never reach a stage where you can visit a water and feel extremely confident you are going to catch a double. Even during those times when you are having a good run, when the conditions are spot on, and you get the best swim on the water. If fishing for big carp, pike and barbel can be likened to a game of rugby, and fishing for smaller species compared to a game of cricket, then fishing for big bream can be measured against a game of chess. With an opponent who cannot scrap as hard as the others when hooked, but has more unfathomable ways of avoiding being hooked in the first place.

MY GREATEST EVER CATCH OF BIG BREAM - 13 DOUBLES IN TWO HOURS

In 1995 I made my personal best catch of big bream, 13 double-figure fish, plus others, in just two hours, a catch that Angling Times described at the time as the best catch of big bream ever recorded. The smallest fish weighed 10lb, and the largest 11lb 10oz. The catch also included a roach x bream hybrid of 6lb 12oz and two tench weighing 6lb 14oz and 7lb 2oz. All the fish were caught in that mad period of just two hours. I wouldn't be surprised if the catch hasn't been surpassed since then, but even so, many anglers have asked me to tell the story of how they were caught.

First, a little about the fishery. It is the same mere, Combermere, that produced my then Cheshire record bream of 14lb 1oz in 1994. In the three years I fished it I learned one thing above all else. It is that I know almost nothing about it, for each year has been different. The first two years produced something like 200 tench, only two of which topped 7lb. In 1995 it produced, amongst dozens of 7-pounders, four over 8lb, and a 7lb 5oz male tench. Two members of the syndicate that control it, none of which are novice anglers, sighted tench they swear were well into double figures. Indeed, experienced angler Tony Miles, who fished the mere as my guest in 1995, spotted a tench that he put at over 9lb.

The first year I fished Combermere I caught bream to 13lb 7oz, tench to 7lb 3oz, and pike to almost 29lb, and little else. Since then the roach and pike population has increased dramatically. The mere is different than any other Cheshire mere in that it is bigger, deeper, and with an infinitely greater variety of swims. It is probably one of the best general coarse fisheries in the country, providing anglers with a most beautiful and peaceful place to fish.

When I caught my big catch of big bream I arrived at the water in the early evening. I was fishing for just the one night session, fired up by the capture of a 13lb 14oz bream only three days previously, which I'd had the privilege to witness and photograph. I headed for a swim with distinct features; a plateau that dropped from a mere 3ft deep to over 10ft. It was the same swim I had taken a low double-figure bream from a week previously.

The author caught this previous Cheshire county record bream in 1994 at 14lb 1oz.

I spent almost two hours in the boat, plumbing the swim and choosing carefully where to place my marker. I wanted to fish down the slope with three rods, one legering near the top of the plateau in 6ft, one half way down in 8ft, and close to the bottom of the slope in 10ft. I placed my marker just beyond the swim so that it wouldn't interfere with any hooked fish. Once that was done I spread about 5lb dry weight of groundbait in the area. This groundbait was 40% fine white crumb, 40% fine brown crumb, 10% crushed hemp and 10% 'Expo'. On top of that I scattered one pint of casters and half a pint of white maggots.

Very often I will spend a whole afternoon prior to a night session just nosing around with the echo sounder or plumbing tackle deciding where to fish. There has never been any doubt in my mind that most big fish are caught long before you wet a line; that every minute you spend ensuring you choose the right swim, and then feeding it correctly, is worth hours, often days, of thoughtless fishing. Given the opportunity, any mug can sit in a swim for days on end and hope the fish will eventually visit the swim and feed on whatever is on offer. But it takes an angler to catch fish without the benefit of wearing them down.

I tackled up with two rods of my own design and manufactured by Harrisons, the 'Graham Marsden Interceptor' range, threading them with 6lb line and terminating in a fixed paternoster rig. This rig has a short, 6in bomb length and a 3ft hooklength of 4lb. The bomb was quite heavy for the 30yds range at 1.5oz, but I wanted the weight, along with heavy indicators, in order to offer the bait on a semi-bolt rig. The hooks were size 6, and each was armed with a large lobworm, which had proven to be the killing bait for most of the bream taken from the water in that period.

It was an uneventful night, which was not surprising, for the heavens opened and it rained continuously from dusk until 4.30 the next morning. The only activity was a few line bites and the odd 'bite' from flying bats. I couldn't sink my lines out of the way of the bats for I would then have been plagued with line bites from fish crossing over the shallow plateau, which is a problem most of the time even with lots of line kept out of the water with the use of high rod rests.

It's an amazing plateau, a huge semi-circle of about 90yds radius, varying in depth from 2ft to 4ft, that drops away quite rapidly all round to depths of 10ft and more. It is so distinct it is felt that it could have been man-made. It is certainly a very attractive location for all kinds of fish, but especially bream, for they love to patrol almost all around the ledge, and often all the way across it.

I made a brew at 4.30, just as the rain stopped, and was ready for the first bite when it came at 4.45. That resulted in a 6lb 12oz roach x bream hybrid, my second biggest, for as far as I know I already hold the unofficial British record for that variety of hybrid at 8lb 4oz from another mere, a fish I caught in 1976. Then I had the second bite at 5.15, a bream of 10lb 2oz, and was rubbing my hands with glee, for the conditions were perfect, and I anticipated catching a few more. The mere had been threatening to produce something really special for a long time. Could this be it?

At 5.45 I hadn't had another bite, not a line bite nor a mere twitch. I couldn't understand it. Especially since I had seen two bream, a hybrid, and an unidentified fish, roll right over my baited area. I felt sure there were fish in my swim, right on the bait, for there were no line bites from fish that moved between me and the baited patch, and the more I thought about it the more I was convinced they were preoccupied with the casters I had put in the evening before. This so often happens with many species; they can become preoccupied with casters to the point of ignoring everything else. The same thing had happened when I had my then 11lb 4oz Cheshire record tench a few weeks previously when for weeks they had been feeding confidently on sweetcorn.

I had two choices. I could tie on smaller hooks and leger caster, perhaps presenting them on rigs more akin to match fishing rather than the semi-bolt rigs I'd used through the night. I could even use the quivertip rod I kept in my bag for just such an opportunity. Or I could do what I had been threatening to do for some time when the opportunity arose, which was to slip out quietly in the boat and float-fish casters for them.

I remembered the time about 15 years prior to that when I was faced with a similar situation on another mere, when I float-fished casters over a ledge to take 16 bream over 8lb, and then 17 bream over 8lb, in two four hour sessions. And then a catch of 27 bream over 8lb in a six hour period, which included the first double from the water. The story of that catch can be read in the book 'Red Letter Days' (Crowood Press). So the decision was made; boat and float won the day.

I pushed the boat over the plateau until I was between two and three rod's length from the baited area, then lowered the mud-weights into the three foot depth. The beauty of the situation was that I was out of sight of the fish which fed over the edge and down the slope (I hoped!). I had tackled up my 12ft 9in 'Interceptor Specimen Float Rod' with 5lb main line to a 4lb hooklength. This terminated in a 14's wide gape hook. I shotted the sliding bodied waggler with a 4 AAA bulk and a No.6 dropper 9ins from the hook. The stop-knot was set to fish the bait, four casters, at 10ft, and when I cast into the 10ft depth at the bottom of the slope I allowed the natural drift to take the tackle to the ledge and lay the line down the slope.

My first cast was at 6am and I ran out of bait at 7.30am, but carried on fishing till 8am. I never waited more than two minutes for a bite. As soon as the line lay down the slope the float slid away. The bream fought really well on the short lines and my first action was to apply as much pressure as I dared to get the fish away from the shoal and onto the top of the plateau where I could play them out and net them with the least disturbance to the swim. As fast as I could land, unhook, weigh the fish, re-bait and recast to the swim I had another fish on.

I loose-fed little and often continuously, with the emphasis on 'little', for I had just half a pint each of caster and maggot. I was tempted to fire in bigger pouchfuls of loose feed, fearing that I would lose the shoal if I didn't, but forced myself to fire more often with less feed. I netted 12 more bream and two tench in those two hours. I kept six of the bream and the hybrid in a pike tube and two keepsacks and returned the rest immediately after weighing. Luckily, they swam off along the plateau and not back to the shoal.

The only time I have ever caught bream like that before was in Ireland, but obviously not of the same calibre. It was ridiculous, almost unbelievable, I felt like I had to keep pinching myself to make sure I wasn't dreaming. Double-figure bream are not caught like that, or at least not at the time. It didn't happen.

One of the 11-pounders in the catch of double-figure bream.

My friends and I went weeks, often months, for one double, and felt proud and elated when we caught one. There were some anglers on the water who had never had a double from there in two seasons, which is not to say they were poorer anglers than me, but I mention it simply to try to put things into perspective.

It may seem somewhat ungrateful and pretentious to say it, but the fact remains that I was a little disappointed that out of 13 double-figure bream, there wasn't one over 12lb. In the three years I fished the water it produced one bream over 14lb, a fish that fell to me, five bream over 13lb, several 12's and numerous 10's and 11's. Apart from one other exceptional catch that included six doubles to 12lb 15oz it was most common for the bream to come out in singles, but that single fish was usually over 11lb. So now you may understand what I mean about being disappointed, for there were four 11's and nine 10's.

What made this water so unique where the bream are concerned isn't so much the size of the bream, but the sheer number of them, and the obvious diversity in size. Other Cheshire meres produce medium size or big bream in a quite rigid weight band. But Combermere appeared to have numerous shoals, and I believed there was a shoal, or group of bream in there, that were far bigger than any that had yet been caught. The most prolific area to see the bream roll is in the shallow area of several acres where the bream spawn each year. This is directly behind Combermere Abbey itself, a no-go area for fishing. Why is it always so?

The author all set for a day's lure fishing on the river Dove where chub, perch, pike and even barbel could be tempted to take one.

Little and often is the best method for the river angler trotting his bait through the swim.

Does this 16lb bream caught by Wol Gaunt behave differently than a 5lb bream?

A big barbel will not allow smaller fish to dominate a swim.

A sonar makes the job of depth and feature-finding so much easier.

Raking the bottom for tench is traditional and worthwhile.

Fishing in the big freeze-up of 1982.

Catching fish takes your mind off anything, even the cold.

The late Professor Barrie Rickards was one of our most successful anglers.

Sunset on a Cheshire mere.

A carp from France's river Vienne, the most powerful fish, pound for pound, I've ever landed.

The unedited shot of the chub.

The edited shot to make it look bigger.

Some days we don't care what our surroundings are like as long as we're catching fish.

Somewhere under the rainbow? Will ESP tell us where the fish are located?

A 27lb carp caught from a boat on an Oxfordshire estate lake.

Immediately following baiting a swim like this from a boat Graham spotted a big bream feeding on the bait he'd thrown in.

Good luck: the pike that won me £25.

The Ribble: an angler has waded across the shallows to fish the deeper water along the far bank.

A double-figure late autumn barbel for the author.

Barbel love high, coloured water at any time of year.

Setting the indicators for big bream.

Hooking big bream is hard enough without having to contend with a prolonged battle to land them!

Carp angling maestro Rod Hutchinson with his 23lb carp.

You had to cast to within 6 inches of the far bank pads to stand a chance.

The modern 'standard' carp set-up.

Carp taking Chum Mixer dog biscuits.

The author with 56lb of pure muscle.

A 30lb mirror fell to my rod.

Ian's 50lb 8oz catfish was the biggest caught that week.

The river Dane where it runs through Holmes Chapel, Cheshire.

An end of season river Dove chub for Graham.

A fine brace of perch for Gary, weighing 4lb 1oz and 3lb 15oz.

Teeth made for biting and crushing, those backward facing teeth ensure that prey can slide in but not slide out.

The nostrils in front of the eye give the pike a good sense of smell and the pores around the eye are part of the sensory system.

My best fish from the Cheshire mere was 29lb.

Piking on the river Wye.

A suspended live or deadbait will usually score on those days when the pike are well on feed.

A 44-pounder and two big 30's caught by these Swedish anglers using stret-pegged roach.

Mark and a typical quality roach that can be caught from many waters.

The author with a big estate lake rudd.

The author with a tench of 11lb 4oz, at one time the Cheshire county record.

Graham fishing the pole for canal tench, he caught his first tench from a canal almost 60 years before this shot was taken.

The gravel pit near Leicester that holds a good head of zander.

My first zander, a really evil-looking, prehistoric creature.

The author with a tench weighing over 9lb.

Tench seem most at home in lily-dotted estate lakes.

Tench will soon return to a swim that has been raked of some of its weed.

Smelt deadbaits were tried and attracted some interest.

The author's late mate, Dave Colclough, with a fine zander from the Leicester pit.

A yacht glides over the zander swim.

Chapter 8

Carp

The coarse angler's most popular species

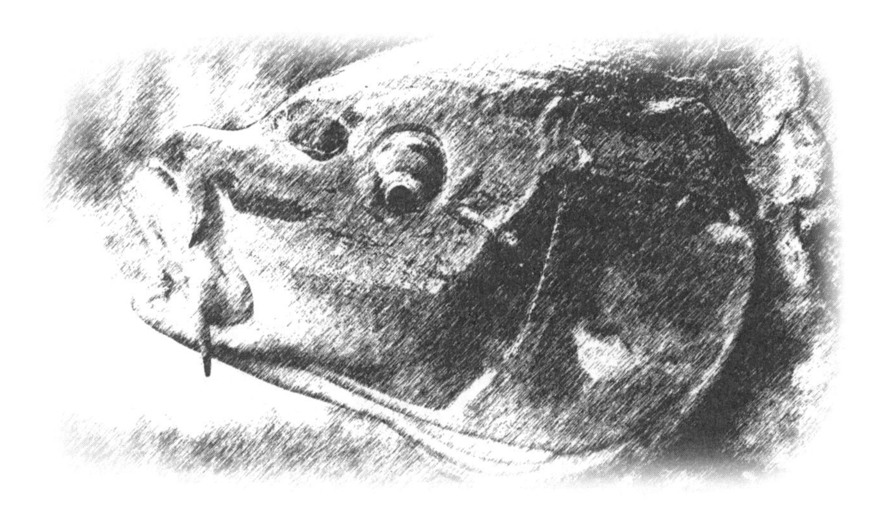

CARP CAN BE CLEVER BUT.... EVERYTHING IS RELATIVE

Carp are clever creatures, make no mistake. Clever in the sense that they're instinctively clever, soon learning just what spells danger. There are too many clever carp anglers catching too few big carp to dispute that, especially considering the amount of knowledge, tackle and bait at the carp angler's disposal.

Of course, everything is relative. If you're trying to catch hungry carp from an overstocked water then the carp are not going to be too clever out of necessity. The need to feed will outweigh the urge to avoid something that arouses their suspicions. It isn't so much that the carp in one water are more intelligent than the carp in another, just that the apparently cleverer carp can afford to be more suspicious.

The same applies to big carp. Big carp (not recent stockies, but naturally grown big carp) have made it big because there is lots of food in the water where they live, and not too many mouths to share it with. They are cleverer too because they have usually been around for a lot longer than smaller carp and have learned more in that time. So if you have a heavily fished, probably understocked water, capable of growing big carp you have a combination of well-fed fish with lots of experience. They are the most difficult of all fish to catch.

Very often rigs are invented to please the angler rather than to solve a presentation or hooking problem.

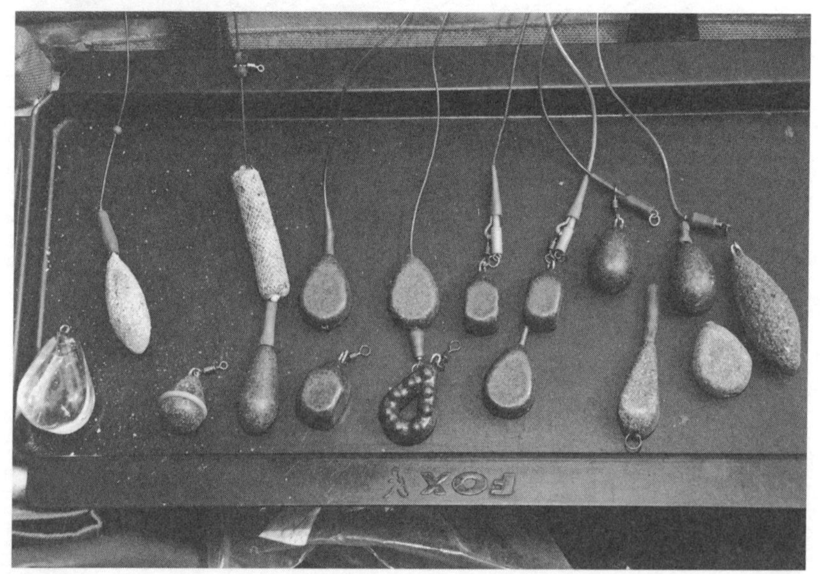

Which is why carp anglers are forever devising different rigs and different baits in an effort to fool those apparently clever carp. I'm not talking about the rig merchants here, who devise rigs for their own sake, but the genuine, innovative angler, who is tackling a genuine problem and trying to devise a genuine solution. As for baits and flavours, well, my own view on that prickly subject is that most of the time it just needs something different. Given a decent base mix of proven materials, a change of 'label' is usually all that is needed. The trick is in finding a label that is genuinely different, for so many flavours are carried by the same material, ie, alcohol, and that in itself is enough to arouse the carp's suspicions when they have been caught on it often enough.

I've said it before, and I'll stand by it again: much of the time too many carp anglers are trying to beat non-existent problems. The number of times I hear an angler say something like, 'I couldn't get a run till I changed to a super-duper, sliding ring, cranked-over stiff rig.' Only to hear another angler say sometime later that he couldn't get a run till he changed to whatever the first angler had changed from. Much of the time it was a simple case of the carp deciding they wanted to feed. That this decision coincided with the time the bait was presented on a different rig wasn't considered by either angler. That happens to all anglers, not just carp anglers of course. It just happens that carp anglers have so many fanciful rigs to play with it happens to them much more often.

I've fished several carp waters where there are regular anglers who swear by popped up baits and others who swear equally as much by bottom baits. Both factions enjoying roughly the same amount of success. All that has happened here, at some time, is that each angler has enjoyed success with one or the other and decided that whatever he used is best, and consequently fishes in that mode most, if not all, of the time. But this needs analysing further, for when an angler has faith in any bait or method he will fish far more confidently, and that in itself gives him an edge and leads to other advantages.

Not the least of these advantages is that he will give his chosen bait and/or method much longer to do the job before he changes to something else. Because he gives his bait longer to work means that the bait has lost more of its flavour (over-flavouring being another common mistake) and that could be all that was needed to tempt the carp to take it. The flavour may have been too strong in the first place, or the carp may be less suspicious of it because the bait is soaked and looking more like the well-soaked freebies it likes to mop up which have been there for several days. It could be more simple than that, in that the carp may have been thinking of taking the bait for some considerable time, and a less confident, more impatient angler, could have whipped it from under its nose before the fatal decision was made.

Some time ago I was carp fishing in France at Le Domaine des Iles with a party of eight anglers. Most of the party were experienced carp anglers, not the least being Rod Hutchinson. As the week progressed it was obvious that the carp were not going to come out easily, which was not too surprising considering the lake we were targeting held big fish in the 40lb plus bracket, for carp of such size, even in France, are never easy no matter what anyone may tell you to the contrary. It was interesting nonetheless, to see what each angler did to try to get that important run that could produce a 40 or even 50-pounder.

Domaine (at the time I fished the place) is noted for being a carp water that demands little in the way of free feed. The vast majority of the carp fall to boilies fished amongst a patch of 20 or less, with particles hardly figuring at all. The standard method is to use a baitboat, ferrying your bait and a couple of handfuls of boilies to your swim, which is generally, though not always, 100yds or more away. There were all manner of rigs being used, from stiff rigs to mono hooklengths, single small baits to double large baits, long hooklengths and short hooklengths, pop-ups straight off the lead and boilies hard on the bottom, braided lines and lead-core lines. No method, no rig, and no bait, however, was succeeding any better than another.

After three days hardly any fish had been caught; just three fish over 20lb, a 23 to Rod and a 21 and 25 to myself. The only other fish to hit the nets were odd singles. Up till then everyone was prepared to sit it out with favourite baits and methods, concluding that the fish were just not feeding. Location wasn't the problem for no area of the lake was fishing better than anywhere else.

We were getting restless. Most of us were taking float rods to the numerous channels that cut off from the main lake, casting baits to odd bubblers and cruising carp that generally didn't want to know. Then Dave Wilkinson, whose previous personal best fish was a 21-pounder, netted a 40lb 4oz mirror. For another day and night we all sat expectantly over the rods again, beavering away, so to speak, yet again with favourite baits and methods. But it soon became obvious the lake hadn't suddenly awakened but simply given up one of its senior occupants just to tease us and remind us they were there to be caught. So it was back to stalking every so often, mainly for something to do now, for stalking wasn't producing any more fish than sitting over static rods on the main lake.

Then Dave caught another one. Another forty, this one 40lb 6oz and a different fish than the 40.4, injecting everyone with a dose of enthusiasm again. And that's how it went for the rest of the week, with odd single figure common, mirror and grass carp, and one or two low 20's being tempted.

It was left to Dave, yet again, to remind us that the most important ingredient of all is being in the right place, for he would be the first to admit that he wasn't doing anything any different to anyone else. He was using the same type of boilie, a fishmeal, that most others were using, and his method was quite conventional with a lead core leader and a popped up 18mm boilie. But this time the wind had struck up, blowing right into his own bank. So he screwed the rubber-duck, bend-over aerial into his baitboat and dropped his bait right under a bush just a yard from the bank and 20yds up from where he sat. All credit to Dave, for he took the initiative, worked out that the only way to get a bait right under the bush was with his baitboat, and did it.

Being in the right swim resulted in a 58lb 12oz carp and two 40's for Dave.

The result was a run so fast it scared the living daylights out of him and gave him a fight that lasted a full two hours. And that is no exaggeration for I stood with him all that time and timed the fight from 12 till 2pm. Most of the fight took place in the 5ft to 6ft of water in the 10yds in front of him, for as soon as the fish came within a yard of the net it just waggled its great tail and surged to the bottom again. It's a good job Dave has a good constitution, for he would never have recovered from the nerve-racking ordeal. He wasn't exactly nursing the fish, but then again nor was he using anywhere near the full power the rod and line were capable of. After the first hour we got a good look at it and we knew it was a 50-plus. Finally it succumbed and the huge carp lay in the folds of the net on the two unhooking mats. I recognised it immediately as the same fish that another angler had caught in January, the lake record at 66lb. It took the 56lb scales down with a bump, so we sacked the fish and set off to get Rod who had a set of 100lb digitals with him, and Bernard, the owner of the lake, had a set going to 120lb. The carp finally weighed in at 58lb 12oz.

A 40.4, a 40.6, and a 58.12 in one week. What a result for anyone. But what a result for someone whose previous best was just 21lb. We were all genuinely delighted for Dave. He did everything right and deserved the free week on the fishery that the fish won him.

That week demonstrated carp fishing -- fishing - in a nutshell. A week when all kinds of rigs and baits were tried, but all that mattered in the end was being in the right place at the right time, recognising an opportunity that a change in wind direction brought, and doing a good job when the fish were hooked. Which does not mean in any way that trying different baits and rigs is a waste of time, just that, most of the time, any sensible, proven rig and bait, will catch if you're in the right spot.

MODERN CARP ANGLING

What is notable in particular about the present day carp scene is that so many things about tackle and bait have become standard. Rods are either 12ft or 13ft, with at least a 2.25lb test curve, and more usually 2.5lb to 3lb. Reels are Baitrunners and/or large spooled reels for long distance casting. Lines are normally either 12lb or 15lb. End rigs are fixed leads, either helicopter rigs or the more in vogue in-line lead rigs. Leads are at least 2oz, more usually 3oz or even 4oz. The hook almost certainly carries a hair, usually fixed to come off the back of the shank opposite to the point, held there with silicon tube. Hook lengths are braids. Rod-pods, buzzer bars and bite alarms are the norm.

Ordinary rod-rests or bank-sticks are not often seen. Mechanical indicators are heavy and set tight against the rod in order to drop rapidly from a drop-back bite. Long range casting, necessary and unnecessary, has become the norm. Boilies, and to a lesser extent particles and pellets, apart from the very odd exceptions, are practically the only baits used.

I'm not knocking that. Or at least I'm not knocking it in a derogatory way. It just seems such a shame, in a way, that carp anglers have been so clever and innovative over the past three or four decades or so the scene has arrived at a point where it is in danger of stagnating because it is known, beyond much doubt, what tackle, baits and approach are best to catch them. It is only very slight variations on a standard theme that are left to choice. No longer is it even feasible to fish a popular carp water (I'm referring to waters with large fish, not the overstocked, man-made ponds) with anything other than standard tackle and baits. You are just very, very unlikely to catch on sweetcorn, luncheon meat and the like. And if you are fishing a water where the fish are very large and runs are at a premium you are wise to fish with alarms and self-hooking rigs to ensure that when the run does come you convert it into a fish on the bank. In the meantime you can read a magazine or a book, listen to the radio, watch the birds, or nod off. And what's wrong with that?

Perhaps the one thing that remains within the scope of water craft is choice of swim, but even that is standardised on many waters, for there are undisputed hot-spots that almost inevitably produce fish to a competent 'rod' given the right conditions. Even on vast waters like Chantecoq in France, and taking into account that you can't fish in all areas, there are certain swims that are far more likely than any other to produce fish, in all kinds of conditions. Yet there are waters where it pays to choose a swim with a degree of sound judgement, where there are no particular swims that are hot-spots at all times.

On most of the carp waters I fish I make a point of walking round the water before I decide where to fish. I look for carp clouding the water or bubbling, or giving their presence away in some form or other. This is then related to current wind direction, and where the wind is going to be later in the day; where the sun hits the water at that time, and then later; approximate water temperature and depth of water; presence of weed, or not, etc, etc.

Although I was a member of a carp syndicate for three years it took until the third year to get a real feel for it. That, more than anything - getting a feel for a water - is the key to success when your bait and tackle are right. Every water has a character all its own and it takes time to learn what that character is all about. Nice and steadily I put the pieces of the jigsaw together, learned which swims were generally best in certain conditions, where the fish usually wandered to at certain times of the day, and where the hot-spots were within the hot swims at the time. I thoroughly enjoying the learning curve. Which is an area in which I get most of my kicks from fishing; piecing the puzzle together and making them fit. And why not? The actual playing and landing of the fish, although intense, is only a small part of a much larger experience that begins with the learning curve.

It's a bit sad when you arrive at the time when the intense learning comes to an end (we never stop learning something, but it does slow down) for it is never quite as enjoyable when you know exactly what to do to catch the fish; when there is little left to think about. Most stillwaters don't change much over the years and there comes a time when you know where to fish and what to do without thinking about it too much. For instance, one carp water I used to fish about 20 years ago, and then fished again more recently with a mate who was a regular on there, hadn't changed a bit as far as the approach to fishing it was concerned.

I knew from all that time ago that in a certain swim you had to cast to within 6ins of the lily pads on the far bank to get the maximum runs per session. That isn't to say you couldn't get a run at all if you fished well away from the pads, but that the difference was usually quite remarkable. The mate I was with knew that you had to cast close to the pads, but I don't think he knew exactly just how close you had to be. A foot was too far away, where 6ins was not too close. The pads grew to the edge of a shelf, and the carp patrolled and fed along the edge of this shelf in what they must have thought was a safe area, hence the reason they were so willing to accept baits in that area but not so habitually in the open water, which they visited often enough, for you could see the tracks and patches of bubbles coming from the shelf. What you had to do was ensure that when you got a run you hit it immediately (no wandering away from the rods) and held the fish tight so that they couldn't enter that labyrinth of stalks which grew as thick as a man's arm. You hooked and held and gave no quarter and more often than not the carp would eventually give and you could pull it into open water.

We fished shoulder to shoulder almost, in the same swim, casting to the same spot. The both of us used 2oz leads, me on an in-line rig and the mate on a helicopter rig with 15lb main line and 15lb braided hooklengths. We both used the same boilies, Rod Hutchinson's Maplecreme, on one rod and tiger nuts on the other. I cast, and then re-cast several times if necessary, until my baits were within 6ins of the pads. My mate wasn't so fussy and left his baits a foot or more away, which is where they landed more often than not.

That was the pattern for most of the day, apart from towards the end of the session when my mate decided there was a difference in how we were fishing. It may have been only 6ins or so, but that was enough, for I'd had six big carp to over 20lb and he'd had none. Just before we packed for home he had one last cast that landed within 6" of the pads. Sure enough, he caught a good fish.

So, knowledge I had gleaned a good many years ago was still valid, and that is the case on most waters and with all species. Only drastic changes in the topography of the water, brought about by drought and encroaching weedbeds in the main, can make much of a difference.

No matter where we fish there is no doubt that it is essential to fish in the right area. And this was brought home to many of us in no uncertain terms when we fished Boulancourt in France one cold and wet May. The carp had gone off to the shallows where the water was warming faster from the weak sun. Unfortunately you could fish only the one bank and the shallows lay adjacent to the opposite bank some 300yds away. We suspected this could be the case before we went so Eddie Bibby and I purchased a baitboat. This enabled us to drop our hookbaits, along with a small heap of particles and a handful of boilies, precisely in the area where the carp were sunning themselves some 250yds away. Many times we were playing fish before we had time to get the boat back to the bank. We never fished at night, had plenty of time off for sight-seeing, and still caught 135 double-figure carp to just over 20lb in a week. That was more than double anyone else's catch. Nothing at all to do with skill, just simply that we were able to place our baits where the fish were, which was beyond the reach of any cast.

Closer to home, my pal Dave Colclough had a bogey water he couldn't crack because he couldn't cast far enough away from the margins which are well trodden with dog walkers. So I went with him with the baitboat and sent out a bait at over 200yds. Within 20 minutes he had a double figure ghost carp on the bank. With any species, on any venue, the first essential is to fish where the fish are.

FLOATER FISHING FOR CARP

Surface fishing for carp and rudd (and dry fly fishing for trout) appeals to me for two reasons: first and foremost it is an exciting and interesting fishing method, and the other thing is that it is riddled with problems which, when solved - if only briefly - offer a tremendous amount of satisfaction.

Fishing floating baits on the surface teaches you a lot about fish, for you can actually watch how they approach a bait. Although the conditions are quite different between the bottom and the surface, much of the fish's behaviour when confronted with a 'suspicious' bait on the top or on the bottom (the refusal, the aborted take, the snatch, and the confident suck) must be almost the same. Which all goes a long way towards teaching you what is going on at times when your bait lies out of sight on the bottom and your indicator tells you that something down there is showing an interest.

free-lines should be free-lined.

As usual, I began by catching a fair number of carp on a freelined crust, and then, when the carp had travelled the learning curve, found I was watching them take all the free offerings and perhaps just one of the hooked ones before they spooked. Close observation revealed though, that they were being crafty and knocking the hooked crust about enough to cause crumbs to fall off it and sink towards the bottom, which they grabbed on the way down.

So I tied up a two-hook rig which had a big hook on the surface carrying a big crust, and a smaller hook 4ins below it carrying a piece of pinched flake simulating a piece that was sinking from the crust. They fell for it hook, line, and particularly the sinker!

I was concerned for some time that the rig could lead to some damage to a hooked fish; the loose hook fouling a snag and tethering the fish to it. But I was using it in a snag-free water and never did have any trouble. I would be wary of this, however, and think carefully before you use the rig. Also, be wary of the fish thrashing in the landing net, causing the loose hook to snag the mesh. What I do is immediately cut off the loose hook before I place the landing net down on the unhooking mat. Tying on a new hooklength is a small price to pay for being able to use an effective method without risk of damaging the fish.

The floater-fishing method I use most of the time is the straightforward controller approach. But like so many other types of fishing, the way you loose feed can make the difference between success and failure. My way is to choose a position where I have my back to the wind and loose feed with trout pellet and hookbait samples (usually Chum Mixer) in the same way I would loose feed with maggot or caster when fishing stick float on the river.

Little and often is the answer, or quite a lot and often if you are fishing a prolific carp water, for they can mop up a hell of a lot of feed if they're well onto it. Whichever - little and often, or a lot and often - the aim is to keep a constant stream of bait bobbing along the surface, to such an extent the carp grow over-confident and therefore careless. Feeding for twenty minutes or so before you actually wet a hookbait is the best way, which allows the carp to grow confident before any of them are hauled off to a landing net, and therefore remain confident for longer.

If you get the feeding technique right, on the right day, you can hook the carp on almost any floater method, within reason of course. They become so preoccupied with feeding, and competing with each other if you get enough carp in the area, their sense of self-preservation goes out of the window to a great extent. Ask any match angler, he'll tell you that correct feeding technique is more than half the battle.

Feed floaters regularly for a while before fishing to get the fish feeding confidently.

BOILIES AND FLAVOURS - CATCHING FISH OR CATCHING ANGLERS?

Boilies, or boilie ingredients and flavours to be more precise, have always been a contentious issue. I constantly waver between a) thinking the whole bait ingredient issue is more to do with catching anglers than it is about catching fish, with carp anglers at the front of the queue, and b) that they do make a great deal of difference. I think I have settled for somewhere between the two extremes. Ingredients and flavours do make a difference, I have no doubt whatsoever, but it is to what extent that is open to conjecture. Some of the rubbish you hear and read about makes you want to puke. And the descriptions on some bait containers rival even the wildest prose of the most imaginative estate agent. To read some bait blurbs you would think that all you had to do to catch a big carp was turn up at any water that holds big carp with your tackle and a bag of that particular bait.

Nevertheless, good bait does make a difference, for there are too many instances of a few carp anglers catching far more fish than most others when they are obviously not doing anything different otherwise. They haven't acquired a magic ingredient, they've simply found a bait that the carp are very attracted to in all the right departments, ie, smell, taste, colour, and, probably most important of all, uniqueness.

They have found a bait that is not yet arousing the suspicions of the carp to the point where they are refusing the bait more often than not. Which is exactly what happens with a bait that has caught a great many carp on that particular water. And the reason that certain popular baits still catch fish even after many years of successful use is due to the very simple reason that they are flavoured with something that the carp, at times, find irresistible. An excellent bait today is a bait that is also flavoured with something the carp find almost irresistible, but that something is not yet well known and therefore is not well used.

Nothing magical, just good bait.

As with ourselves, I assume, some of the tastes that carp are attracted to are acquired tastes, in that some of the baits we try may not be too appealing to the carp the first few times we introduce them to a water. This is often a good thing, for those baits that take a little longer to establish usually last that much longer before the carp decide they've had enough. The best way of establishing a new bait is to throw in plenty of it, not in huge piles at odd times, but in lots of smaller doses, scattered over many areas of the lake, as often as you possibly can. And although this may seem obvious, don't make 20mm boilies for this taste-establishing period, but rather 14mm or even smaller. Unless, of course, there is a problem with 'nuisance' fish that make 20mm boilies essential. Make these boilies a little harder than normal so that they last longer too. And the final piece of advice I can give on this matter is that you should fish an already established bait on your second or third rod while running-in a new bait. That way, if you go through a particularly blank spell, you won't be piling all the blame on your new bait.

Yet no matter how sophisticated carp angling tackle and bait becomes it is still the thinking angler, the one who has decent water craft and the desire to occasionally move from behind his bank of bite alarms, who will catch more fish than anyone else. When carp fishing moves into the next millennium and electronic gadgetry rules, the basic principles of fishing (find the fish, and offer them a well presented, attractive bait) will still apply.

NUTRITION RECOGNITION IN CARP BAITS

Although I've headed the following with the words 'carp baits' it generally applies to baits for all species. I've directed it specifically at carp because it is carp anglers who have pioneered the modern day thinking about baits and propounded the theories upon which modern baits and flavours are based. And for that we owe them a vote of thanks, for at the very least the theories are a basis upon which to launch a train of thought. Nevertheless, that should not, and will not, prevent me from questioning some of the theories that have now evolved into accepted 'fact' with many carp anglers.

How nutritious are these boilies, and can the carp tell?

One theory is that in the long term a carp can recognise the difference between a nutritious and a non-nutritious food item. It is said that if a carp does not get what it needs, nutritionally, from eating, say, a boilie that is little more than flavoured stodge, it will have to go in search of other food items in order to supplement its diet. The conclusion being that if carp are offered a highly nutritious boilie they get all the nutrition they need from it and have no need to go in search of supplements; they will continue to feed on that particular boilie indefinitely.

I don't know enough about nutrition in fish or any other creature, including humans, to dispute that, but my knowledge of nutrition is no better or worse than that of most of those who continue to sustain the now accepted carp bait theories. But I've always wondered how fish can instinctively recognise all this nutrition, or lack of it, in a ball of man-made food, and yet we humans, supposedly the most intelligent creatures on this planet, need research scientists to discover what is nutritious, and labels on food to tell us if it's any good for us. Almost every food package you pick up today carries a list of ingredients, E numbers and allergens. Shouldn't we be able to instinctively recognise the good from the bad just like fish are supposedly able to do? Why do we need a label and they don't?

How is it that the human appetite is triggered solely by smell and taste to the point where a person will wolf down a bag of greasy chips but reject a stack of lettuce leaves that will (according to scientific research) do us far more good? And yet a carp can, according to what we're told by the bait gurus, identify and avoid low nutritional food, then go off and search for other food that will supplement a poor diet. The theory says it does this only after eating the poor value food for some time, but nevertheless, that kind of nutrition recognition is beyond the capability of any human being that I know of.

I'm honestly not being facetious here, but I've always found the nutrition concept regarding carp baits hard to come to terms with. Some of it makes partial sense and some of it doesn't; common sense that is. I understand that the carp's feeding behaviour is a matter of instinct and that human feeding behaviour is, at least in the civilised world, research and label led, but that doesn't explain why carp in a rich environment don't just go and eat everything they fancy (just like humans) and become unhealthy lard arses like those of us who still eat according to smell, taste and appetite.

Ah, but they do!

The majority of the biggest carp caught do look like unhealthy fat-gutted creatures; the equivalent to the human couch potato. Most of the big carp that anglers target have unnaturally fat, bloated guts that fly in the face of the theory that says carp have this marvellous natural instinct to recognise what food is good for it. So if this natural instinct is so good, good enough to recognise the difference between a ball of stodge and a ball of nutrition, why isn't it good enough to tell the fish it is eating too much of something and getting too fat for its own good? Yes, I know this big gut factor is bred into them to some extent, but not wholly.

"Perhaps it does know it is eating too much but ignores it, just like many overweight humans do," the HNV bait expert may reply.

OK then, so why doesn't the carp ignore the instincts that tell it to reject a stodge boilie and scoff a HNV boilie? It just doesn't make sense to me to believe that a carp instinctively rejects a poor food

Red, pineapple-flavoured boilies, or yellow strawberry flavoured boilies – not many of those around!

value boilie in favour of a nutritious boilie, but continues to eat to the point where it has an unnaturally fat gut. Either its eating instincts are highly tuned or they're not; either those instincts are highly tuned and heeded, or they're not. Something, somewhere, about this widely accepted theory regarding carp baits, just doesn't add up.

It was following a conversation about food factors, flavour and bait that inspired me to take another look at the latest findings regarding smell and taste in humans. I know that is, to some extent, a waste of time as it may have very little to do with what carp can smell and taste, but it's no more a waste of time than the millions of words written about smell and taste in carp by laymen (anglers) who have nothing more to go on than what bait caught the most fish last year and maybe even the year before. To be fair, a few have gone into the topic in some depth and gathered as much information and evidence as they could, but most are just repeating what others have written. At least by looking at what we know about smell and taste in humans we're dealing with facts and not mere conjecture, and if nothing else, it may give us a few clues where carp are concerned.

Due to us becoming increasingly health and fitness conscious, nutrition in humans is a current hot topic and there is an absolute mass of information about it. Go on the internet and you can easily spend a week doing nothing else but read about healthy food and nutrition and still only scratch the surface. The basic premise is this: the flavour of food is determined by a number of different factors including taste, smell, colour, temperature and general appearance. It had long been accepted that there were four basic tastes: sweet, sour, salty and bitter. But now we have a fifth element known as umami, a Japanese word meaning savouriness, and most specifically to the recognition of glutamates common in protein rich foods, monosodium glutamates (MSG), of course, long being used in Asian foods and the element that gives you the sensation of feeling hungry again just an hour after eating a generous Chinese meal.

So what's all that got to do with carp baits? Well, even where human nutrition is concerned we're still discovering new things (umami for instance) about smell, taste and appetite and in many ways still only scratching the surface. So how can it be possible to draw so many of the many quite inflexible conclusions we have drawn about baits and flavours where fish are concerned when it's obvious we know so little? Some anglers state that x ingredient is best in winter and y flavour is best when the sun sets on an October evening. Others say that flavours don't make any difference; that it's all about having a good base mix.

How do they know that? Short of fishing multiple rods in the same swim at the same time, pitching multiple baits, flavoured and non-flavoured, against each other for at least several years, can you draw a tentative conclusion. And even then changes in conditions and other variables will prevent any meaningful results. It's all baloney! Very rarely do many of the statements made about baits include essential words such as 'apparently', 'possibly' and even 'probably'. Oh no, it appears that many anglers think the popular bait theories are written in stone.

Right, now let's bring colour into the equation and see just how we automatically relate colour to taste and flavour. What colour is a pineapple flavoured boilie? Yellow of course, because pineapples are yellow aren't they, so what else would they be? And yet most of the flavours used in foods, and especially in carp baits, are clear liquids. So why don't the bait makers leave the boilie the natural colour of the base ingredients with the flavour of pineapple? Because colour is important, the bait maker will say, and colouring it yellow will enhance its appeal. Appeal to whom though? The fish or the angler?

Most anglers will tell you that the colour red is the most appealing colour to most fish. And I wouldn't argue with that, having caught my fair share of different species on red maggots, red boilies and other red baits. Most anglers will vote for red being a more appealing colour to fish than is yellow. Those same anglers will swear that pineapple flavour is one of the top flavours for carp. No question about it.

So let me ask you this: why do we not have a pineapple flavoured boilie that's dyed red? Have you ever seen one? No, neither have I.

But why not? Are we pandering here to what colour humans associate with pineapples? And if so, why? Do we think that a carp may be visually attracted to a red boilie but turn away from it because it smells of pineapple and it's not yellow? How many real pineapples do you think a carp comes across in a year; in a lifetime? Quite probably none. So on that reckoning it won't know that a pineapple is yellow. In fact it won't know that what it's smelling is the essence of a pineapple. All it may know is that it quite likes the smell, and possibly the taste, of pineapple, even though it won't know the identity of what it's smelling and tasting.

But we don't have any red boilies flavoured with pineapple. In fact I've never seen a yellow strawberry flavoured boilie. It's all nonsense isn't it. We haven't moved on too far really from the early days of bottled carp flavours when one of my favourites, mainly due to the amusement factor, was called 'Mown Grass'.

Of course there must be elements of truth in the general carp bait theories, but what annoys me are the categorical statements made by some, just as though they know that what they're saying is an actual fact. Some make statements that are downright laughable, where they would have had to have had a conversation with a carp, or been a carp in a previous life, to know if what they're saying is absolute fact, or even close to being a fact.

Moreover, everyone assumes that all carp behave the same, with the same preferences in taste and smell and colour. Isn't it just possible that, like humans, individual carp have individual preferences, some liking sweet, some preferring savoury.......?

Who knows? I certainly don't.

Chapter 9

Catfish

You want a fish that fights like a tank? You need a catfish!

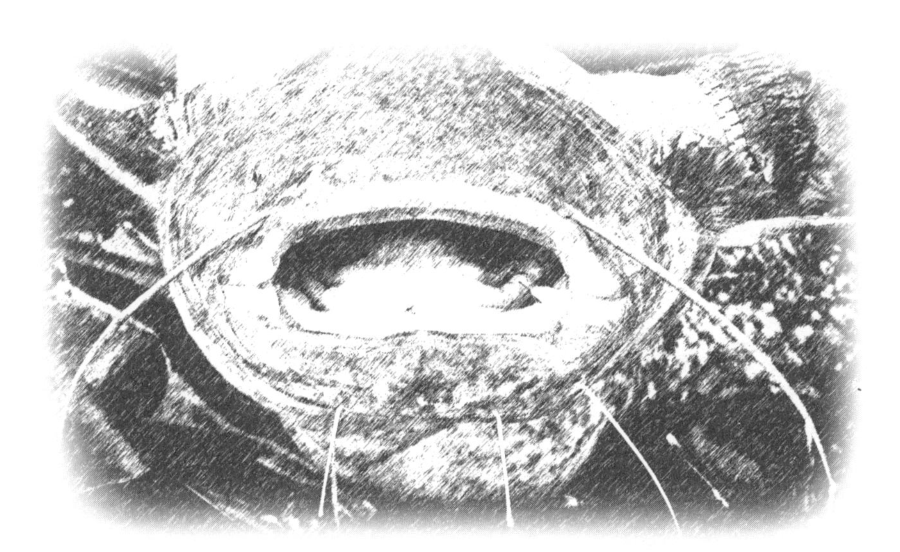

THE WELS CATFISH

What has surprised me since I became really interested in catfish are how many anglers there are who have never caught a one, but who are also greatly interested in them. Many of the emails I receive from anglers wanting to know about the fishing in France want to know about the cats. And many of the die-hard carp anglers I talk to, some of whom think that any species other than carp are something you have to avoid to get to the real fish, want to talk about catfish.

There is no doubt that the species has captured the imagination of many anglers, and even though some will never actually have a go for them, they want to hear about them.

Catfish have been around for a long time in small numbers, in fact they were first introduced in Britain in 1880 but remained as a rarity until fairly recently. Now they are more widespread in Britain than most anglers realise, for many waters have been stocked illegally and the owners are playing it low profile. But in the not too distant future catfish will be quite common and then, obviously, more anglers will have a go for them and realise what a great sporting species they are.

Let me confess right from the off that I am not a catfish expert (are there any British catfish experts yet?) but I have caught enough of them to over 50lb to be able to give anglers sufficient knowledge to enable them to go out and catch one or two. Then, later, if they want to venture to the river Ebro in Spain, or the river Saonne in France, where they have a chance of fish topping 100lb, or even the great Russian lakes where they can top 600lb, they will at least have a basic knowledge and won't be floundering completely in the dark. But let's have a look at the fish first, and see what makes it tick.

The Species

The family name for catfish is Siluridae, and there are a dozen or more varieties, including Europe's most popular one, silurus glanis: the European wels catfish. This species has six barbules, or whiskers (hence the name catfish) two long ones growing from the upper jaw and four shorter ones sprouting from the lower jaw. They have a long, eel-like body, a very long anal fin and a tiny, adipose-like dorsal. The skin of the wels is similar to the eel in that they haven't got obvious scales, and the colouring is generally a mottled creamy grey, but like any species this can vary somewhat from one water to another. The wels has a large mouth, stretching from ear to ear, so to speak, and with a grin to match. This huge mouth is full of tiny teeth that feel like a feline cat's tongue, with two larger, chunky teeth in the throat for crushing its food. The small teeth slope backwards and are used to grip and manoeuvre the food to the throat teeth for crushing prior to swallowing. Like most big fish they can pack the weight in the belly when over a certain size. How big do they grow to? In Britain the biggest accepted weight they have grown to so far is less than 60lb, for catfish bigger than this are generally believed to be illegal imports. On the continent they can easily top 100lb, and the granddaddies of them all reside in Russia, where they have been caught in trawler nets at more than 600lb. It is generally accepted that they grow to even greater sizes in these Russian lakes, possibly approaching 1000lb.

The catfish is a scavenger and as such will eat practically anything edible, such as invertebrates, worms, maggots, fish portions, pellets and boilies. Its natural food is live and dead fish, with other animal fodder, such as reptiles and rodents, a close second.

Although most often seen as a nocturnal feeder, catfish will happily feed during daylight hours when the conditions are favourable. Dull days and coloured water are a good combination for daylight feeding cats.

Tackle

I don't have any specialised catfish tackle, and except for fishing big lakes and rivers for giant cats of 100lb-plus, when tackle of the sea fishing variety wouldn't be out of place, I don't think you need any. I use the same rods I use for carp and pike, which are 12ft long with a test-curve of 3lb. But any rod from 10ft to 13ft capable of handling line in the 15lb to 20lb bracket will be fine. Any decent fixed-spool reel that will hold at least 200yds of 15lb to 20lb line is okay, as is a small multiplier.

The teeth of catfish are not particularly sharp, but they are extremely abrasive, capable of wearing through conventional nylon line and braids very quickly indeed. However, do not use a wire trace, primarily because wire can damage the soft mouths of cats, and secondly because they can detect it too easily. An abrasion-resistant braid is best, and the most popular, proven one, is Kryston Quicksilver. The 35lb and 45lb test strengths are favourite, depending on the size of cat you think you may have a chance of catching. Single hooks are used for cats; large, very strong, sharp, single hooks – not trebles or doubles, for with these you run the risk of damaging their mouths and possibly locking their jaws together. For big cats use size 0/1 and 0/2 when using livebaits and deadbaits, and size 1's and 2's for other types of bait.

Rigs and methods

The best rig of the lot for catfish, where it is possible to use it, is the simple freeline rig. This is just the baited hook on the line. It is ideal for fishing in the margins and any short distance. But don't use it for fishing more than a couple of rod's length, for it makes it too easy for the cat to swallow the bait without you knowing anything about it. For greater distances use a conventional link-leger setup, with a 2ft to 3ft long hooklength, and the lightest lead you can get away with to cast the distance necessary. This will provide the essential fulcrum point that will register drop-backs when the cat picks the bait up and moves towards you.

Perhaps surprisingly - for we tend to think that scavenging fish, especially those with long whiskers, are strictly bottom feeders – catfish take much of their prey at, or near, the surface. The prey is usually live fish, and floating dead or dying fish, which they can home in on from great distances with deadly accuracy. The problem is that you never know for a fact if they're going to be in surface bait-taking mood, or bottom bait-taking mood, but being as most of us fish with at least two rods, where we are allowed, it is sensible to fish one bait on the bottom and one near to the surface. One popular catfish rig, however, makes it easy to fish the bait at varying depths. All you do is construct a simple running leger rig and then tie a 6in length of 6lb mono to the hook that has a small polyball attached to the other end. This serves two purposes, it makes the livebait work harder and prevents it from sulking on the bottom, due to the constant pressure of the polyball trying to float to the surface, and does in fact force the livebait to swim close to the surface in between bouts of struggling to lie on the bottom. It is an odd-looking rig, and one tends to think that tangles are inevitable, but in reality it is a very efficient, tangle-free rig.

Although I prefer the polyball rig I have seen a number of catfish caught by anglers using conventional (other than a wire trace) suspended live/deadbaits under a pike float. When catfish can be seen taking fish close to the surface I suppose it is as good a method as any when they are well on feed and not being too cautious about how natural their food behaves.

Hair-rigging also has a place in catfish fishing, not so much because of the presentation, but due to the simple fact that it allows you to use a completely unmasked hook, giving you much better hooking power. This is a great plus-point when fishing what can be a very large bait on a relatively small, single hook.

Lure fishing, sink and draw, and wobbled deadbaits, either cast and retrieved or trolled are very popular methods on the continent for catfish and are rapidly becoming more popular here. It has to be said, though, that we don't (not yet anyhow) have the size of waters holding catfish in Britain to make trolling a feasible proposition. When we have then we need to study the methods of a continental angler by the name of Oliver Portrat who has used mobile techniques to catch hundreds of huge catfish – and this man rarely, if ever, fishes at night.

Baits

Popular baits are large bunches of lobworms, live and dead freshwater fish and sea species. Anglers fishing for huge cats of more than 100lb in weight think nothing of using a 4lb carp as bait, but for most of the cats found in this country a 4oz to 12oz fish is plenty big enough. In recent years big halibut pellets of 25mm or larger have become very popular, not surprisingly considering the numbers that are thrown in by carp anglers. On the Ebro in Spain they're being fed into the river by the sackful so that visiting anglers from the UK are almost guaranteed to catch. Chunks of fish and meat such as liver are good too, and cats have a particular liking for squid, although in some waters squid have been so popular the cats appear to be wary of them. My best catfish of 56lb, and several others I've caught, fell to squid that were fly-blown and stinking. Squid and fish and meat portions can be threaded onto the hook with a baiting needle, although I often prefer to just hook them lightly in the tougher bit at the head. Live and deadbaits should be lip-hooked or fished on a hair-rig. When lip-hooking, slide a tiny piece of rig foam or elastic band over the point of the hook, just past the barb, to prevent the bait from sliding off. Lobworms are best hooked once about an inch from the head. Any of these baits can be fished hard on the bottom, or popped up with the use of a polyball or air injection. Pellets and boilies are best hair-rigged.

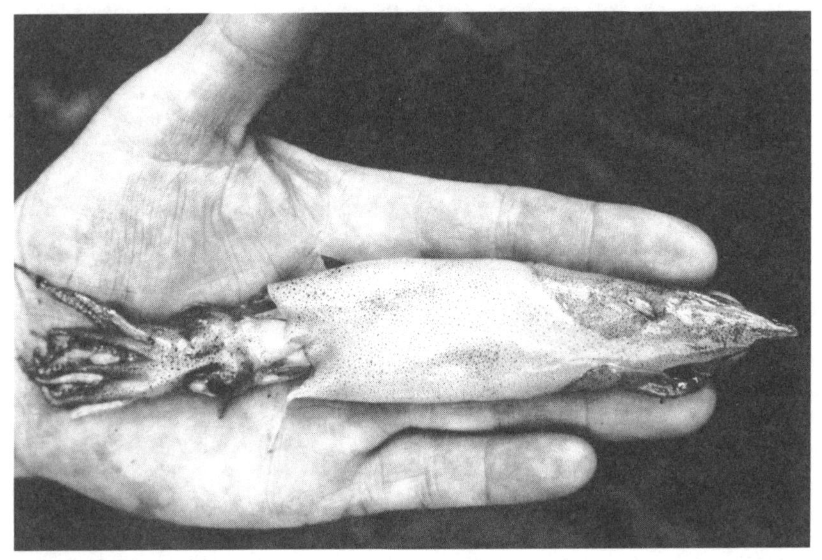

Squid is a popular catfish bait.

Bite Detection

In spite of their not-too-attractive appearance (ugly sods are a popular description) and the brute strength they display when hooked, catfish are otherwise extremely sensitive creatures. They have tiny eyes and obviously do not rely on optical power too much, but when it comes to smelling and feeling they are amongst the best. Those long barbules (the whiskers) are no doubt responsible for the detection of food, but they must also provide the catfish with a very efficient means of detecting hooks, lines, friction and resistance. This is also why braid is better than wire, why the end rig should be as resistance-free as possible, and why the bite detection system should be as sensitive as we can make it.

A light bobbin, or an ultra-sensitive swinger; one that is only just heavy enough to counteract any undertow, with a little extra weight to take up slack line from a drop-back bite, is the best indicator to use. Any type that allows the line to run freely, without trapping it, is fine. Use this indicator in conjunction with a bite alarm and watch for drop-backs - which is a trait of catfish - as well as runs. Don't use the baitrunner facility on the reel, but rather use an open bale-arm so that the line can run with minimum resistance.

A large landing net is essential when your fishing position does not allow you to land the fish by hand. Specialist catfish landing nets with 6ft arms can be purchased if you intend to take up catfish fishing on a more than casual basis. On a flat, or only slightly sloping grassy or sandy bank, cats can be landed by sticking your hand in their mouth, gripping the bottom jaw, and sliding them up the bank onto an unhooking mat. Use a glove if you feel better about it, but their teeth are soft, and not that sharp, and you're very unlikely to get hurt. But don't take my word for that and wear a glove or net the fish!

Most often the margins are the best areas to fish for cats, right in alongside any vegetation which they love to forage amongst. Cats will patrol all along the margins, especially at night if the water is clear, but will feed during the day on some dull days and when the water is coloured. Return the fish as soon as possible after weighing and following a quick trophy shot with the camera. Catfish may not be the prettiest fish in the world (although beauty is in the eye of the beholder) but they are amongst the best for their powerful fighting qualities. Hook a catfish and you know you've hooked a wild creature with the shape and muscle to give you a hard time.

INTRODUCTION TO CATFISH

My introduction to fishing for catfish came about during a trip to a small French water, Authon. It was a week when most of us recorded a personal best. A week when all of us laid eyes on a species we had never seen before in the wild.

Best of all, it was a week when we saw more than one grown man tremble at the sheer power of a fish. The story is about catching carp as well as catfish, but it's worth re-telling in full as there were so many incidents, and a trip where most of us, in our minds at least, joined the Catfish Appreciation Society.

Authon is a venue consisting of two small estate lakes, Autels and Cailleaux, just a half mile apart, in mid-France. We had heard on the grapevine that several anglers had returned from there the previous year singing its praises, which was enough to encourage 18 of us to book both lakes for a week in mid-April.

The ferry trip was from Portsmouth to Le Havre, and it was a good trip due mainly to the fact that it included a berth, allowing you to enjoy a good night's sleep and wake up fresh for the drive from Lehavre to Authon du Perche, about 150 miles across some beautiful French countryside. The painful part for we northerners is the drive from our neck of the woods to the south coast, which is about four hours to Portsmouth for most of us. But as the well-known phase has it, 'no pain - no gain'.

Saturday

We arrived at the waters about mid-day, half an hour or so behind Terry 'Singer' Knight (he can stitch up swims faster than any sewing machine) and in spite of being tired we soon erected our bivvy homes for the week and tackled up three rods each on the respective waters we had been allocated. There were nine of us on each water, but on our water, Cailleaux, we shared it with two anglers from the Manchester area.

Cailleaux, covering about 5 acres, with an average depth of 4ft to 5ft, was a little disappointing at first sight, for we had imagined it to be similar to a small estate lake back home, with their typical landscaped wildness - you know, neat but natural. Instead it was part of a fishery complex, complete with fish farm, at the side of a road busy with tractors. Although it was mid-April and the greenery had yet to blossom. By the end of the week, however, we loved the place. Autels, slightly smaller than Cailleaux, was certainly a more natural water, but generally shallower. Both were said to be similarly stocked, namely carp to 40lb plus, and catfish over 50lb. From what we had heard we could expect to catch carp mainly in the mid-double to mid-twenty class, and the odd big cat if the water was warm enough.

The previous week's anglers were just leaving as we arrived. They told us that they'd had a good week, catching lots of carp over 20lb, with two over thirty. But no cats, for the simple reason that they hadn't fished for them. They also claimed that on our lake, Cailleaux, it was essential to cast within one foot of the far bank to get regular runs. That was daunting to begin with, for I was at the wider end of the lake, and the 120yd distance to the far bank was stretching my casting capabilities, for although my casting accuracy is fine, I would never win anything for distance. I was not on my own, all five of us at the wide end had the same problem. So we baited and fished a good 10yds short of the far bank.

That first day we eventually had to give in to sleep, but it was a promising start with several doubles from 15lb to 19.8 caught.

Sunday

One of our party was determined to fish for cats, and that first night drew blood with a kitten that weighed a little over 9lb. It was a significant fish, however, for it triggered us to make greater efforts to catch them. By mid-morning we hadn't had a run on the carp rods, and we were all wondering the same thing - was it really essential to have the bait tucked into the far bank? The situation was crying out for a baitboat, and we didn't have one.

Necessity is the mother of invention, however, so we soon came up with a scheme to get round the problem. Although we were not allowed to fish from the far bank, we were allowed to walk round there to throw bait in. So we attached the baited end tackle to the tip of a 12ft rod, and carried the bait over the top of the hedge at the dam end of the lake, and dropped it into the margins along the opposite bank by hand. It was a better method than casting, for there was less disturbance, it was more accurate, and the end tackle was almost guaranteed to lie straight and tangle-free. And the fact that every time we dropped a bait in we also quite tightly surrounded it with particles, chopped boilies and whole boilies made it a particularly deadly technique.

It certainly seemed like it was a fact that the bait did have to lie very close to the far bank, for within minutes of the baits resting there we were into fish. First there was a 14lb common to me. Then myself and Richie Lee had 30lb mirrors, at the time a personal best for Richie. Terry hooked and lost two fish in quick succession. Then I lost one. We soon learned, however, that it needed a double strike to set the hooks properly at that range, where line stretch can be a problem. John Charlesworth was suffering, he hadn't yet had a run. We heard that they'd had carp to 27lb on the other lake.

Late that evening, outside my bivvy, where me, Terry, Richie, John, Eddie and Alan gathered to try a drop of grape juice and chat about the day's events, we decided to go in heavy with particles the following day.

Monday

Plenty of excitement in the night at 2am. Terry had a run that didn't stop when he hit it, taking line that made the reel scream like a wailing banshee (or was that Terry?). Tackle was 15lb main line, 45lb Quick Silver hooklength, and a size one Gold Label Continental Penetrator hook. A simple running lead, along with a small polyball attached to the hook with 6ins of mono to lift the bait completed the set-up. Ten minutes later, following a scrap that forced the comment, 'these make carp seem like bream', I lifted the net to enclose a catfish that weighed 32lb. Another personal best. And what a tremendous fish. A long, lean, muscle machine that had taken a roach livebait. There wasn't a man amongst us now who didn't have at least one catfish rod out at night for the rest of the week.

It was very quiet all morning from daybreak. We had caught a few double figure carp between us. The particles were in and we hoped it wouldn't be too long before the fish found them. I was fishing 1 ½ boilies on each of two rods and three peanuts on the other. I'd fed the swim with lots of chopped boilies, some halves and whole ones, over a bed of mixed particles. There wasn't a problem with small fish attacking the boilies, which enabled me to use the half boilie to see if the extra flavour it released would attract more attention.

Eddie and Alan had a small cat apiece.

I must have done something right, for at 1.30pm there began a tremendous period of activity for me. I kicked off with a 25.6 mirror that came to a boilie rod. Then a 22.8 common at 2pm to peanuts. Half an hour later an 8.14 sturgeon accepted boilies on one of my rods. Then all went quiet, with the carp clearly visible close to the surface in the middle section of the lake, just basking in the warmth of the sun. But at 7.30pm I was away again, this time a 25.2 mirror on peanuts, Then a 24.4 common on boilies just 15 minutes later. An hour after that another 24.5 mirror to boilies. Eddie and Alan had a small catfish apiece.

It must be my birthday, I thought. And then I remembered. It was! That day I was 54 years young, and still as daft as a brush about fishing, fishing daft hours, with daft mates who were still taking the piss out of me for being 'lucky'.

I said a silent prayer, to whoever may have been listening, before opening the first bottle of wine that night, 'Please, let me be just as daft when I'm 64.'

Talking about wine reminds me of a little scam Eddie and I had going on Terry Knight all week. Each night, in the dark, as the gathering sat outside my bivvy Eddie and I would open a new bottle of red wine and make a great show of tasting it and commenting about the exquisite bouquet, its nose, its subtle tones of this and that fruit, and all that crap associated with wine. We would gargle with it, swallow it, and say what a wonderful drink it was, this new wine we were trying. Then we poured Terry a glassful and he would say, 'Oh yes, very nice. What's this one called?' What he didn't know was while mine and Eddie's glass of wine was genuinely a good wine from a bottle, his was from a 5 litre red plastic barrel that cost about two quid. It was little better than red vinegar. In fact I've tasted better brews from Sarsons. What made the whole wind-up even better was that he plied us with a good brandy one night in return for our generosity!

At the other lake young Jim Hulse had caught a 45lb cat.

Tuesday

At 7am I was having my first brew of the day. A nice cup of Indian Prince, my favourite tea. At 11.30am Terry netted a common of 19.8 and then a smaller mirror soon after. I was thinking that peanuts caught a few fish yesterday and now that the fish had had chance to get more of a taste for them it may be a good idea to put two rods on nuts and one on boilie. So that's what I did. At 11.40am Terry caught the carp of the week at 34.12. Not the prettiest carp I've seen, but its weight made up for it. At 11.50am I netted a 14lb mirror on the single boilie rod. Still nothing to nuts. At 2pm Eddie netted his own fish of the week, another personal best. It fought like a sack of spuds, but what the hell, a 19.4 grass carp was a great fish.

Richie and John were fishing the dam end with float rods, casting right to the edge of the bushes where we had continually seen carp bubbling and topping.

Nobody had bothered with them until now because they always looked like small fish. Small, that is, compared to the standard we hoped to catch that week. But when you fish 8lb line to an 8's hook loaded with sweetcorn, on a through-action 1.25lb test-curve rod it's fun all the way. Richie and John, and young Tommy Chubb, caught a succession of double-figure carp through the week to a best fish of nearly 19lb.

At 8.10pm I got my own fish of the week at 32.10. While this fish was being photographed Richie asked Terry how many 20lb commons he had caught, to which he replied, 'very few.' Old Tel had forgot that I knew he had caught none, so he had loads of stick for the rest of the week with us continually asking, 'How many 20lb commons have you had Tel?' And answering ourselves in chorus: 'Very few.'

At 10.20pm, while we sat toasting the successes of that day outside my bivvy, young Mattie and Darren came running up to tell us that one of the Manchester lads had caught a big cat of 52lb at the far end of the lake. I got down there just in time to get a quick shot before it was returned. What a superb creature. It fired us all, and we went back to the rods hungry for pussy. And when John had a screamer of a run just half an hour later on his live roach, and hooked something that bent his 3 1/2lb pike rod like a young sapling - only to come adrift - it meant there was little sleep that night. But there was more to come anyhow.

Wednesday

I woke from a half sleep, switched my bivvy light on and glanced at my watch. 3am, and John was screaming. 'Big cat! Big cat! I've got a big cat on. Some ****** get out here!' I was at his side in seconds, the big net in my hands and my headlamp switched on, tilted down so as not to shine directly at the water. Eddie, then Terry, followed soon by Alan and Richie, watched the events as they unfolded. It was a still, very slightly misty night, a clear sky, but as black as a bag. The only sound to be heard was the screaming clutch as John held tight to the rod with both hands, the butt jammed into his groin. The screaming went on for ever, or seemed to, and then, mercifully, came the occasional swish, swish of a reel gaining line. Voices chipped in, John's, quivering: 'Oh God. Oh God, it's a big ******.' Then mine, and other voices behind me: '...Kinell. ...Kinell. It IS a big ******!'

I glanced down at John's knee and lit it with my headlamp. All eyes followed and we could see it, quite literally, jumping up and down. He was shaking with a mixture of fear, trepidation and elation. And then a most terrible stench pervaded the air, and all around hands were wafting it away from noses and accusations were being hurled at each other. John piped up: 'I can't 'elp it lads, it's me. It's worked me.' Everyone tumbled around with laughter at that and relaxed a little.

It must have been 20 minutes before the big cat showed signs of tiring. It came to the surface and we saw the great length of it in the torch beam. Then it was time to net it and we realised we had a problem. I got the head into the net, but there was no way I could get enough of the tail in to enclose it safely in the mesh. Luckily, the big cat was played out and lay quiet while Alan and Terry got down to the water's edge and managed to fold the tail inside. They unshipped the handle from the net and between them carried the cat up the bank. It weighed exactly 50lb. John just couldn't stop laughing. Elation and relief poured out of him, and we were all glad for him, for he hadn't had much luck with the carp. He kept repeating, 'Oh my pussy, oh what a lovely little pussy. You're the nicest moggy in the whole world.' He kissed it while we photographed it, and wafted away that awful smell.

Later that day Richie recorded a few doubles and a 21.12 common. I had a 14.4 common on peanut, and Terry an 18lb and 19.12 common (to a chorus of 'How many 20lb commons have you had Tel?.......... Very few.'). Alan, Eddie, Darren, Mattie, Tommy and John had a double or two. Then later that night both me and John had the scales stripped off our roach baits from aborted cat runs.

Thursday

At 2am I netted a 17lb cat for Terry, and we heard that the Manchester lad had caught another big cat of 42lb that had fought harder than his 52-pounder. Richie had another personal best, a 33lb cat in the night. Two thirties and two PB's in a week can't be bad. A 15lb mirror came to one of my boilie rods at 5.45am, then I caught my first grass carp ever at 6.30am, only 8lb but a first is a first and very welcome. Nothing much happened through the day, apart from the odd double, mainly to the float rods along the dam. Most of us sat in the hot sun, eating French stick loaded with cheese from the local Intermarche, washed down with occasional sips of red wine.

John and the big cat that 'worked' him!

Evening came quite rapidly, bringing that flurry of activity from night anglers everywhere. The splash of fresh baits being cast, and the music of bite alarms being set. Everyone was on the go for a short spell, and then all went quiet as the atmosphere settled into one of mild tension, hope, and anticipation. The quiet solitude outside my bivvy didn't last long though, for the usual gang turned up, bottles under arms, Alan with his crate of beer. Tonight was to be a serious session. It was the last night we could have a drink, for tomorrow night, Friday, was too close to the long drive back to Le Havre on Saturday morning.

Terry brought his bottle of cognac, which Eddie and I proceeded to help him empty, plying him with Red Barrel wine (a La Vinegar) in exchange. We opened a bottle of champers to celebrate the victories that week and it mixed well with the cognac. A few hours later old Tel's chair fell over with Tel still in it, so we tucked him into his sleeping bag, reeled his rods in, and went to bed.

Friday

Two cats were caught in the night, a 13-pounder to Eddie's rod, and a '21' to Alan's. Again I had missed out. No cats for me, and no carp either that night. An hour or so after daybreak Ian came round to say he'd caught a 51lb cat on the other lake, so we went round to photograph and video it. The weight was checked, for there was £65 resting on the result, for most of us had wagered a fiver on the best cat and the same on the best carp caught that week. John was particularly anxious, for he thought he had the cat money sown up with his '50'. Ian's fish had lost half a pound in the hour or so it had been in the sack, weighing 50 1/2lb, and took the money. Another magnificent fish in a week of magnificent fish.

Apart from that big moggy, Friday faded away on a relatively quiet note, with a few big doubles coming to leger and float tackle. Part of the day was spent packing away as much gear as possible, ready for the big 'pack-up' in the morning. Good weeks like we had had are always tinged with sadness when you are faced with leaving the water a thousand miles behind you.

Chapter 10

Chub

A fish with a big mouth and an appetite to suit

THE EVER-OBLIGING CHUB – MOST OF THE TIME!

Chub are probably the most obliging freshwater fish that swims when it comes to bait choice, there is very little that is edible that they won't accept at some time or other. And yet there are some days when they are so fussy they will home in on one particular bait to the exclusion of all others, and if you haven't got that bait with you that day, then hard luck, you'll be the one with a dry net! I've met quite a few anglers who found that out to their cost, for they were fishing with just the one bait, either bronze maggot or caster, which is fine on many days, but not every day, and especially when the river level has been up and down like a yo-yo.

I really enjoy float fishing for chub, and it is my first choice on my local river Dane (or any river where the swim is suited to it, and the fish are numerous enough to make the effort worthwhile) so I invariably take at least a pint of maggot or caster and begin on the float. The Dane has a good stock of dace too, and roach in some areas, so if you fish light enough you usually catch a mixed bag, which is great, for I love catching dace and roach, as well as chub, and it makes it all the more interesting when you don't know if the next bite will be from a 4oz dace, or a 2lb to 4lb chub. In odd swims it could be a 5lb-plus barbel. You just never know.

More often than not maggot and caster will be their usual productive selves, but it is those odd days when the chub are being fastidious that you have to be prepared for. And that means taking maggot, caster, bread, worms, cheese and luncheon meat. You could take a lot more than that of course, such as sweetcorn, cheese paste, hemp and tares, etc, etc. But you have to draw the line somewhere, otherwise you would need a rucksack just to carry the bait, and spend more time changing baits than you would actually fishing.

The essential six, as I call them: bread, cheese, luncheon meat, worm, maggot and caster, are a large enough variety of baits for anyone to carry, especially since bread can be used in three forms: flake, crust and paste, and if none of those tempt a chub on any day, then it can only mean the chub are not feeding at all, so it wouldn't make any difference what baits you had with you. Except one, perhaps. If there is a magic bait where chub are concerned then it has to be wasp grub, but I don't include wasp grub in my essential six for the simple reason that I can't get enough of it to use on a regular basis. But it must be said that although wasp grub can be a brilliant chub bait, it does not guarantee fish. Anyhow, what happens on the Dane on quite a few occasions is that maggot and caster fails almost completely when the water is carrying any colour, apart from the odd dace, roach and gudgeon. This is not too unusual, for in coloured water the larger and smellier baits have the edge. Favourite amongst many anglers is luncheon meat, but my own personal favourite when the water is carrying any colour is a large lobworm. Any other time, when I'm not fishing light with a float and maggot or caster combination I automatically reach for the bread, with flake on a long tail or a crust fished up to two inches off bottom.

What is unusual is the number of days when the chub refuse to be caught on one large bait in preference for another. What generally happens is that we fish all kinds of large baits when the water is coloured, each angler having his own personal favourite, and each catching his fair share of fish on his choice of bait. This makes sense, for each angler has come to prefer a certain bait because he has done well on it in the past, in the conditions he is faced with that day. In effect, it means that the fish don't really have a favourite bait, but rather anglers do, a bait they will use with a great deal of confidence, which in itself is a great fish-catcher.

It doesn't always work out like that though, for there are times when the chub decide they are going to like only one bait on some days. And what makes it worse is that it is not the same bait each time. Most often it's bread, either flake or crust. Followed by lobworm. Then just occasionally they want luncheon meat. The angler who catches the most fish on a particular day is the angler whose favourite bait is wanted by the chub on that day. Not for the reason that other anglers are not willing to change baits once they know what the chub want, but simply for the reason that they don't fish the bait as efficiently as the angler who is comfortable with that bait.

I'm pretty sure that most anglers fish much the same as me, in that if the chub are taking, say, luncheon meat, one day, and my preference is for lobs or bread, then I would frequently be trying lobs and bread through the day just to see if I could catch on them. It results in much wasted time when I could have been pulling one or two out on the going bait.

The author float fishing the Dane.

It's uncanny really, for chub are not usually the kind of fish that are so fussy. Normally, it is a case of finding them, sticking any decent bait under their nose, and wondering when, rather than if, you'll get a bite.

The Dane is no different than any other rain-fed river, in that when the water is coloured - which means it goes a muddy brown - the chub are usually suckers for lobworms, and if no other bait tempts a bite on a coloured, rain-fed river, a lob almost certainly will. When the water is clear, bread (apart from maggot and caster) is generally the preferred bait. But all that can be out of the window, with bread at times being the sought-after bait when the water is coloured, and lobs and luncheon meat being hot favourite when the water is reasonably clear.

There have been times when I haven't known where the hell I was with them, and if I hadn't had a bite in a reasonable length of time, it was a case of going walkabout, to see what others were catching on, if they were catching at all.

There is usually someone along the length who has tried the right bait and is pulling out a few fish.

THREE APPROACHES TO BIG CHUB

There are three basic approaches to catching chub. The first way I call the 'Feed and Wait Approach'. This entails choosing a swim, sitting on it, and feeding it for the duration. The second way I call the 'Walk and Feed Approach' This entails walking the length, or a good piece of it, feeding each swim, and then fishing each swim, beginning with the first one you fed. The third way is the least complicated of the lot. I call it the 'Walk and Fish Approach', which is as simple as it sounds, meaning I walk the stretch and fish and feed each likely swim as I go. Let's look at each approach in more detail.

The Feed and Wait Approach

This approach is ideal for established swims, those swims with a proven track record that you already know very well. You will know they are capable of producing several good fish on a day when they are well on feed. You will know exactly where to cast in each of these swims, and what rigs and baits are productive, and you will have already learned how much feed to put in for the best results. They are swims, really, in which you know you can afford to invest plenty of time.

You set up in such a swim knowing you are there for the duration of that session, using a comfortable chair, and laying everything you need around you in easy reach. You can take along a few luxuries, such as a small radio, and settle down for a good day's fishing. You feed the swim, cast in, and wait, sitting back in the sure knowledge that that is all you can do now, except to ring the changes with bait, and top up the swim with feed, as the day wears on. There is nothing else you can do, apart from something radical that you may want to experiment with, otherwise you know from past experience exactly what is required to catch chub from the swim.

The Walk and Feed Approach

This is the best approach for short session fishing where you arrive at the river an hour or two before dusk with the intention of fishing an hour or two into darkness. You have selected a length that you know well, and are fishing the time when chub are most likely to feed. Before you set out you soaked a bucketful of stale bread and then stiffened it with dry groundbait. You added enough groundbait to make it just stiff enough to squeeze together so that when it is thrown into the swim the majority of it sinks to the bottom, but is soft enough to break up easily when it gets there.

On arrival at the water you shrug off your tackle at the first swim you come to (providing you know it is safe, or will be able to keep it in sight) and then set out with your bucket to prebait up to perhaps a dozen swims along the length. You feed no more than two or three good handfuls of groundbait into each swim, for the idea is to give the chub no more than a taste, an appetiser if you like, so that they already have their bibs on when you drop a special morsel of crust, flake, cheese, or whatever bait you know they usually like best, armed with a hook, onto the dining table. By the time you return to your tackle, that first swim you baited should be well primed, with the chub mopping up the last crumbs of the groundbait and anxiously grubbing round for more. Your first hookbait will be like the sausage that follows the beans.

Or at least that is the theory, and I catch enough fish following this walk and feed approach to suggest it is often the right thing to do. After all, most of the swims you visit along that length should have chub feeding in them, not only feeding, but feeding confidently and safely on the prebait with not a hooked or spooked fish in sight to destroy the illusion.

But I have reservations about this approach where big chub are concerned, and whenever I fish a stretch where my target is 5lb-plus chub I prefer the last, but not least, of the three options.

The walk and feed approach.

The Walk and Fish approach

This technique is similar to the latter approach, except that you fish each swim without the advantage (or disadvantage, depending on your point of view) of prebait. I usually prefer this approach because I believe that prebaiting more often leads to catching the smaller fish in a swim than it does to catching the largest. Unlike the thinking of many experienced chub anglers, I think the first big bait introduced to a swim is more likely to be picked up by the biggest chub in that swim than is a bait that follows other baits, hooked or otherwise). For some time now it hasn't made sense to me to think that the bigger fish hang back while the smaller ones take their pick of what is in the larder. The biggest fish haven't got to be the biggest by being the last ones in the food queue!

I'm not saying that the technique of wading your way through the small ones first is not an option, especially where you are fishing waters like the southern chalk streams where you can tempt the fish into leaving the sanctuary of a 'safe' area and then selectively casting baits to fish you can see. What I am saying is that northern spate rivers don't often run clear enough to be able to see the fish, and even when they do it isn't a great advantage to you when you're fishing into darkness!

So the 'Walk and Fish' approach simply means that you walk to each swim and drop a big bait right into the thick of it. If there are any big fish around they aren't likely to let the smaller ones beat them to it. It isn't a case of the smaller ones being quicker off the mark, it is more a case of the bigger ones being dominant that matters. If a smaller fish tries to take a bait from a bigger fish it is going to get a thick ear, so to speak. That's the law of the jungle, including the aquatic jungle. Survival of the fittest, the strongest and the biggest.

Another thing, when fishing for big fish, especially big chub that are more easily spooked than many other species, it isn't a good idea to hook any other fish in that swim first, for the fact that other fish are being hauled from the swim in panic is a dead giveaway to the bigger fish that something is wrong! No, I reckon your best chance of catching a big chub is to drop a big bait right into a swim that has not been 'interfered' with in any way for some time, where you either know, or suspect, big chub are present, and then move to another swim once you have hooked a fish, of whatever size.

Which does not mean that you cannot revisit that swim later in the same session once the dust has settled. In fact I may revisit swims several times in a session if a sufficiently long enough period has elapsed between each visit. At least an hour, say, after hooking a fish or disturbing the swim in any way.

Whatever approach you decide to try it is best to keep your tackle as simple as possible. One rod for the roving techniques, and possibly two for the static approach (one rod to fish a well-proven bait and rig in a known hot-spot, and one to experiment with rigs, baits, feed and feeding techniques, and for allowing a bait to lie in areas other than the known hot-spot). Both rods don't necessarily have to be used at the same time, although it depends on the size of the river and the type of swim.

The main line I most often use is rated at 6lb, and the hooklength 5lb, although I won't hesitate to go stronger when I know big chub are lying close to snags. Over the years I've experimented with all kinds of end rigs for river legering, but still come back to a simple running bomb or feeder. I've tried all kinds of booms, paternosters and all manner of fancy rigs with tubing, bangles and beads all over the place, but simple is still best. But at least I tried them, and will probably continue to try new ideas rather than be left wondering if I'm missing something. After all, it is difficult to claim you are using the best of anything unless you've tried them all.

Keep everything else to a bare minimum if you are following one of the wandering approaches. A waterproof cushion rather than a chair, a small ruckbag, a small tackle box with a few compartments, and a selection of baits, including bread, cheese, luncheon meat and lobworms, the four all-time favourites.

CHUB ON WASP GRUB

It seems there are at least some anglers out there who are not sure exactly what wasp grub are, and the odd one who hasn't got a clue! One angler who I met while out fishing said he thought a wasp grub was a worm flavoured with something he'd seen in a bottle in the tackle shop! Yes, there are flavours that are supposed to smell like wasp grub, and 'supposed' is

Wasp cake and wasp grub.

the operative word, for man-made wasp grub flavour and the real thing are about as similar as eau de flatulence is to Chanel No. 5.

There are different species of wasp (Hymenoptera) most of which are solitary, but the one we anglers are interested in is categorised as a social wasp. These live in colonies of up to several thousand members and are divided into three castes: egg-laying queens, workers (sexually undeveloped females) and drones (males). It is the females (as always!) that have the sting in the tail for which they are famous. They build paper-like nests consisting of from one to several combs (layers) in a papery sheath. Wasp grubs are the larvae of the wasp which are laid in the individual cells in the honeycomb (cake). The grubs can be anything from about 15mm to 20mm long and 4mm to 5mm thick. Wasps make their nest in cavities in walls and trees, but more usually they use a hole in the ground, most often in the sandy soil of a hedgerow.

Wasp grub and cake have a unique smell. It is a pleasing smell even to us mortals; not exactly honey-like, but more of a musty, semi-sweet, pungent, waxy aroma, if that makes any sense. It is no wonder it has not yet been imitated by a bait flavour company. But no matter how pleasing the smell is to us it is far more pleasing to fish, especially chub. On the right day they can't get enough of it. Wasp grub and cake is the nearest thing there is to an irresistible bait. It stops short of being magical in that there are days when it is ignored with the same disdain as any other bait. But on the right day, on that day when the chub really want it, they queue up for it like starving men in a soup kitchen.

The best example I can think of to describe how addictive wasp grub and cake can be was the time I was asked by a weekly angling journal to catch chub for the camera on my local river Dane. In a 2.5ft deep swim, from low, clear water, with a reporter and photographer wandering the bank behind me, I took over 70lb of chub to over 3lb on float and leger in three hours. As I threw in the special wasp cake groundbait (I'll tell you how to make it in a mo) the chub were battling with each other to snatch it from the surface before it could sink. My hookbaits were taken just as quickly.

Wasp bait is a real killer bait, and it is probably just as well that it is not easily available. Apart from chub wasp bait will take many species of fish. I remember that wasp bait was an especially good catcher of brown trout for me and my pals over 50 years ago when we used to fish the upper reaches of the Dane at night during school holidays, and I've also hooked the odd barbel when fishing the bait on the Severn, the Dane and the Wye. It does, however, appear that it is the chub, in particular, that is addictively attracted to it. And contrary to some opinion, wasp bait is an all year round bait, working just as well in winter as it does in summer - on the right day.

Where do I get some from?

The most asked questions are, 'How do I get hold of some?' And, 'Can I buy it?' As for the former, yes, you can get hold of some if you have the right contacts, or are willing to track down and take the nests yourself. And the answer to the latter is that a few tackle shops sell wasp bait occasionally, but it is an uncertain business and one where demand by far exceeds supply. I get hold of my wasp bait in two ways. The easiest way, and the one I rely on most, is to cadge it off a pal of mine, who is a pal of the local Pest Control Officer, who is called out to remove wasps nests from locations where the wasps are causing a nuisance. Failing that I ask friends and relatives to look out for wasps nests, and then take them myself.

How to Take a Wasp's Nest

Before you attempt this operation be sure you have the confidence to do it; that you are not allergic to wasp stings, and be very wary that you will be using toxic gases that must be handled at all times with yours and other's health and safety very much in mind. You will need a mole smoke, which can be obtained from most garden centres or online, a torch, a bank-stick, a lighter or box of matches, a spade, a pair of garden gloves, and a bin liner.

Ignore all nests except those that are found in ground that can be easily dug up to expose the nest. Most often this will be in the sandy soil of a hedgerow. Go to the nest in the late evening, just after darkness has fallen, when all the wasps will have returned for the night. The idea is to kill them all while they're in the nest. There is no point in trying to kill them at any other time when wasps will constantly be returning to, and departing from, the nest.

Tape the mole smoke to the bank stick, light it, and then wait for it to reach full burn. Now plunge it into the nest entrance. Wait for it to stop smoking, and make sure none of the surrounding vegetation sets alight. Once you are sure that everything is safe; that the mole smoke is burnt out and nothing else is alight, leave it for the night and return the following morning armed with your spade, gloves and bin liner. For extra safety take a spray-can of wasp killer to kill the odd one that escaped the smoke, and to finish off those that have enough life to get their own back. A good idea also is to take a spray-can of sting relief for those that get past the smoke and the spray (very rare, but you may as well play it safe).

With your gloves on pull the smoke out of the nest entrance and wait a few minutes to see if any wasps fly out. If the smoke has done its job properly there shouldn't be any, but give any odd ones a squirt with the killer spray. Now dig out the nest, being careful not to damage it with the spade. Drop the lot into the bin liner and seal the neck with tape. Now spade the soil back into the hole you've made and leave everywhere nice and tidy.

When you get back home put your gloves on again and take the nest out of the bag. You need the gloves at this stage for there may be some half dead wasps that can still sting. Get rid of these and then split the nest into the different layers of cake, placing the best layers (those which are full of whole white and grey grubs) into one or more margarine tubs or biscuit tins (Tupperware containers if you're posh) and the worst (those with no grubs or fully developed wasps) into other tubs. The good stuff is for hookbaits and the rough stuff is for making groundbait. Any that you don't need immediately should be stored in the freezer.

Making Wasp Cake Groundbait

Being as wasp bait is not too easy to come by it is wise to make it go as far as possible, but not so far the unique smell of it is degenerated to the point where it becomes ineffective. The idea then is to mix the rough wasp cake with as much other material as we can get away with, and the best 'other material' I've found is pulped brown bread.

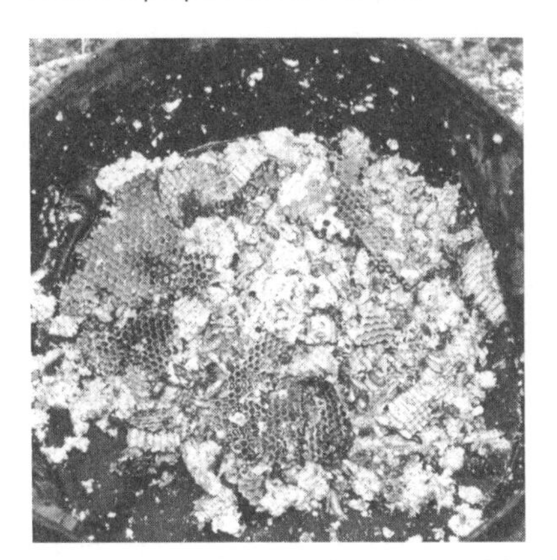

Place some rough wasp cake in a mixing bowl and squeeze the rough cake to a pulp. Add the already prepared brown bread and then some dry brown groundbait to stiffen...but only just stiff enough to throw.

Take equal amounts of wasp cake and sliced brown bread (visually equal, nothing fancy) and place the bread in a bowl, covering it with water. Leave to soak for at least 10 minutes. While it's soaking, pulverise the cake to a pulp and crush any odd grubs to liquid, using your fingers. Squeeze the bread between your fingers until it reaches an almost liquefied state, run off the excess water, and then squeeze out as much water as you can. Thoroughly mix the bread and wasp bait together, and then stiffen with fine brown groundbait to the right consistency, stiff enough to throw but soft enough to dissolve as it sinks and when on the bottom.

Float Fishing

A standard match rod set-up is fine, except that it needs to be stepped up slightly. I use a 13ft match rod, closed face or centrepin reel loaded with 3lb line, a 2.5lb hooklength to a 12 hook. Float can be a waggler or a double-rubber float such as a Stick, Avon or Chubber, but most often it should be the double-rubber type for the simple reason that wasp bait will not stand up to casting, and therefore has to be used at short range. You will be using just the grubs for float fishing, and a 12 hook is necessary because of the difficulty in keeping wasp grub on the hook, and the line is heavier so that the 12 hook can be planted without fear of breaking off. Choose a float, whatever the type you use, that will take a shot or two more than you would normally use in a particular swim. That way the tackle can be swung out, and the line mended during the trot down the swim, with less effort, and therefore with less chance of throwing the bait off the hook. Bulk shot the float at about half depth, with one dropper shot about 6" from the hook. That's all you need to do.

Feed the head of the swim with three or four golf ball-size pieces of groundbait straight away, then have a few trots down. More often than not, on a good day, the chub will be onto the bait instantly and it isn't unusual to catch a fish first trot down. Now feed the swim as you would when caster fishing; little and often, a tiny piece every trot down.

The 12 hook should be a fine wire type, for the grubs are extremely fragile and almost liquefy the moment the hook penetrates them. Some will stand up to being hooked better than others, so what you do is keep hooking a grub on until there is sufficient on the hook to present to the fish. Sometimes three good ones will do the trick, other times it will take six poor ones.

On very good days the chub can be worked up to a feeding frenzy and will take the groundbait and hookbait before it has had chance to sink many inches. If this happens slide the shot and float right down and trot the bait down really shallow. It may look ridiculous, but it works, and that's all that matters. And keep the feed going in, a small piece every trot down.

Legering

Your usual quivertip rod and the reel that goes with it are all you need. The reel can be loaded with 5lb line to a 4lb hooklength, but this can be 6lb/5lb where bigger chub in snaggy swims are expected. For legering you will be using grubs whilst still in the nest material (cake) as hookbait. There is nothing stopping you using neat grub as for float fishing (or vice-versa) but I like to fish for better quality chub when legering wasp bait, and a big chunk of cake can usually sort them out. The end rig can be as simple as a single SSG direct on the line, or a simple linkleger that offers quick changes of leger weight. The hook can be as big as a 2, but shouldn't be any smaller than a 6, for the cake is just as difficult to keep on the hook as is the neat grub. Hook it on as you would a big crust; into the open side of the comb, through, and then back into the closed, papery white side, or with a bait band tied to a short hair, making sure the bait band is big enough and not too tight or it will slice through the cake.

Wasp cake banded to the hook.

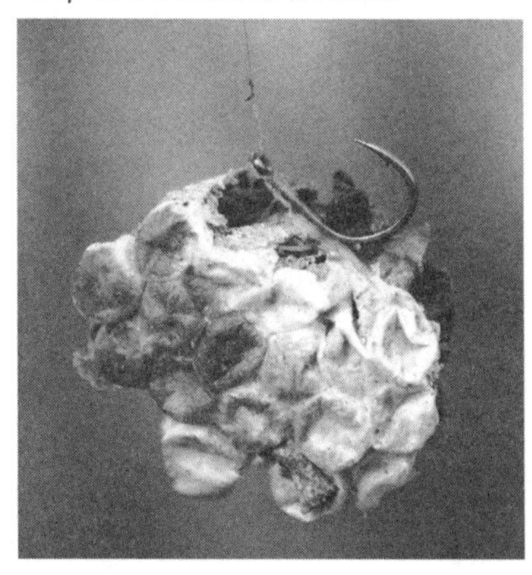

Again, you won't be casting very far, for the cake won't take it. I try to choose a swim where all I have to do is lower the bait into a spot under my own bank from behind cover, and then move upstream, away from the swim, by several yards. Failing that, I choose a swim where all I have to do is swing the bait in, pendulum fashion, from my fishing position.

Squeeze the groundbait into a more compact, dense ball for legering, so that it drops rapidly to the bottom and feeds where your hookbait lies. Alternatively, use a bait-dropper to release a piece on the bottom, or an open-ended swimfeeder. I should point out, however, that on the best days the chub attack bait-droppers and swimfeeders when they are mad on feed and you end up striking and missing a lot of fish, or foul hooking a few. Better to feed by hand whenever you can.

Bites are usually strong and confident, but not always. Sometimes the chub feed so confidently on wasp bait they suck it in and don't move off too far. This calls for some experimenting on the day, to get the timing of the strike just right.

Don't expect miracles from wasp bait, but on the right day you may think it really is a miraculous bait!

CLOSE THE SEASON WITH CHUB

Generally speaking chub are not a difficult fish to catch and the goodwill from this species reaches its peak in the last few weeks of the season. No matter if you fish for a bag of chublets, or are more inclined to sit it out for a special, chubbier chub, you can be almost certain that your season will end on a successful note if the river is in anything like good condition.

Obviously, there are no guarantees, which is why I say you can be 'almost' certain of success. We are dependent on those inconsiderate weather men.

They have to pull their finger out and give us some decent conditions for the last few weeks of the season. If they can't give us ideal conditions, then at least let the weather be settled, even if it has to be settled into regular frosts, or regular anything. That way we have got a damn good chance of netting some good fish before we have to hang up our river rods for three months.

The most difficult choice I have to make where chub fishing on my own local waters are concerned is whether to visit a stretch where the fish are above average size for the river and sit it out for something a bit special. Or fish a more prolific stretch and enjoy lots of bites and good sport for most of the day. As it happens I'm lucky enough to be able to fish two or three times a week and I can, if the fancy takes me, regularly follow both options.

My local rivers are the Dane, the Dove, the Ribble, the upper Trent and the upper Severn, although 'local' may seem inappropriate in the case of the Severn and the Ribble considering the closest stretch I fish is some 45 miles away. The Dane, on the other hand, is a mere 10 miles, with the Dove and the upper Trent somewhere in between.

Chub fishing on the river Dane can be brilliant, providing you don't have the need to be pulling out 4lb plus fish fairly regularly. If so, then the Dane is not for you. Dane chubbers catch good bags of fish ranging from less than 1lb to a little over 4lb, with the average size in most swims around the 2lb to 3lb mark. Of course there are odd bigger chub in the Dane, but not enough to make fishing for them exclusively a realistic option. Which does not say that you cannot fish with heavier tackle in snaggy swims for the bigger than average fish. Not at all, many times I go for an hour two after dark to try and catch some 4lb plus chub. The biggest difference between that and doing the same thing on the rivers further afield is that the chub, on average, are likely to be a pound or two bigger. It all depends on my mood at the time, or what takes my fancy. Or something much more basic than that, such as simply not having the time to spend on travelling. A couple of hours chubbing on the Dane definitely beats no chubbing at all.

Chub fishing on the Severn is most certainly getting better. This is due in no small part to the barbel boom being over, in that scores of these magnificent fish are not multiplying like rabbits to establish a colony. That's over now. They are just another Severn species, well established, their numbers more or less settled, and a range of sizes from babies to fish in double figures. Only the higher reaches of the upper Severn are still undergoing change, with barbel steadily colonising the area. It has taken the barbel several decades to settle as well established citizens of the Severn, but in the process they played havoc with the food availability and spawning sites for the already established species, particularly chub. Our friendly chub suffered for years, but now that the barbel have stopped their rampaging the chub are making a steady come-back. Severn chub weighing over 5lb are no longer a wistful dream. They are such a reality now that I fish there almost expecting to catch one, rather than merely hoping. The same can be said for many stretches of the Ribble, Dove and upper Trent.

Other than the average size of the fish, the main difference between river Dane and chub from the other rivers is that the Dane chub are caught like clockwork. You can visit most stretches in the week and find someone, somewhere, pulling out at least a few chub. Nine times out of ten the angler will be using stickfloat methods with either maggot or caster as bait. Maggot and caster are certainly part of the staple diet of Dane chub, to the point where they cannot resist them, no matter how often they are caught on them, and how soon after they are caught they are offered them again. I think it has reached the stage on the Dane now whereby the chub think it is part of the feeding ritual to be hauled from the water at some point during a meal. Perhaps they feel that they have missed out somehow if they are not given a lift in a landing net every so often during the week, and always on Saturday and Sunday. There must be many popular waters just like the Dane.

It is a different story on the other rivers, especially the upper Severn. Many stretches go for several weeks without being fished at all by a coarse angler. On many stretches maggot and caster are still a strange creature that the chub are not overly interested in. Bread is far more attractive, and a chunk of flake trotted down a swim is far more likely to be taken. And that is one of my favourite methods on the upper Severn, in suitable swims. Feeding with mashed bread and trotting flake under a chunky float is one of the old favourite, and still deadly, upper Severn methods.

Mashed bread for float and feeder fishing for chub.

You have a job to imagine anything more simple. All you do is save your old bread until it goes stale. Take it to the river and mash it to a pulp with lots of water in a bucket or bowl, squeeze out the excess water and then stiffen it a little with dry groundbait. Not too much, for you want the particles to break away and follow the current just like the piece of flake you're going to send down riding on the back of a hook. You tackle up with a match rod, 12ft to 14ft (whatever is your personal favourite) and a fixed-spool reel, or centrepin, loaded with 4lb line. I use a bodied waggler if I'm fishing mid-river and beyond, or a Chubber float fixed top and bottom for near bank to mid-river swims. A 10 or 8 hook is tied direct to the main line and all the shot is bulked a little below mid-depth, and a single dropper, which is at least a BB, a foot from the hook. In very fast swims the dropper is dispensed with altogether and all the shot bulked no more than a foot from the hook.

Feed the swim every cast with a ball of mashed bread about as big as a chicken's egg and hold the float back hard at times to make the flake flicker and rise and fall in the flow - just like all those particles of loose-fed bread that dance in the current. A piece of flake as big as a five pence piece is about right, for on the upper Severn (and upper Trent, Ribble and Dove) you will be fishing for 4lb plus chub, with an excellent chance of 5-pounders, and always a chance of the odd chub going over 6lb.

If you have your sights set firmly on the bigger fish then there is no doubt that the best time to fish the rivers that hold the biggest chub is from an hour before dark to several hours after using leger tackle. There are many stretches of my big chub rivers, especially the deeper, slower reaches, where there is not a big head of chub, but the ones that inhabit the stretch are mainly in the upper 4lb to 6lb bracket. You fish them with the thought firmly in your mind that you are fishing for one fish, but hopefully a really big fish. You hope that you will catch a good fish as soon as possible, for that means you then have plenty of time to move to another swim to try for another big fish.

The drill is to bait two or three, or more, swims, and fish each in turn, depending on how events unfold. The thing to remember is that you are likely to catch no more than one fish in each swim, and that is on a good night. If you catch a fish quickly you then move straight away to the next swim. If you see some interest in the bait but fail to hook a fish you stay in that swim, trying to convert the interest into a bite, for as long as it takes. If you see no interest in the bait then you move after, say, half an hour. It is a fact that, more often than not, if you are going to catch a chub from any swim it usually takes the bait within five minutes of casting into it.

I should mention too, that there are times when the ploy of prebaiting several swims is inferior to fishing each swim from a standing start. The difficult bit is deciding which approach is best on the night. My usual approach is to have ten minutes in each swim first, before any loose feed of any kind is introduced, see how it goes, and then prebait each swim and start again. Very often that special fish will hit that first chunk of flake or crust within minutes of it sinking to the bottom. Big fish don't get big by hanging back and allowing lesser fish to steal food from under their nose. At least not on those stretches where the fish are not well educated.

My legering tackle for big chub consists of medium strength quivertip rod. The fixed-spool reel is loaded with 6lb line, and the hooklength is 5lb. Hook is a wide-gape, size 6. The rig is a simple running leger bead with, a clip-link to allow for quick change of the bomb, stopped with a rubber bead up against a swivel stop. Heavy baits like cheese, luncheon meat and lobworm are fished about 15ins from the hook, bread flake about 9ins to a foot from the hook, and bread crust just two inches away; the crust being popped up from an SSG shot. I use a bomb that is just, and only just, heavy enough to hold bottom in the swim I'm fishing. Then, a little flick of the rod tip will cause it to roll, if that is what is needed at the time.

The tip of my rod is fitted with an adapter to hold a Betalight which allows me to fish into darkness without any need to illuminate the quivertip. But do treat yourself to a headlamp if you haven't already got one. Then you will have hands-free illumination of everything else you do: baiting the hook, landing and unhooking fish, and walking back to the car at packing up time, which can be quite dangerous along some river banks.

I fish to the same pattern when I fish the Dane in the evening, baiting several swims and trying each - if necessary. Obviously, if I begin to enjoy some good sport in the first swim I fish I stay there until it dies. The big difference between the Dane and the big chub rivers in this instance is that the Dane chub are much more prolific and it is possible to catch several from the one swim.

Whatever river you are fishing it is important to take a selection of baits. Bread is my favourite and I would be reluctant to fish for chub anywhere without having a loaf with me. Swap between crust (popped up about two inches) and flake, which will dance enticingly on a 12ins hooklength. Luncheon meat is another must, and boilies are always worth a try, although it can be a case of muck or nettles with boilies and chub, in that there doesn't seem to be anywhere in between - they either go well, or not at all.

Cheese paste is a must for me. Many times just the fact that I have a tiny pinch of cheese on the shank of a hook otherwise loaded with bread makes all the difference. It is great too, for counter-balancing the buoyancy of bread. Lobworms can be great in coloured water, providing the temperature is not too low. There are lots of other baits that chub find perfectly acceptable too, possibly some will work better in your rivers than the ones I've covered. The only way to find out is to experiment.

There isn't a better fish to fish for than chub in the last few weeks of the season.

CANTANKEROUS CHUB

I've fished a great many rivers in this country where the chub have, at times, just about thrown themselves on the hook. On numerous visits it was a simple case of fishing the right swim and pulling chub out until the swim was empty. Any method would do. Any bait would do. And if you didn't do something really stupid, any angler would do. They were so easy to catch it was ridiculous.

They were visits that could lead a less experienced angler to believe that chub are dead easy, and if it hadn't been for the equally numerous visits I've made to many different rivers, when the chub have been extremely hard to catch, I would have believed it myself. They can be the most contrary, cantankerous blighters you could wish never to meet, and if I didn't love the species so much I'd consider spending less time fishing for them and more time fishing for a more predictable species.

But that's just one of the great aspects of chub, for you never know when you've got them by the short and curlies. Many times you think you have, and then they let you know who's boss by not feeding when you fully expect them to, in conditions that were made for chub fishing. And then feeding totally uninhibited when the conditions say they should be lying torpid on the bottom.

The easiest chub to catch are those in rivers which are heavily fished, especially those that are match fished on a regular basis, for although it is necessary to fish very fine with tiny hooks and small baits, the chub have come to rely on the vast quantities of bait introduced as loose feed each week, and dodging the hookbait is, to them, a way of life. The most difficult, and unpredictable, chub are those in rivers where they are under little pressure, grow to good size, and inhabit only the most suitable swims rather than every swim that is deep enough to cover them.

The upper Weaver holds some good chub.

Locating big chub in small rivers or the upper reaches of larger rivers is not usually difficult, for the quality chub swims stand out a mile and shout at you as you pass. The course of the river twists and turns, and varies greatly in depth and character. The deeper holes, undercuts, glides, rubbish rafts and the like that make up the classic chub swims are all there, and most of them hold a big chub or two, with just a few holding bigger chub than others. That is probably the most difficult bit as far as locating big chub is concerned; finding those odd swims where the biggest chub are. The nice part is that once found, they stay found, at least until floodwater changes the character of the swim.

Incidentally, one of my favourite chub swims is a piece of slack water along the margins, maybe only a yard or so wide and a few yards long, where, in periods of extra water (but not too much) the river flows very, very slowly back on itself. This water will have a distinct crease where the flow of the river butts up to the slack. If this slack water and crease lies under some kind of cover, beneath the branches of a tree or bush, and is 4ft to 6ft deep, then we are close to utopia.

Baits for big chub are not a problem either. They usually prefer a big bait, and big crusts and chunks of bread flake, along with cheese paste, are top of the list. Following that are big lobworms and luncheon meat. Slugs and wasp cake (and wasp grubs) are very effective, especially in summer.

There is no question that bread in all its forms, but especially flake and crust, is a bait that is second to none for chub in all rivers, lightly fished or otherwise. Many of the bigger chub are too wily to get caught during daylight, especially on bright days, but as soon as the light begins to fade a big crust or fold of flake is readily accepted at dusk and a for a few hours into the night.

But not always, for when there is some colour in the water they will feed during the day. In fact they will feed heavily on some days when the water is coloured, to the point where they stop feeding as soon as the light fades and retire for the night! Many times I've taken advantage of the coloured water to successfully float fish for big chub through the day, thinking that I would swap to leger tactics as soon as the light faded in the evening and catch a few more, only to find I couldn't get a single bite. This light factor with big chub is most certainly a crucial issue, for they definitely are not inclined to feed in bright light – unless, of course, they are feeding under, or from under, the heavy cover of weed. In clear water you can watch chub slip from under the fronds of waving streamer weed to accept a slug or lobworm that is trundling by, only to slide back under the weed as soon as they've claimed their prize.

From what I've written so far you can be forgiven for believing that it is only a matter of fishing the right day, in the right swim, with bread, in order to catch chub from most rivers. Many times it is! But it is those days when it is neither a good feeding day, nor a bad feeding day, but somewhere in between, when the cantankerous chub decides it is not going to play with the same ball as us, that we have to delve a bit deeper into our bag of tricks to get a result.

Try a spray flavour on flake and crust when chubbing.

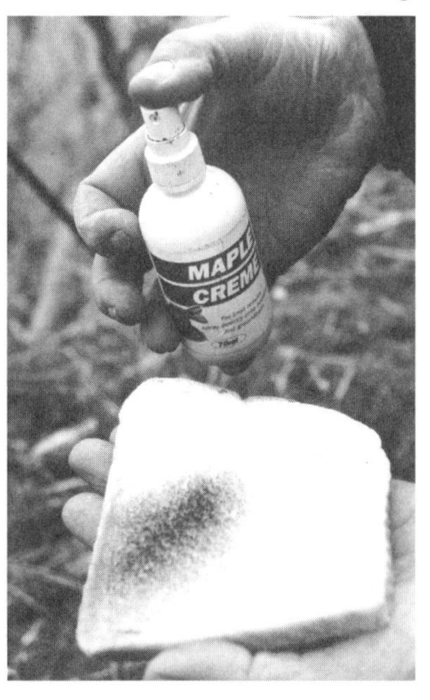

I have often said that flavouring baits is not always the best thing to do when the free feed you introduce is not flavoured. That a flavoured bait lying amongst a sea of unflavoured baits could have the opposite effect of what you are trying to achieve. I've said that flavouring baits should not necessarily always be the first line of attack. Often it is better to follow up with baits smelling and tasting of something other than their natural flavour, after first trying naturally flavoured baits.

So when the chub are not responding to conventional tactics and baits we have to turn to something a little different. This can be one of those times when a bait flavour and/or colour can make a difference. One of the things I've found with chub is that they have days when they seem to prefer a savoury flavour and other days when the same chub in the same swim appear to want a sweet flavour. Crayfish and Monster Crab flavours have worked well for me in the savoury line, and my first choice in sweet flavours for chub is Maple Creme. I prefer to use the sprays when fishing with bread, for then I can spray the hookbait just before I hook it on, using just a hint of flavour, or I can whack it on, almost soaking it, if I want to try the heavy-handed approach.

Using the same spray I can give the soaked bread I use for feed a dose of flavour too, ensuring that my hookbait is just a more heavily flavoured version of the feed they find in the swim. I don't overdo it with soaked bread, for it is obviously not just an attractor but an out and out food supply. I don't mind feeding them a little, for the idea is to give them a taste for bread, and make them look for more, homing in on the hookbait, which is a more substantial, and therefore, tempting, offering. I also flick in a few pieces of flake so that they get the idea that these hookbait size pieces can be found if they look for them. Using punched flake can also make a difference on some days.

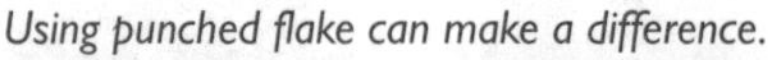

Using punched flake can make a difference.

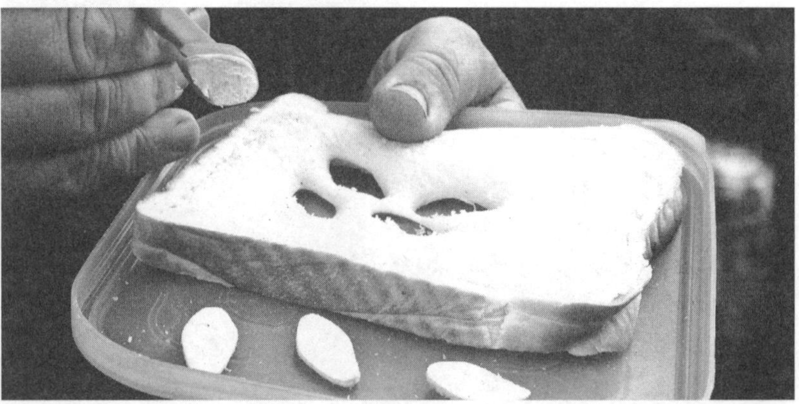

Finer lines and smaller hooks can have their say in turning poor bites into good bites. And touch-legering can be essential rather than obligatory. On cold, winter evenings, touch-legering may not be a viable proposition and in that case I have to rely on a quivertip. Better still, however, is to hang a light bobbin on a bow in the line from rod tip to water surface in those swims where this is feasible. One of my favourite chub swims I mentioned earlier, the slack at the side with a crease adjoining, is a classic one for hanging a bow. Obviously, there should be sufficient light to see the bow, for the idea is to watch it for bites. You can strike at bites that have not yet reached the rod tip. This is sensitivity at its best. Most of the time, though, when the cold isn't de-sensitising my fingers, I feel for bites, combining touch-legering with watching a quivertip.

Perhaps I should explain a little more about touch-legering for chub before I go on to something else. Touch-legering is not used solely for detecting bites. It can, and in my case, is, used for enticing bites, and for encouraging seemingly strong bites to develop.

There are times when every chub angler will experience what appear to be good, strong bites, only for the strike to result in a complete miss. The rod tip or quivertip bends over quite steadily, or, when touch-legering, you can actually feel the chub pulling strongly at your fingertips and you feel as though it is impossible not to hook the fish. You strike so confidently the end tackle is likely to finish up in the trees around you or in the field behind you because you struck with no inhibitions. Changing line strength, hook size, and bait size, up or down, usually makes little or no difference. The only thing that has any success is to feed more line to the chub. If you are hanging on to a loop of line between butt ring and reel, or butt ring and second ring, then you feed this line to the chub as it pulls, striking when the limit of the line is reached. The bigger the loop of line you begin with the more you can feed to the chub before you attempt to plant the hook. This has to be experimented with on the night, but 2ft to 3ft of line is usually about right.

Touch-legering with a loop of line also means you can twitch the bait towards you while still keeping in constant touch with the bait. Inching it back can do the trick, or snatching a foot or more back can often be a better bet. Again, you need to experiment at the time. More often than not the chub will seize the bait in mid-twitch or mid-snatch, often ripping the line from your fingertips. Holding the line, or touch-legering, is an excellent technique for many reasons, for most species at times, and should not be dismissed as some quirky tactic used by those who wish to appear to be on a loftier plane than we mere mortals.

Finer lines and smaller hooks rarely make much difference to chub that are not hammered week after week, except perhaps when float fishing in daylight. But when legering they don't seem to be bothered about 5lb and 6lb lines and 6's hooks, which is just as well considering that many of the chub swims I fish for big chub are snag-ridden, calling for strong-arm tactics once the hook has bitten home. But, in swims where it is possible to get away with lighter tackle, it is always worth a try when the bites are finicky, not so much with lighter lines but with smaller hooks that better present smaller baits.

Most of the time I use a very simple rig, just a run-bead direct on the line, stopped with a rubber bead up against a swivel-stop. The run-bead has a link attached to facilitate a quick change of the bomb to cope with different swims when I roam along the stretch trying different swims.

The rig for float fishing bread for chub is dead simple. A Chubber float big enough to take the shot required for the type of swim, the bulk shot about mid-depth, and a dropper about 6ins from the hook. More sophisticated rigs are just not necessary on stretches of river where the chub have not been hammered.

Chapter 11

Perch

Bold and beautiful, the perch, praised and pursued by Gary Knowles

Gary is a true all round specimen angler with an outstanding list of personal bests which is even more impressive when you consider he lives in the big fish desert of North West England. A regular and respected contributor to national and specialist angling publications for many years Gary has a wealth of perch fishing experience having targeted the species from venues ranging from farm ponds to glacial lakes, this together with his boundless enthusiasm and determination has helped him catch numerous specimens of over 4lb on a variety of methods.

Arguably the most beautiful of our indigenous fish and certainly the most striking, there can be few anglers that have not come across perch at some stage of their lives. They inhabit rivers, streams, lakes, lochs, ponds, canals and even ditches so it's no surprise that in our formative years most of us will have caught them weighing just a few ounces then fumbled with a disgorger to try and extract a hook which was probably situated nearer its vent than its mouth. It's these early memories that have left me, like a lot of anglers, with a real soft spot for the species, a species that can be ridiculously easy or unbelievably difficult to tempt.

Perch are found in all types of waters, including canals.

I remember the first 'big' perch I caught, I was about 11 years old and along with four mates I had caught the bus to my local Pennington Flash, a huge expanse of water for a snotty kid like me but it was a step up from the local canal and I was determined to up the size of my best perch by catching one of the rumoured monsters that some of the 'grown ups' had told us inhabited its depths. The choice of bait used to tempt one of these leviathans seemed to be open to debate, giant lobworms were the choice of some whilst others swore by the use of live minnows fished below a cork float. As if this wasn't confusing enough the more adventurous anglers insisted that neither of these was as effective as a silver or copper 'Toby' lure.

Whilst my mates decided to continue with the standard float-fished maggot I'd tackled up with my granddad's old fibreglass leger rod complete with a homemade swingtip and, as advised by Mr Crabtree, a fat lobworm was my bait. After hours of inactivity the tip shot upwards and I was soon playing what had to be one of the legendary monsters, and it was. All my mates left their rods and came to see me slip the net under the biggest perch we had ever seen; it must have been all of a pound and a half. We decided to a man (or rather boy) to pack in there and then and take the fish home to show our parents, so the unfortunate fish was placed head-first in a small bucket of water and we set off for the bus stop about a quarter mile away. Fortunately for the fish the bus driver, despite admitting it was a fine specimen, refused to let us on the bus with the dripping bucket, so I was forced to run back to the lake and promptly release the confused, but probably unharmed, fish back to the lake.

Although I wasn't aware of it at the time this had been a great lesson in my angling education, and I suppose a first step into specimen angling as I had begun to target bigger than average fish by selecting methods, bait and tactics best suited to tempting them. And 30 years later nothing has changed, I still love to fish for perch, and I still aim for the biggest I can, in fact the size of some of the fish I have since caught probably wouldn't have fit into that bucket, even if the bus driver had let me take a seat!

So where do you go to target a big perch? Well, I said at the outset that they are found in a variety of venues, and this is undoubtedly the case, but in my experience there is one major factor that contributes to a water having the potential to produce outsize specimens and this is an abundance of food. Now this may be blindingly obvious but I don't just mean adequate amount of suitable prey, I'm talking a glut here. Look at some of the recent catches of specimen perch and you will see that a lot have come from overstocked, commercial fisheries, and I'm talking of tiny, chocolate-coloured puddles that have only been dug a few years earlier. There cannot possibly be any other reason for their massive growth rate other than gorging on freshly stocked and probably badly handled and dying silver fish. However, before we go too far down this line I had better point out that I won't be writing about catching perch from these types of venues because I absolutely hate these places and would rather take up golf than spend my weekends on one of these puddles. But if you don't mind the crowds and the nonsense that goes with fishing these small commercials then good luck to you, if you sit it out with a small livebait or deadbait you have a reasonable chance of a really big perch, but it's not for me.

So onto more traditional venues, where fishing more 'natural' waters such as gravel pits, lakes and even rivers and drains there are two simple rules to locating perch - features and fish. With regard to features look for anything that breaks up the margins, and these can be either natural or man-made, overhanging or fallen trees are a winner, as are random clumps of weeds or reedbeds, locks, bridges, dam walls and particularly jetties with submerged piles. There are other obvious hotspots but if I'm honest there is only one real key that I use for location and that is to find the silver fish. Yes, all the structures mentioned earlier are good areas to target, and for sure these are all often frequented by perch, especially if shaded, but if the water holds any number of silver fish, and shoals of fry at various points of the season, then I would focus all my attention in finding these. If you do, you can pretty much guarantee the perch won't be far away. Remember first and foremost they are predators, and the number one food source of a big perch is fish.

This approach caught me plenty of fish on my local waters, but not of the size I was after. Every season 2lb plus fish would grace my net but a 'three' seemed a million miles away, and after a lot of effort I decided there was a simple reason I wasn't catching the monsters I'd seen in the angling press: they weren't in the waters I was fishing!

The upper Gt Ouse.

This is an important lesson in any form of specialist angling, you need to set realistic targets, and the size of fish I was catching were big fish for the North-West of England and, although I'm sure a lot of people were happy with fish of this size, I wasn't, it was time to travel further afield. My mind was made up, whatever it took, however long it took me I was going to have a 'four' and the fuel pump at the service station was about to become a regular acquaintance.

When it came to producing outsized perch one venue stood head and shoulders above all others and that was the upper Gt. Ouse near Buckingham, and it was here that my dreams became reality. Incredibly on my first ever visit to the water I caught what was then, and still is, my personal best perch of 4lb-10oz. The sheer size of that fish remains etched in my memory and the circumstances behind its capture remain an inspiration for me each time I fish the venue, no-matter how difficult the conditions or the fishing appears.

Along with my brother I had arrived at first light and chosen a spot on the main river where a large Alder overhung the margins and I began the day fishing on a slight inside bend where the large reeds shielded the near bank and stretched at least 40 yards down from where I was positioned. Using lobworms on a light, almost wand-like quivertip rod I hooked a couple of average sized perch and a small pike but also missed a couple of bites. Having spent the previous few winters chub fishing I soon learned to pay out line to a taking fish to ensure minimal resistance was felt and the fish 'hung on' to the bait for a few extra seconds. Although I now usually float-fish lobworms, as I will describe later, when using a quivertip it is vital you allow some slack line when using large baits such as lobs if you are to hit the bites. The reasons for this are twofold. One, often a perch will actually drop the bait if it feels the build-up of resistance and secondly paying out a little slack line allows the perch to properly inhale the full lob and ensure the hook is actually in the mouth when the strike is made.

On this particular day we decided it didn't seem to be happening in the spot we had chosen and around lunchtime decided on a move. About three miles upstream of where I was fishing a small brook entered the main river and having wandered upstream a little I was delighted to see small fish breaking the surface. As I noted earlier, if there were prey fish here I was certain perch wouldn't be far away and this was the only sign I needed to fish this area hard for the rest of the session. I chose a pretty featureless swim close to where the fish had showed themselves and this time I was positioned on the outside of a slight bend which careful plumbing had shown that at 4ft it was slightly deeper than the surrounding water.

I fished with full concentration all afternoon without the slightest indication, and then, just as the light completely faded, the tip pulled round about half an inch or so before I released the foot of loose reel line I had held in a loop. I waited for the line to tighten again and struck into what was obviously a good fish. The size of that first big fish shocked me that day, and I don't mind admitting we were a little overwhelmed by the sight of it. The lessons I learned that day were that when fishing for these awesome fish your 'luck' could change in an instant, but perhaps most of all I realised, especially when the water is running clear, the window of opportunity can be very small, lasting for as little as half an hour on some occasions.

I have visited the Ouse many times since that day and have gradually refined my tactics. I now feel pretty confident of a good fish on each visit.

Nowadays my standard approach is to fish with two rods, a float rod fishing on the inside and a legered bait on the far bank. Practically all my attention is paid to the float rod with the bite alarm on the second rod allowing me to fish this as a 'sleeper'. If possible I like to fish with livebaits on the second set up and, as transporting livebaits is no longer an option, this often means spending a few hours fishing for bits before the serious stuff starts. Although many would consider this a waste of valuable fishing time I certainly don't. As I touched on earlier, if the river is running low and clear and the conditions are bright, then often the lobworm attack will be next to useless until dusk, but the livebait does often give you a chance during the day, and I have now caught quite a few 4lb plus fish on livebaits in such conditions.

Firstly though, let's look at the float set-up in more detail. When I first started fishing the Ouse I was always looking for a decent feature on the near bank, an overhanging tree, bush or larger than average clump of reeds, but although this remains a good starting point on most stillwaters, on the Ouse I'm no longer hung up about this. I'm pretty sure the fish patrol regularly along both margins, so constant baiting will eventually attract the attention of any fish moving through the swim and this is probably why for me featureless swims have proved to be much more productive over the years. This success could also be due to the fact that a lot of anglers still religiously fish to the features, and as the Ouse perch are now subject to angling pressure perhaps the perch are beginning to wise up to this and to treat 'feature swims' with some caution.

To bait the float swim I use the same cheap fibreglass whip that I take along to fish for livebaits. Tying a short length of 10lb mono to the end of the whip and a small bait-dropper to the other I can leave this set up throughout the session allowing me to quickly and effectively keep a supply of bait trickling into the swim without breaking down my float rod. Until recently I used a softer actioned match rod but I have found the extra power of a specialist 13ft float rod helps me pull fish out from under my feet into the central channel where there are little or no snags to worry about.

As I am fishing literally within inches of the near bank it is important to stay low and keep below the skyline, and for this reason I will present my bait a good few yards downstream of where I'm sat to reduce the chances of my 'skylining' my own swim. The size of float will depend on the amount of flow but I do like to use a buoyant float such as a peacock waggler and leave a good couple of inches proud of the surface, which allows me to monitor the crayfish activity, as the float will constantly be dipping an inch or so if they are present, and the buoyancy also stops the float from being dragged under as I'll be using enough bulk shot a foot or so from the hook to keep the bait stationary in the flow.

If conditions are tough, ie, cold, clear conditions then I'll often change this float set-up around to present a livebait as I feel this gives me a much greater chance of action. To do this I change to a 2 or 3 SSG chubber float and set up a small fixed paternoster with the lead set to just touch bottom and the livebait working a foot or two shallower on a 6lb fluorocarbon hooklength. Yes, I know pike are present but I honestly can't see a single size 4 or 6 hook causing much of a problem to a pike should a bite-off occur. In truth I've hooked a few pike on this rig and have landed about 95% of them as invariably the quick strike results in the hook settling nicely in the scissors. My hooks for both lobworms and small livebaits are wide-gaped fine wire Kamasan B983 in a size to match the bait.

It's important to bait the swim properly so I'll regularly place a dropper or two of red maggots and chopped worm tight to the chosen area, the rate of this bait introduction will increase if the crayfish activity is substantial, although an extra helping or two will always be introduced half an hour or so before dusk regardless of the cray's activity.

Gary nets a big perch on the Ouse.

The far bank rod is the one that I always prefer to fish with a livebait. This time I used a sliding paternoster rig which allows the perch to take a small amount of line before feeling any resistance. A small ½" polyball is used to keep the bait off the bottom and the bobbin used will be the lightest possible the flow will allow me to use, with a nice long drop to ensure a taking fish feels little or no resistance. As mentioned earlier, by using an audible bite alarm in conjunction to the bobbin I can let this rod look after itself whilst I concentrate all my efforts on the float rod. Occasionally I catapult a few red maggots over the bait to try and draw a few silver fish into the area but that's about it, this rod remains a sleeper, albeit an often very productive one.

If the water has colour in it then I expect bites at any time of the day, and will often forsake the far bank rod and spend a little time roving. To do this I try and cover as much water as possible by dropping in every 15 yards or so and fishing each spot for just ten or fifteen minutes before moving on. In fact the biggest brace I had came to this method when I took fish of 4lb 1oz and

3lb 15oz from the same tiny swim in less than five minutes, which is probably as close as I'll ever come to a brace of 'fours'.

If the water is clear then it's important to understand that due to the perch's obvious preference to feed in low light levels often I'll only be fishing effectively for the last few minutes of daylight and as such my whole day will be geared around having everything just perfect for this short period of activity. Incredible as it may seem the window of opportunity I spoke of earlier can last for as little as half an hour each day and it is not unusual for me and a couple of mates to all be blanking, only for three or four texts to bounce back and forth in just a few seconds as we all land fish within a couple of minutes of each other. In fact, during one trip my mate Steve, fishing about 50 yards upstream of me, saw me strike into a fish, looked back at his float, only to find it gone. Incredibly, both of us landed fish weighing exactly 4lb.

This only serves to illustrate how focussed you need to be as the last half an hour of daylight approaches. It really can be frustrating if you don't get this right. I remember one visit when on dusk I had three good takes, two to the float and one to the livebait rod all in the space of 15 minutes and missed them all. I had been waiting for eight hours for that chance and blew it, the chances are that one or two of those would have been from big fish so you can see how devastating it can be if you don't take that chance, especially if you then have a three hour journey home. Fortunately I was due to fish the following day also and the next night I had just the one chance to float-fished lobworm, and luckily I put this on the bank. It turned out to be from a lovely marked fish of 3lb 2oz. Not one of the Ouse monsters but I was very grateful for a reward for what had been a couple of really tough days.

Being a predator, and one which predominantly hunts by sight, perch can also be very receptive to lures. Over the years I picked up a few good fish by accident when pike fishing but it's much better using gear which is more suited to perch, not just because it is more effective but also it is much more fun on balanced gear. There is nothing complicated about my lure set up; I use a light 6' 6" jigging rod and a small front-drag fixed-spool reel loaded with 15lb braid (my preference is for Power-Pro) which balances perfectly and is light enough to hold (and cast) all day with ease.

Before we move on (and apologies to the more experienced anglers) I feel it's well worth offering a few tips relating to loading braid onto fixed-spool reels, as if this is not done correctly, fishing with fine braid can be an absolute nightmare.

Firstly it is important to start the spooling with a few layers of mono, this grips the cone of the spool and doesn't slip as braid would under tension, I then join the braid to the mono with two, four turn grinner knots, which are then lubricated with saliva and gently tightened, the tiny knot is then trimmed and wound by hand to the bottom of the spool before the braid is loaded. Unlike mono I find fine braid needs to be wound on the spool under a decent amount of pressure. If like me you have a wife who would rather stick pins in her eyes than help with anything angling related then you'll usually be loading the braid yourself.

To do this I place the reel on the rod and drop the spool of braid in a bucket of water, then, using a damp cloth, clamp the braid against the rod blank about 18" up from the reel and slowly wind the braid up to the level required. Another important point with braid is unlike you would do with mono, do not fill the spool right up to the rim, this is an absolute guaranteed way of ensuring you get wind-knots every other cast. I like to leave at least 2-3mm of lip exposed; this does not seem to noticeably affect the casting but it does drastically reduce the number of wind-knots I get. These can also be avoided by closing the bale-arm manually after each cast and make the first couple of winds under tension to ensure the braid doesn't spool loosely, which is another big cause of the dreaded wind-knot.

Another 4-pounder, this one 4lb 10oz.

Although I've mentioned that I'm happy to use mono when livebaiting for perch this is most definitely not the case when lure fishing. As you can never be 100% sure that a water contains no pike, I'll always use a wire trace when using lures. This may detract slightly from the action of some lures but I still catch plenty of fish so I'm not unduly worried about the use of one, especially considering the quality of some of the trace material available these days. Apart from the traditional seven-strand variety of trace which you can get in quite fine breaking strains there are also a couple of Kevlar and steel-woven materials that have been pioneered by anglers fly fishing for pike. The real plus however of using a trace is the amount of bonus pike I have caught when lure fishing for perch, I have been fortunate enough to have landed fish of over 20lb on this light perch set-up and although not ideal, it can be really good fun.

The choice of lures is immense, and seemingly growing by the day but there are quite a few that have stood the test of time. When the perch appear to be pretty active I like small orange or red 'Vibrax' or 'Mepps'-type spinners and coloured spoons as well as small fat-bodied crankbaits. If the perch are playing hard to get then I'll revert to a soft plastic lure, again there are plenty of these to chose from but my preference is for small weighted shads or twin-tails. These soft plastic lures come in a wide range of sizes and some of the smaller ones, particularly when the perch are fry-feeding, can be very effective. Although a steady retrieve often works with these lures I usually prefer to twitch these along the bottom, hoping to pass one right past the nose of a decent fish and provoke a response whether the fish is hungry or not.

These weighted shads and grubs are also particularly good when used as vertical jigs. For those not familiar with the term you won't be surprised to hear these are lifted vertically off the bottom and 'jigged', hopefully right under the nose of a lurking fish. This is ideally carried out from a boat but it's also a fantastic and very effective method for working a lure around jetties, locks, trees and boats from the bank. Keeping the lure as close to the bottom at all times the lure is lifted slowly no more than a few inches as you work your lure around the targeted area, bites are usually savage and if you are lucky enough to find fish grouped together results can be both instant and spectacular.

A prime example of this happened a couple of autumns ago. I was fishing a large stillwater and came across a mass of tiny perch shoaled up under a long wooden jetty. After a few minutes watching I saw the fry spraying across the surface and, hoping that they were being attacked by cannibalistic perch, I started to work a lure around the pilings. Straight away I took a couple of average sized fish, one of which coughed up a little perch, proving my theory correct. Still hopeful of better things I moved to the very edge of the structure where the water was at its deepest, and whilst jigging a small lure right around the very edge of the pilings, I hooked and landed five fish weighing between 3lb 7oz and 3lb 15oz in as many casts. Perhaps once again reinforcing the point I made at the very beginning of this chapter, that when perch fishing, location is everything.

A generation has passed since I caught my first 'monster' from Pennington Flash, and yet in terms of perch fishing very little has changed. Although my tackle is amongst the best available I'm still catching fish on what are basically the same methods, albeit slightly more refined, and just as they were thirty years ago lobworms, lures and livebaits remain the top baits. However, time stands still for no man and as the next crop of youngsters are busy catching goggle-eyed perch from farm ponds, I've now become one of the 'grown-ups' viewed with reverence by the next generation of aspiring and enthusiastic anglers.

Whatever happens in the future it is clear that perch fishing is undoubtedly cyclic and in my lifetime I don't think there has ever been a better time to target a big specimen of the species. Huge fish are being taken from venues as diverse as large glacial lochs to tiny commercial pools, so now's your chance, get out there and turn those childhood dreams into reality.

Chapter 12

Pike

The ultimate freshwater predator in the UK

PIKE - THE ULTIMATE PREDATOR, IS DEADLY, BUT EASILY DAMAGED

Often known as the freshwater shark and equipped with a lethal set of teeth and eyes like the devil that look straight at you and straight through you, the pike in reality is a pussy when it comes to survival. Poor water quality, persecution by the ignorant, excessive pressure by the angler, and poor handling by the inexperienced, all add up to a tough time for pike as they are extremely fragile when compared to other species. Which is why I begin this chapter with the latter important warning and now a recommendation: if you are an inexperienced pike angler please try to begin your pike fishing adventure accompanied by an experienced piker who can show you how to catch pike, and equally important, how to handle them with care and confidence once you have them on the bank. There is nothing at all to be frightened of when unhooking pike providing you use the right technique and have the right equipment. A pike can be back in the water very fast indeed following unhooking, and even weighing and photographing if it is a notable specimen, in no time at all.

Pike are fascinating creatures, well worthy of intimate study. I once gave a slide show in which there were a number of close-up pictures of parts of pike we don't normally look at too closely, ie, sensory glands, eyes, etc. I then went on to talk briefly about these and other less obvious differences between pike and all other coarse fish. The comments afterwards suggested that although there were a number of very experienced anglers in the audience I was touching upon things they had little knowledge about.

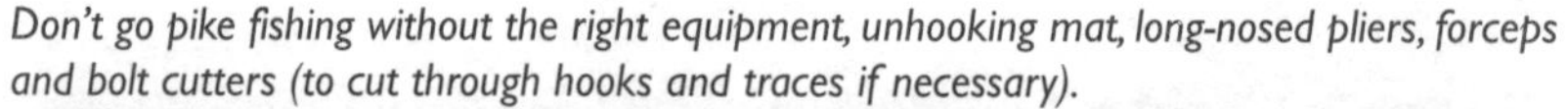

Don't go pike fishing without the right equipment, unhooking mat, long-nosed pliers, forceps and bolt cutters (to cut through hooks and traces if necessary).

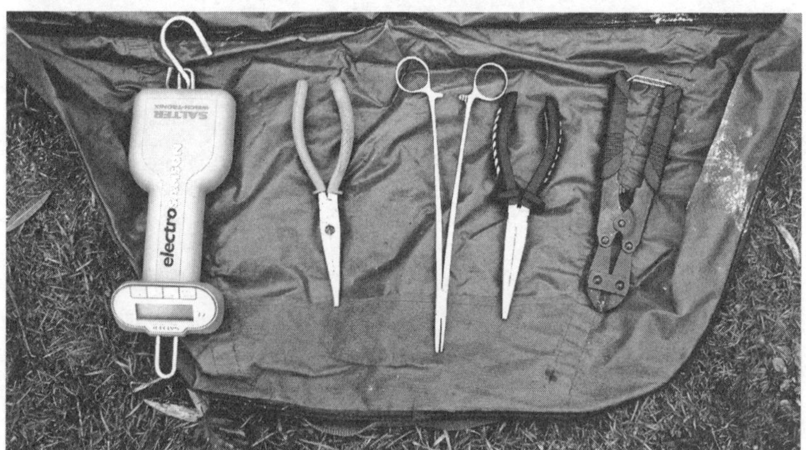

One of the most intriguing things about close-up, or macro photography, is that it does most certainly lead you to study those little details more closely and at your leisure. For at the time one catches a fish the concern is always to get it back in the water as quickly as possible, taking time out only to weigh it and take a couple of quick trophy shots. Recently, for my own curiosity, and for a wood carver who wanted some detailed pictures to refer to, I began to take a close-up shot of some feature of the pike each time myself or a pal caught one. But before I mention any of the less obvious details of the pike, let's just take a look at the whole body colour and shape.

The first thing we notice is that it is long and slim. Add to that the fact that the pike has an almost circular cross-section, and you have a fish that is more streamlined than most others. There are few creatures with more effective camouflage than the pike. That dark back, the mottled (or striped) green/yellow or yellow/bronze flanks, and the white belly combine to blend in with any aquatic background. The next time you see the sun shining into a clear lake that is slightly rippled, look at the bottom in a shallow area. You will see a mottled pattern playing across the bottom, a pattern that matches exactly the back and flanks of a pike. In young pike, and those that live predominantly in reedy waters, that mottled pattern may incline to stripes. The pike is very adaptable.

The streamlined body has a dorsal and anal fin set well back, very close to the tail, which produces a thrust that propels the pike through water with an awesome burst of speed. The emphasis is on acceleration rather than sustained speed, for the pike is an ambusher, not a chaser, and one can imagine this camouflaged executioner lying in wait, or slowly, ever so slowly, gliding through weed to within striking range of an unwary victim, then seeing the fins twitch, and the subtle stiffening of the body before it unleashes its lethal self like a bolt from a crossbow.

Surprising as it may seem, the first thing one notices about a pike, in or out of the water, is not the teeth, formidable though they are, but the eyes, which are

The first thing you notice is the eyes, unlike other coarse fish, the pike has binocular vision.

set well forward in the head and have a degree of binocular vision. They seem to look right at you, fixing you with a stare that gives you great sympathy with a roach that may have met that stare on the wrong day! Like the predators of the aerial world; the hawks, eagles and falcons, pike too must have superior vision to be able to spot a victim, and to precisely judge the distance between them so that an attack can be launched with deadly accuracy.

In spite of the tales one often hears most pike do not have huge teeth in those flat, crocodile-like jaws. In fact, only the longer, lower jaw has a row of fang-like teeth around the edge.

The kill is made more from crushing than it is from biting. The hundreds of other teeth are relatively small, hinged and backward-pointing, allowing a hapless victim to slide down the hatch with consummate ease, but have a snowball's chance in hell of sliding out again! All the teeth have one thing in common - the sharpness of a surgeon's scalpel, which I've been able to vouch for more often than I would have chosen. Always through my own carelessness of course, and not, as many non-pike anglers would have you believe, because the pike bites like a dog when on the bank. Would you be trying to bite something if you were drowning? Neither is the pike when he (or she) is on the bank and deprived of oxygen. Any snapping of the jaws is a purely reflexive action and not a deliberate attempt to bite anything or anybody.

Esox Lucius, the pike, does not rely entirely on its visual sense to locate prey. There are cases on record of totally blind pike surviving well enough to remain fit and healthy, and night fishing for pike, although not popular, is certainly productive. The pike's sense of smell must, therefore, have a lot to do with it.

The nostrils (olfactory sacs) are large and just ahead of the eyes, and appear capable of detecting the smell of a deadbait from a long way off. Deadbaits, and in particular sea species, give off more smell than livebaits, and the oily species such as sardine and smelt must emit the most scent of all, hence their proven success as deadbaits. Although there is little scientific evidence about the sense of smell in pike, there is, however, more available about the sense of smell in salmon (isn't there always!) and their sense of smell has been demonstrated to be responsible for their uncanny homing instincts. I don't expect the salmon's olfactory sense to be any more powerful than that of the pike, which means it is very strong indeed.

Like all fish, pike have ears too, not like ours which we can see plainly, but inner ears, which are gristly sacs of fluid residing in capsules at each side of the head. Balance is one of the functions of a fish's ears, but they are also able to detect sound waves and vibrations passing through the water. Where the ears leave off and the sensory pores along the lateral line take over is, though, another question. Unfortunately, there is a distinct lack of research in this and many other fields regarding fish, particularly where coarse fish are concerned, but it does appear that the ears and lateral line of a fish are linked.

Pike have more sensory pores than any other coarse fish. As well as those that run along the lateral line, there are openings along each side of the lower jaw, around the gill cover, and around each eye, extending along the top of the head. Who knows exactly what these sensors can detect. Most of us assume they are a kind of radar that pick up vibrations, or changes in water pressure resulting from nearby movement, but what other function could they have; is there a link to the olfactory sense too? Can they taste?

One thing is for certain, the pike is well equipped to detect prey. If he can't see it, he can smell it. If he can't smell it, he can hear it. And if none of those produce a result, there's a good chance he can feel it.

What a fascinating creature - the ultimate predator indeed.

THE FINER POINTS OF PIKE FISHING

There are days when pike can be incredibly easy to catch, as there are such days with every species. Unfortunately, when pike are feeding ravenously they invariably make it known, often in spectacular fashion, and this leads to many anglers thinking that pike are always particularly easy to catch. We know pike are feeding when they strike close to the surface; when small fish leap through the surface, fighting for their lives. We see keepnets suddenly developing a life of their own as a marauding pike strives to get at the fish it contains. And the sign of feeding pike we all know only too well, when the small fish we are playing suddenly becomes a big fish as it is grabbed on the way in. Many non-pikers reckon they spend too much time trying to avoid the attentions of pike. Certainly, it must seem that way when they lose yet another fish and hooklength before the prey reaches the safety of the landing net. To the non-pike angler it must suggest that pike are always much easier to catch than any other species.

Experienced pike anglers know that this is far from the truth. It is just as easy to notch up a run of blanks when fishing for pike as it is with any other species!

Sadly, however, many anglers, and I would go so far as to say the majority, foster this attitude towards pike fishing even following several years of seriously fishing for them. It appears that they follow two or three basic methods, usually lure fishing, straight-legered baits, or simple float-suspended baits. The more ambitious try sunken float tactics, driftfloating, and various means whereby a natural bait is wobbled, sunk and drawn, or twitched back to the bank or boat. It isn't that, however - the ability, or wish, to try other methods - that sets many pike anglers apart. It is the fact that they give far more thought to the finer points, those little things that can make all the difference on a bad day.

The author returns a 24lb 5oz pike.

And isn't that the time that sorts the men from the boys, so to speak, a bad day, when the fishing is tough, and you have to cut through the basics and do something that can turn failure into success? All right, you may catch only one fish that day, and a small one at that, but when everyone else is catching nothing, or you are faced with the prospect of a blank, that one fish can give you as much satisfaction as a netful on an 'easy' day.

I remember once when John Charlesworth and I sat on the banks of an Irish lough, following a day when John had lost a big pike and I hadn't had a run. The day before we had caught a 9-pounder, six big doubles and a beauty of 24lb 5oz. We remarked that the 9lb fish from the day before would go down very nicely just then, as we packed and contemplated the prospect of going back to the digs without a fish to speak of. As we spoke my alarm sounded and I landed another 9lb pike. I went back to the car with a smile on my face. Yet a fish of similar proportions caught the day before had hardly warranted a mention.

What are the finer points then? And I can almost hear some of you: "Finer points? Is there any such thing in pike fishing? Finer points, when 20lb and heavier wire traces are used. Sounds like a contradiction in terms to me."

I suppose it does take a bit of accepting that a ferocious looking, generally big, tooth-infested creature like a pike can take food rather delicately, to the point where it can rival the wariest bream in the twitch-bite stakes. Yet we don't give such a concept a second thought where other species are concerned, even though the pike, unlike other coarse fish, has a lateral line that stretches all the way to its nose, and probably is more sensitive to what goes on around it than any other freshwater species. We don't think twice about changing a 2 ½lb hooklength for a 1 ½lb hooklength, or a 16's for an 18's hook when we're fishing for roach or bream, yet how many pike anglers swap from, say, a 28lb wire trace to a 20lb trace, or size 6 trebles for 8's trebles to get more bites? Very few that I know of.

A change in the environment in which pike live can make an awful lot of difference to how they feed. I don't mean the usual changes that involve just the immediate conditions, such as water temperature, but changes that creep up on you yet have a much more devastating effect. They can cause what appears to be tremendous personality transformations in pike, converting them from ravenous beasts to pretty picky feeders in the space of a season or two. Take one of the Cheshire meres I fish quite regularly for pike, where the catch expectations have changed somewhat dramatically over the years. At one time it was nothing unusual to go down there and net six or more pike in a day. Not big fish, but decent enough sport as Cheshire meres go, for the meres rarely produce big pike consistently. Most of the pike were in the 6lb to 8lb bracket, with an odd double or two, and there was always an outside chance of an upper double or a twenty. My best fish from there, far and away bigger than the average, was 29lb and is still the best from the water as far as I know since proper records have been kept.

The year following that big fish there were no twenties caught that I know of, although a number of upper doubles made an appearance. The pike were noticeably thinner, however, and there were quite a few caught that had the length of a 20-pounder, but weighed several pounds less. Another year later and the pike were still being caught in numbers, but were thinner still. Even the jack pike were scrawny, with a pike's head and a body like an eel. Another year brought another change for there was a massive explosion of small fish; roach, perch, bream and hybrids. Not fish that were spawned that year, but from about four years earlier, fish that were now big enough to take angler's baits instead of the more microscopic creatures that they had fed on previously, and so had not been caught.

This eruption of small fish, hundreds of thousands ranging from an ounce or so to a plump 10oz, with a considerable number of fish in the 10oz to 1lb bracket, had an incredible effect on the pike. Or, at least, I believe it is this food fish explosion that is responsible for the latest trend in the pike's feeding habits, in that they no longer had much of a feeding habit on pike angler's baits! Everyone struggled to get a bite. But when we did, and the fish was landed, instead of the fish looking like a 12-pounder, yet weighed as little as 9lb, it looked like a 9-pounder and weighed as much as 12lb. They were fighting fit and as fat as butter.

But there is always a 'but', and this one came in the shape of poorer catches.

Difficult to catch wasn't the word for it. Where before we were netting anything from one or two to six or more pike a day, a single run was being classed as a success, whether the fish was landed or not! That's how hard it was. But the problem was that most of us, and me included for a spell, were still fishing as though the pike were starving, and always hungry enough to accept any kind of offering on any type of rig.

Much of the time the pike were simply not attempting to take baits. When the water is full of food fish of all sizes, and extremely limited effort is required on the part of the pike to partake of a meal, and a good meal at that, why the hell should they take that stale deadbait that lies on the bottom? The use of livebait wasn't proving any more successful either. And why would it, for when any water becomes rich with natural food it also becomes a difficult water from which to catch fish. Why would it be any different with pike, when the water in which they live becomes rich with the natural food upon which they live?

No, I haven't forgotten that there are many waters with lots of small fish where the pike are still readily caught. But the difference with this water is that it had a massive stock of food fish of all sizes, from fry of two inches long, to big roach and perch topping a pound, with hybrids and bream from 1½lbs upwards, and all sizes in between. The bottom line is that whatever size of food fish is preferred by the pike they were there in abundance.

We also suffered from the knock-on effect caused by the pike taking our baits so freely in the past. Very few who fished the water used livebait, not because of any moral or political reasons - for the real piking world is quite different to that written about by some anglers - but simply because it was illegal to use live fish from another water, and you couldn't catch any from the same water. So everyone used sea species deadbaits, and everyone caught lots of fish, for the pike were so hungry they couldn't resist them. Their hunger was so desperate it overcame the underlying wariness that must still have been warning them that they were in great danger of being removed from the water. Most of the pike must have been caught scores of times in that three year period, and although the hunger pangs were dominating all their natural instincts, were they remembering the lessons they learned during that fasting spell? Was it still in their memory banks that sea fish spelt danger?

Right, the finer points. What are they in pike fishing?

Accepting that pike do not always attack a bait with a display of fireworks and a run to rival Linford Christie is the first requirement. And then recognising the time has come when you generally need to be more subtle when pike fishing is the second.

The first thing that was noticeable on the Cheshire mere I described earlier was that a fair number of pike were still picking up the bait, only to drop it pretty quickly when they sensed (or remembered) that it was suspicious. Many times these pick-ups were not noticed, for lines would stay clipped up to drop-off indicators, bobbins would hardly move, and when they did those fishing off the baitrunner waited for the spool to begin revolving,

Lines would stay clipped up to drop-off alarms.

which of course it never did. That's a mistake anyhow, for even when pike are well on feed it is better to fish an open bale arm when legering, for there will always be an odd time when even the little resistance from a baitrunner will be enough to cause the fish to drop the bait. It is not like bolt-rig fishing for carp, where the baitrunner is somewhat irrelevant to the sensitivity once the carp is on the move.

Many times it was discovered a pike had picked up your bait only when you spotted the teeth marks on the bait after you reeled in for another cast, or to pack for home.

The answer to dropped baits can be tackled in two basic ways. The first method is to increase the sensitivity of the rig and bite indication, and the second is to offer baits that they are less wary of. Along with the first method of increasing rig and indicator sensitivity rides the fact that pike anglers have got to get it into their heads that it is totally unnecessary to allow a pike to run, or even hold the bait in its mouth, for any length of time before striking. Quite apart from the fact that any hesitation about striking a pike that has picked up the bait can result in deep-hooking, the greatest risk you take otherwise is in allowing more time for the pike to reject the bait. I think this delay between bait pick-up and striking is responsible for more lost pike than any other single reason. Logically too, if we are going to employ more sensitive techniques in order to spot those pick-ups from pike that normal techniques miss, then it makes sense to immediately react to any indication of a bite. Anything less, and we may as well not bother to try and spot that moment when the pike takes the bait into its mouth, and just sit there waiting for that full-bloodied run that may never happen.

First, though, make sure you use fresh baits. There is not a rig, technique, or anything else that matters if you're offering bait that is stale. It won't be rejected by the pike, that's for sure, because the pike won't accept it in the first place. If you can't get hold of fresh-caught deadbait and, like me, have to use blast-frozen deadbaits most of the time, then buy them from a reputable company. Try bait flavours too, often they can tip the balance between a rejected bait and an accepted one.

Let's start with the end tackle of my legering set-up. I use a very simple rig comprising a 15lb main line to a 65lb link-swivel. Above this swivel is a rubber bead, then a leger bead with a bomb attached. Two to three feet above this is a large float stop, whose purpose it is to prevent the lead from running back up the line when I cast. It does not interfere with the run from a pike for the simple reason that I have usually struck at the fish before the stop reaches the swivel. The only times I haven't struck before then is because the run was faster than I was, and then it usually doesn't matter anyhow, for the pike is hooked because it ran the stop fast up to the bomb and hooked itself.

I most often use a heavy lead of at least 2oz, which may seem to you to be far from a sensitive set-up. For some time now I have been convinced that reasonably heavy leger weights offer the most sensitivity - with any rig and any species - and the free-line rig offers the least, which doesn't matter if you're fishing in the margins and even more so if the water is clear and you can see the bait being taken.

Hook size is important. On a really good day the pike will take size 2 hooks and think nothing of it. On a less than good day a 2's hook can have the same effect as having a couple of Rottweilers attached to the bait. The biggest hooks I use for bait fishing are 6's, most often I use 8's and 10's, and occasionally 12's. These should be barbless or micro-barbed. I compromise by flattening the barbs on my micro-barbed hooks to leave just a little bump that offers enough grip to make me feel better about it, but offers hardly any resistance when unhooking the fish.

The most sensitive bite indicator we can use is dependent on the distance we cast. At short range a loaded float is best, but at long range we need more of the float above surface in order to see it and therefore degrade the advantage of using a float. When a loaded float is used, the rod, following casting, should be placed in two rests and the line tightened until it is fairly tight all the way to the bait, and the float is sunk almost to its tip. The moment the bait is interfered with in any way will register at the float, usually by rising through the surface, and the instant you see anything happening is the instant you should strike. Don't give the pike any chance, any more time than necessary, to eject the bait. If you have been in the habit of 'letting a pike run' you will be surprised at the number of fish you hook. But I wouldn't be surprised if your hooking success took a turn for the better.

If the range at which you need to fish inhibits the use of float-leger methods you need to look at the bite registration system you're using on the pod or rod rests. For most applications the mercury tilt-switch type of drop-off alarm is fine, but when the fish are in a really difficult mood an extremely sensitive conventional bite alarm is better. I still use a drop-off visual indicator, which is a large, egg-shaped polyball painted fluorescent orange that incorporates an adjustable Gardner line clip and a length of cord to attach it to the pod or rod rest. For this sensitive type of application its main use is to hold the line tight. The important part now is to set the alarm at its most sensitive, and the vibration sensing alarms are best in this instance. Set correctly the line does not have to be plucked from the clip to register a bite. Any extra tightening, or any slackening, of the line will trigger a response.

As for the use of float-suspended baits, live or dead, I much prefer, when the pike are in dour mood, to offer the bait coming up from the bottom. Use a polyball attached to a livebait, or a buoyant insert in a deadbait. Very often it is enough to insert just enough buoyant material in a deadbait to make it hover on, or very slightly off, the bottom - critically balanced. It makes it so easy then for the pike to suck it in.

So, don't assume that pike are not feeding at all, or not interested, the next time you're having a bad day. Try some extra sensitivity, especially if you have evidence that they're picking up the bait. After all, you wouldn't just give up, or stick to your regular method if you were fishing for any other species. Would you?

A PIKING WEEK IN IRELAND

We were in Ireland, pike fishing, and I've never in my life seen so many changes in weather conditions in the space of one week. The best day, for us at least, if not for the fish, was flat calm and sunny, the day beginning with the sun sweeping away a thick mist and ending with a sunset you'd kill for. The worst day we woke to a blizzard; snow that was being thrashed and plastered to the ground by a wind that took no prisoners. That lasted most of the day. They were the extremes. In between we had heavy rain and calm, heavy rain and gale-force winds, heavy frosts, and one day when it was perfect; quite mild with just enough wind to chop the surface. The most amazing thing of all was that the two extremes of weather followed each other, first we had the blizzard followed by the flat calm and sunshine, all in the space of 48 hours.

Pike fishing on Lough Gara, on the west coast of Southern Ireland.

This was on Lough Gara, Co. Sligo, a water lying about 40 miles from that huge expanse of sea we know as the Atlantic Ocean. Which means there is very little except water and space between Lough Gara and the USA, where anything can be brewed and thrown at Ireland's west coast. Some good, some bad, but mostly bad. And this was late November, early December when the conditions anywhere in Britain and the Irish Republic are transient. Which is to say a little of the autumn remains but enough of winter has arrived to give us a taste of both.

The usual gang had gone across the Irish Sea to take up cudgels with Gara's pike, something we do once or twice each year, and while we didn't catch as many fish as we normally do, we did learn a hell of a lot about how different conditions affect pike in regard to location, method and baits. That is the real advantage of fishing every day for a week or more, when the weather is as changeable as a chameleon's skin: you see the patterns; the trends. When you normally fish only at weekends, or for a day every so many days, you only know what happens on those days you actually fish, when the equally interesting bits are those days in between that lead up to either a good day or a bad day.

It has been my contention for a long time that all weather conditions, as far as fish are concerned, are not as important on the day you fish as they are over a period of time leading up to that day. It is the trend of the conditions that matter more than what the actual conditions are on the day. And the more settled the conditions have been, for the longest possible period leading up to the fishing day, the better. For instance, the best day for fishing may be on a cold, frosty winter's day rather than a mild winter's day, if the cold day had followed several like it, and the mild day was a one-off in an unsettled period; although the mild day following a number of cold days will still offer an opportunity for the fish to feed.

And while this applies to all fish, it is a little different with pike in that they are opportunist feeders much of the time, willing to take a little food when the conditions are unsettled and they are not really hungry. This is especially true in winter, when the shoals of fodder fish are not as active and the pike have to work harder to find them. When prey are found, or stumbled across as must happen pretty often, they take a bite to eat, so to speak, hungry or not, which is a good idea when you don't know how long it will be before your next meal, and where it will be coming from.

Although Lough Gara covers, in total, an area of about 3000 acres, it is really three large lakes joined together by narrow channels, the three parts known as Upper, Middle and Lower Lough Gara. All three parts are generally shallow, averaging about 5ft to 6ft, but with a few areas of deep water going to 40ft or so. Locating pike in such a vast expanse of water - no matter whether it be Gara or anywhere else - could seem like a daunting prospect, but it only has to be done once. By that I mean that once you have found where the hot-spots are they usually remain hot-spots, and that 3000 acres then shrinks to more manageable proportions. We fish several areas in all three parts of the lough, which ones depending on the time of year, weed growth, etc.

There are hot-spots within those hot-spots, and over the period we have fished Gara we have narrowed down the places we fish to just a few bank stretches of no more than 300yds to 400yds apiece, and several boat fishing areas. We know them well enough now to remain confident that the fish are there even on those days when we are not getting any takes; that it is only a matter of time before someone gets a run. This being so we can concentrate our efforts on baits and bait presentation, knowing that any absence of takes has nothing to do with general location.

Precise location is another matter, however, for there are times when the pike are patrolling along, and just beyond, the edge of the weedbeds, and other times when they are much further out, beyond casting distance, harassing the tightly packed shoals of roach and bream. That was how it was for much of the time on the last trip, when we had an absolutely marvellous week, with both the weather and the pike smiling favourable upon us. That week the pike were chasing roach and bream, and you had only to spot the tell-tale swirls from the roach to know exactly where to find the pike. They had surrounded the roach and bream with the precision of a military operation, and were busily picking them off almost at their leisure. Then the operation was complete when we, the ultimate predator, slipped out like the Spanish Armada and in turn surrounded the pike. At times there were several shark-like dorsal fins and long, black backs, slicing through the surface as the pike attacked along the top. It was an awesome sight to behold, surpassed only by that moment when the float disappeared when a pike grabbed a roach wearing a sharp overcoat made from treble hooks.

Nothing like that was happening this trip. The pike were in dour mood, and while a few fish, including a couple of twenties, were taken from the hot-spot on the bank, John and I were struggling in the boat with suspended baits. It seemed to be a case of drop the bait within sight of a pike and you had a chance, but picking a spot and then waiting for something to happen didn't work much at all. We'd had a couple of doubles each over the two days we had boat-fished and were ready to kick the boat into touch and fish the bank. In fact I'd already told Eddie that he could have my place in the boat from the next day if he wanted to have a go afloat. John couldn't make his mind up one way or the other. I was ready to relax on the bank behind a set of leger rods for a change.

Just before we were due to haul up the mudweights and head for the bank we spotted something break the surface 100yds away in the shallower water. Not a significant upheaval of water, but more of a disturbance that you would expect to see from a roach or small bream. In for a penny in for a pound, we thought, and slipped over for a spell. The first thing we found was that it was only a little over 2ft deep, and therefore set the floats accordingly, so that the baits hung just off bottom. Within ten minutes John was attached to a pike that took off as though it meant to head down the river a mile away. I pulled the mudweights into the boat so that there was no danger of the pike running the line round the ropes, and John took up station at the fore end of the boat and allowed the fish to tow us around for a minute or two. It was good fun, and soon knackered the pike. It weighed 26lb 2oz and made John's week. I was regretting my decision to give up my place in the boat, but stuck to it. It turned out to be a good decision in the end.

The worst day's fishing during this particular visit to Gara, as far as fish caught was concerned, was the best day as regards conditions on the day. When the early morning mist cleared it turned mild, with a light breeze to ruffle the water. The sun was quite warm at mid-day, to the point where top suits and jackets were removed, and it felt good to be there. But we never had a fish between us. That was because the day before we had received a skyful of snow. And because last night it had rained like it can only rain in Ireland, washing all the snow into the rivers and lakes, and brought Gara up about a foot. That's some water over 3000 acres. No wonder we didn't get a bite, in spite of how good the conditions were on the day.

By the following day a few inches of that extra water had been run off and the pike were feeding again. Not with any enthusiasm, however, and only in the one hot-spot. Anyone who was fishing in that area was in with a chance, while anyone out of the area was in for an extra tough time. Unlike the last trip, when freshly killed roach suspended under floats were the top bait, this time they wanted legered deadbaits, and mainly sea species giving off a smelly oil slick at that. Naturally oily baits such as sardine, smelt and mackerel were best, although half herrings were good, liberally injected with a proprietary pike-attracting oil. I scored best with fish oil-injected mackerel tail, deliberately fishing a small bait with plenty of flesh exposed in order to give off maximum oil and smell. I also popped up my baits, for the weed was more prolific this year following the dry summer, and my intention was to make it as easy as possible for the pike to find the bait. A mackerel tail oozing oil was appealing to their sense of smell, it being popped up above the weed was making it easy on their eye-sight, and its smallness was tempting them to partake of a little food they may not have been too enthusiastic about taking in the first place had it been larger.

That's another thing about pike and pike fishing. We think nothing of using a smaller bait when other species are reluctant to feed. Why should it be any different with pike? Yet it is very rare to see a pike angler swap a large bait for a small one following one, or even more, aborted takes. I've seen more than one angler carry on throwing, for instance, a huge, whole mackerel into the swim following several dropped runs. Half a mackerel, or even a tail or head could have made all the difference.

Anyhow, because of my tactics (or in spite of them, who knows?) they caught me the fish of the week, a pike that beat my previous best by 10oz.

It was 11am on Saturday, the last day of the week, just a couple of hours or so before we had to pack for home. I'd gone three hours since daybreak at 8am without so much as a pick-up, and then the mackerel tail went. As I played that fish the bait on my other rod was taken. I struck that with one hand as I kept a tight line on the other fish with the other hand. Then I opened the bale-arm and replaced the rod on the rod rests, allowing the second fish to run while I played the first one. As I played that first fish I kept glancing down at the rod that lay in the rests and could see the line peeling off the spool at a great rate of knots. In spite of fishing two or more rods quite regularly, it is not very often I find I am attached to two fish at once. Which is not surprising when you consider we fish multiple rods on difficult waters in order to increase our chances of getting just one run, never mind two. Normally, too, we are with at least one other mate, who can take charge of one rod while we deal with the other. This week I was with five mates, so what was the problem?

Only that Terry and Alan had gone off to fish another piece of the lough several miles away, John and Eddie were quarter of a mile across the water in the boat, and Ron was in his bivvy 300yds along the bank, probably fast asleep. I know I was getting hoarse shouting for him at the top of my voice and not getting any response. As well as losing my voice I was losing my cool, for I was getting nowhere with the fish I had on, for it was attempting to bury itself in a weedbed with a determination matched only by my own resolve to stop it going too deep. And all the time line was still peeling off the spool on the other rod.

I gave that first pike a tremendous amount of stick, not realising at that stage in the proceedings just how big it was. I was anxious to pull it through the weed and keep my rod bent into it and haul it into the landing net before the second one ran deep into any of the distant weedbeds. I almost literally popped it out of the weed and was hauling it towards the net with no regard whatsoever for its hugeness. Then overwhelming relief as Ron appeared by my side and took the landing net off me. The pike's head came out of the water. I grabbed the other rod as Ron engulfed the pike in the mesh of the big landing net.

Another big fish, no doubt about it. Felt like a 20-plus, but hard to tell on the end of 250yds of stretchy line. But more important, not weeded. I'd recovered about 100yds of that line when all went slack, and I brought back a huge ball of weed. The pike had obviously gone into and then out the other side of a weedbed, dragging a chunk of it with it. It came off probably because I was using barbless hooks. But that is the price you can pay for barbless in such circumstances. The plus side being that if the fish had weeded solid and I'd had to pull for a break, the pike would have easily shed the hooks and not run the risk of becoming tethered.

In the meantime Ron had unhooked and sacked the first fish and was proclaiming that it could be a thirty. I'd had a glance of the fish, but hadn't registered anything approaching that kind of weight. The scales, however, announced that Ron's estimate was pretty close at 29lb 2oz.

The fat lady really had sung when I netted this 29lb 2oz pike!

It was an important fish for three reasons. 1. It was my personal best. 2. It was my best fish from that water. And 3. It stopped Terry (Singer) Knight from claiming the fiver off each of us for fish of the week for his 26-pounder caught on the second day. It was particularly sweet because he had given me a load of stick in the pub the evening before, telling me how good he was and what he was going to spend the money on. 'The fat lady hasn't sung yet, Tel.' I told him, but not really expecting to beat him with only a little over a half day left to fish.

POSITIVE RIVER PIKING

A few decades ago pike were something you fished for when you couldn't fish for anything else, or you stuck a pike rod out to fish for itself while you concentrated on the 'real' fishing. If the river was up and the stillwaters were too cold for roach and bream fishing, you got the pike rods out. Fishing for pike was marginally better than not fishing at all. At least to some anglers, but there were plenty who stayed at home rather than fish for pike.

Of course, there have always been a few pike fanatics, but they were in a very tiny minority compared to the fans of other species. Angling journals had few, if any, features about pike, and the anglers who wrote the pike articles were regarded as quirky, or 'different' at least. And, at best, all you could buy in a tackle shop that was specifically pike related was a Fishing Gazette bung and a Jardine Snap Tackle. The rest you had to make yourself.

When you caught a pike you lifted it from the water with a gaff, which was slipped through the soft tissue of the bottom jaw by those few anglers who intended to return the fish. And then you prised its jaws open with a spring-loaded, pointed gag (which almost dislocated the jaws of smaller pike) while you tried to get the rank-barbed trebles out with a pair of pliers. If, like many anglers of that time, you never returned pike, it was thrown up the bank and left to die, or taken home for the pot. The rules of many clubs demanded that pike were never returned, and the maxim of most anglers was that the only good pike was a dead one. Unspeakably cruel acts were meted out on them with boots, rod rests, etc, all stemming from incredible ignorance. What a way to treat a fish that can give you as much sport and pleasure as any other species, and more than most.

Why the hell did we do it, and why the hell did it take us so long to learn that pike are not the enemy, but a major player in the big angling picture?

How different today. Every coarse angling journal (apart from other single species ones) covers pike in as much depth as any other fish. There is a major organisation, the Pike Anglers Club, catering solely for fans of the species. All major tackle manufacturers have a range of pike fishing tackle. You can buy pike floats to suit all purposes, and almost as many gadgets and gizmos as there are for carp fishing. Today, pike fishing is treated with the same respect as any branch of angling, and while there are some old, pike-hating dinosaurs still out there, the majority of anglers accept pike for exactly what they are: a beautiful, awesome fish with as much right to be in a mixed fishery as any other species.

Pike have enough stature and respect now to demand as much thought about how to catch them as goes towards catching all other species. No longer is it a mindless exercise whereby you impale a minnow or gudgeon on a set of trebles riding under a bung, and then chuck-and-chance-it wherever you happen to be fishing for something else with your No. 1 rod. Not long ago I was thinking about this as I fished a river for pike, using a float-fished dead roach with all the same concentration and tackle manipulation that I would give to float fishing caster for chub.

I was using a 12ft, 3lb test curve rod, a big fixed-spool reel, 15lb line, and 20lb wire trace fitted with two size 8 semi-barbless trebles. Not by any stretch of the imagination can you call that a delicate, refined set-up. However, big, bold and brash the tackle may have been, but above all it was well balanced. You need a heavy rod to cast a heavy bait and to plant treble hooks in big pike. You need heavy line to do that job too, and a wire trace to go with it. Treble hooks are necessary to fish a sizeable baitfish properly. And the whole combination is needed to land big pike. Although the outfit is heavy in every sense of the word, it doesn't mean that it can't be handled with flair and finesse.

Float fishing for river pike is something I've done a lot of, and the more of it I do the more I realise that good presentation of the baitfish is of paramount importance, no less so than the good presentation necessary with any bait for any species. Get that wrong and one of two things will happen: the fish will not see the bait at all due to it being presented outside the feeding area (and that includes fishing at the wrong depth). Or the bait may be behaving wrongly and causing suspicion. The answer to the former is simple: you experiment by

Trotting for pike with a roach deadbait.

presenting the bait at various depths until you find the depth at which the pike are feeding. The latter can be a mite tricky, but more of that soon.

The usual spots to fish for river pike are the slacks. In slack water - and I mean really slack, with hardly any more flow than you would get in a big stillwater when there is a big blow on - there isn't a problem. Or no more problem than if you really were fishing a big stillwater, for the baitfish can be swimming in each and any direction. Remember that what I am referring to applies to both live and dead baits, for a suspended deadbait has to give the illusion that it is live, otherwise it would be floating at the surface or lying on the bottom. Presentation is therefore quite easy; the leading treble in the root of the pectoral and the upper treble in the root of the dorsal: the hooking method used by many pike anglers no matter what the situation is. It is when fishing flowing water that presentation has to be given a lot more thought.

And think on this: pike can be found more often in the flow than in the slacks when they are hunting food. They will be where the prey fish can be found, and when that prey is dace, roach, grayling, perch and small chub the most likely place to find them is right in the flow, or at least at the edge, along the crease. Pike won't hang around in the slack water if there are no prey fish in the slacks. Indeed, I've caught pike from some of the fastest currents I've ever fished for any species, especially in some really racy grayling swims.

Pike are no different than any fish when they're hungry. They can be incredibly stupid. There are days when big fish of all species will take a crudely presented bait. How often have you gone through a rough patch, struggling to catch a decent fish for weeks on end, and then seen a complete novice extract a big fish on a tackle, rig and bait that made you want to throw up? Too often probably. And then you have to remind yourself that the more sophisticated tackle, rig and bait presentation you are using is designed for those days when they are not so hungry and exercising their usual caution. They are the days when you are successful and the novice blanks. So, a suspended baitfish, set to fish at practically any depth, and hooked to hang horizontally, will score on those days when the pike are hungry enough to throw caution to the wind. They will be hunting food in each and every direction and willing to accept anything that comes within striking range.

There are four float-fishing methods I use to fish for river pike and you can never be sure which is the best method on the day until you have fished for a while and experimented somewhat. The first method is the conventional suspended bait under a float for fishing the usual slack water at the side, or in water flowing so slowly the current is negligible. The second method is a paternostered sunken float, the third is similar to fishing a slightly overdepth stickfloat and used in any kind of flow, fast or slow. And the fourth method is a kind of stret-pegging, where you fish the bait several feet overdepth, leave it float-legered for a while, and then randomly feed it down the flow, along the bottom, in erratic stops and starts to float-leger the full length of the swim, which can be up to 50yds or so.

Method one, the usual, conventional technique used by everyone at some time or other, is the first choice. And why not? There is no point using the more difficult methods for flowing water if the pike are lying in, or on the edge of, slack water and open to some easy pickings. So, I hang a bait - live or dead, depending what I have with me, but preferably live - from the trebles, under a sliding pike float, and set off for a walk along the river, dropping the bait in every likely looking slack pocket I come across. I use a powergum stop-knot that grips the line enough not to slip as it shoots through the rod rings, but will slide easily without kinking the line as I adjust the depth for each swim I fish.

The second method, a paternostered bait with a sunken float, I use when I take a break for a brew and/or a sandwich, or when I wish to exploit a particular spot, usually right on the crease. Set the bait to fish at whatever depth you think is right - I usually start about 6ins off bottom - tighten to the float, and clip the line to the rod. That way the pike can snatch the line from the clip on its first strike, when it is least likely to feel anything untoward, and is then free to take off with the bait on an unrestricted run, which, of course, you hit immediately.

Method three is a brilliant technique for flowing water, allowing you to cover a stretch of water up to about 50yds. It can be hard work with a heavy rod and reel but is well worth it on the right day, for the returns can be a bit special. Use a slim pike float; the pencil variety, that will hold back in the flow without too much resistance. It can be a sliding float as normal, or fixed top and bottom like a normal stick float. Sliding is better, for the line coming from the top centre of the float gives you better control and, of course, it is easily adjustable when you wish to alter the depth. To fish the method correctly you need to fish overdepth and be over-shotted, for remember, you will be holding back against the flow, which will keep the float well above surface. Fish about a foot overdepth, and where, say, a 1/4oz bullet is normally sufficient, use 1/2oz. This should be positioned just above the trace, which should be about 15in to 18ins long, and held off the knot to the trace swivel with a rubber bead. You can also add SSG shot to the trace itself if necessary.

Use a deadbait, a roach or dace of about 3oz to 4oz is ideal, and I've had great success with small herring, joey mackerel and smelt too. There is no point in using a livebait for you will kill it in no time anyway from repeated trotting and retrieving. To begin with mount the bait on a pair of trebles so that it hangs tail down, the top hook through both lips and the bottom hook about half way down one flank. Bind the fish on with knitting-in elastic, a few turns around the shank of the flank treble. This is a very fine elastic with a diameter about the same as 2lb line, and can be bought from most haberdashery shops. It is important, at least in this first instance, that the fish hangs tail down, for you are about to try to imitate a fish that is swimming against the current, as they do. River fish occasionally turn downstream, but generally they swim against the current and drop downstream a short distance tail first.

When trotting the bait down the swim it is this action you should try to simulate. Hold back the float and allow the bait to drop downstream a little slower than the pace of the current; stop the float completely and allow the bait to rise in the current, then let the float go so that the bait sinks and runs downstream. Vary the technique by holding back for longer (to allow the bait to rise right to the surface) and for short spells (to allow the bait to rise to mid-water or thereabouts). You can really play around with the technique to make the bait run through the current at varying depths and with various actions.

Another variation of this same method is to shallow up to only a few inches overdepth and with the bait mounted head down. Now trot the bait down the swim, holding back frequently to allow the bait to rise a few inches, and then drop back to the bottom. The baitfish will appear to be standing on its head on the bottom, as if feeding, then dropping downstream to feed again.

With either variation you will be maintaining a tight line to the float, but most of the time the takes are surprisingly gentle. The float normally sinks slowly away just as though you have snagged the bottom. Obviously, the pike has grabbed the bait and lay on the bottom to allow it to slip down its throat before moving off. I strike at all float 'stoppages' just in case a pike is the culprit and to ensure that I do everything I can to avoid deep hooking.

The final method, stret-pegging, or at least a variation of it, is one of my favourites. I've done a little of it for some years, but I saw the method fished superbly by the Swedes when in their beautiful country a few years ago to do a slide show with Mick Brown. The locals used the stret-pegging method on the mouth of a river that flows into the Baltic Sea and caught a 44-pounder and several others over 30lb whilst we were there.

You tackle up the same as for trotting, but this time with the float set to fish several feet over depth. Most important is to use enough lead on the line - but only just enough lead - to keep the bait on the bottom. This time you can use a livebait if you wish, for you will not be casting and retrieving the bait too often.

It is best fished from a boat, but can be fished very effectively from the bank when you can fish more or less directly downstream. You swing the bait out and allow it to sink to the bottom and then tighten up to the float. The bait will be resting on the bottom with its head facing upstream, just as a fish does. A slight lift of the rod will cause the bait to dislodge from the bottom and then drop slowly downstream until you stop it, but a yard or so at a time is about right.

Each time you stop it you can leave it there for long or short spells. The time to especially watch for a take is when the bait has been lay in one spot for a while and you make it twitch and glide downstream. Pike have this habit of eyeing a bait for a while before they pounce, and they are often provoked into pouncing when the object of their attention makes an unexpected move!

Again, there is some scope for varying the action of the bait, but the method is basically a means of float-legering a bait for varying periods in many different spots down the length of a swim. There is, of course, no reason at all why the bait should not be mounted in any direction, but I've found that mounting it head up is the most effective.

DRIFTFLOAT FISHING FOR PIKE

Many pike anglers prefer a mobile approach, ie, artificial lure spinning, deadbait wobbling, and trolling, while other pikers generally favour a more static approach, such as legered deadbaits, paternostered, suspended deadbaits and livebaits. Both will venture into less favoured methods, but usually only if the preferred one has failed.

Fortunately though, there is a technique that is both static and mobile, which should be to everyone's taste. It is driftfloat fishing, which is implemented from a stationary position (bank or boat) with tackle that is mobile. The basic principle is to get your back to the wind and use a live- (where permitted) or deadbait suspended under a special float that has a large vane. This large, square vane acts as a sail, allowing the wind to push the float, along with the bait beneath, up to and over 150yds from the boat or shore. It is possible to drift to distances over 200yds, but anything over about 150yds begins to become unmanageable, with too much stretch in the line to allow positive striking with the possibility of poor hooking.

Why would we want to fish with a driftfloat?

If there is just one hot-spot you want to fish, and you can cast to it, then there is no good reason for using a driftfloat. A driftfloat is useful when you want to search a long stretch of water, for, remember, a bait under a driftfloat doesn't just fish that bit of water at the end of the drift, it fishes all that line of water as it travels to its limit. It is a great method for searching lots of water from the bank, or from a moored boat. It can often be used to work a bait into quiet bays which you don't want to disturb with a boat. It can be used to send baits to swims which are otherwise inaccessible due to fishing not being allowed from the nearest bank, or from a boat. Many times I use the method to deliver my baits to the perimeter of islands that are beyond even a long cast from the mainland. The possibilities are endless to anyone with only a little imagination!

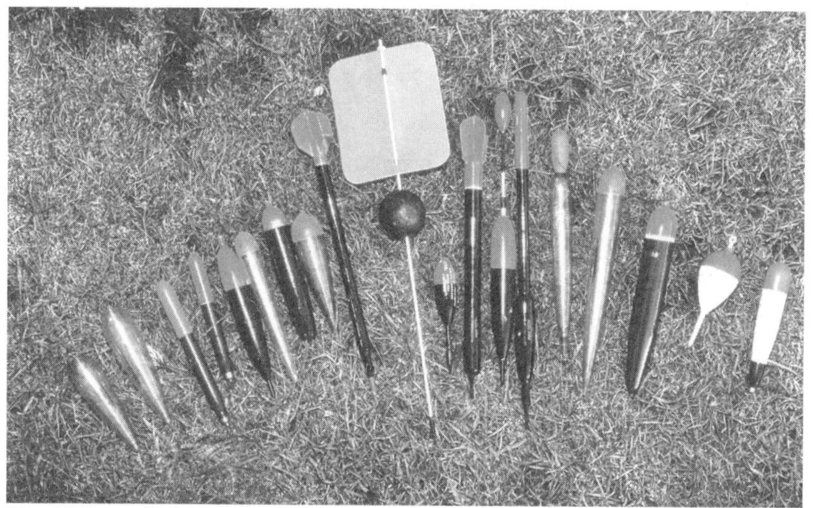

The driftfloat is in the centre of this array of pike floats.

The Driftfloat Rig

The float has a wire or glass-fibre stem with a link-swivel fixed at the bottom, a ring, or eye, that pushes into a float rubber at the top, and a sliding polystyrene ball on the stem. The vane has a hole at the bottom through which the stem goes and is held in place at the top with an elastic band. This allows for easy changes of vane of different colours for varying light conditions. The float can be used fixed or sliding just like any other float. In fact, apart from the quick-release ring at the top of the float the set-up is exactly the same as that used with a conventional float. The quick-release ring is so that on striking the float becomes detached from the top and collapses, with the idea that it now puts up much less resistance when being retrieved - with or without a pike in tow.

The Driftfloat Technique

It is better, but not essential, you use a long, powerful rod of 12 - 13ft with a 3lb test-curve. Such a rod makes it easier to pick up a lot of line when striking to set the hooks or when 'mending' the line. The reel, a fixed spool or multiplier, must be loaded with at least 250yds of line. This length of line is required to allow up to, and occasionally more than, 200yd drifts, with sufficient line left on the spool to allow a big fish to run on hooking. Braided line is best as it floats more readily and is therefore easier to lift off the surface. Braid also has virtually no stretch and this too helps with 'mending' and striking. It is impossible to fish properly with a driftfloat if the line sinks, the float will not drift, and the strike will be impaired to the point of being useless. Braid is thinner than mono pound for pound, so a braid with a strength of at least 20lb can be used.

One of the problems of driftfloat fishing is that the depth at which you fish the bait is usually a compromise, in that on many waters the bait will be drifting over a variety of depths. Very often you find you have to cast into shallow, weedy water of less than 6ft deep, meaning the float has to be set to fish the bait at less than that depth to avoid it dragging bottom, only for the depth to drop to 15ft or more following a drift of a few yards. This means the bait will be fishing at a depth of less than 6ft in more than 7ft of water, which is clearly not always a desirable situation. When the wind is very strong and the bottom not snaggy you can sometimes get away with setting the float to fish the bait deeper than the depth of water at casting range, and then allowing the float to drag the bait along the bottom until it reaches deeper water and hangs clear.

On waters where there is no great variety in depth then there is no problem, and in most cases you'll find that you can set the float to fish the bait at some compromise depth that is acceptable to the pike.

Ensure that the bullet and the combined weight of the bait are heavy enough to lift the vane of the float off the surface and cause the float to stand upright following casting. There is considerable drag between the vane and the surface, especially on not-so-windy days when the vane and the surface are more prone to 'sticking' together. When the float stands up make sure the line is free to pull off the spool, sometimes giving the rod tip a flick in the early stages to loosen the coils on the spool, for these will be sticking a little if you've greased the line well. Once the float is well under way, with plenty of wind in the sail and a good bow in the line, there will be no problem.

Much can be done to guide the float more or less where you want it to go, within reason, of course. A braided line will lift easily off the surface and can be 'mended'; flicked from one side of the float to the other. This will steer the float to left or right, and a straight line behind the float will keep it on a fairly straight course.

Take as much slack out of the line as possible by winding down to the pike immediately the float disappears, and then strike very firmly. I have never found any need to wait for runs to 'develop' whatever method I'm using, and there is a very good reason why you should not delay when driftfloat fishing, apart from the obvious one of hooking the pike too deeply. The driftfloat, once submerged, offers considerable resistance to a taking fish, and the longer you leave the fish to feel this resistance the more likely it is to spit out the bait.

No matter how big the pike you will find that playing it in the early stages is easier, for there is so much drag in the long length of line cutting through the water. Only when most of the line has been retrieved will you feel you are in direct contact with the fish, and by then it should be so exhausted there isn't a lot of fight left in it. Unless, of course, you hook the fish when the bait has drifted only a short distance.

Not a Method for all Occasions

Driftfloat fishing isn't a method that is used most of the time, for there has to a be at least a little wind to make it work, and that wind has to be behind you. Also, whenever you can approach your fish from bank or boat, and fish for them with conventional float and short line it is much more efficient than long range fishing. Driftfloating should only by used when you can't get near enough to the fish with conventional methods, or, when you wish to search a lot of water from a stationary position.

PIKE FISHING WITH MARINE DEADBAITS

Pike hunt by using three senses: sight, sound and smell. The vast majority of pike anglers everywhere take great advantage of the pike's sense of sight by using artificial lures and by fishing deadbaits spun, sink and draw, and wobbled. We rely on the pike seeing these animated baits and attacking them. We also try to appeal to the pike's sense of hearing by using lures that rattle, for instance. When I refer to the sense of hearing I am including the pike's ability to pick up vibrations through the sensors along the lateral line.

Yet it seems that it is mainly the English pike specialist who goes all out to catch pike by appealing to their sense of smell. It is certainly a peculiarity of the English, for other Europeans, and the Americans, Canadians, and Australians all prefer to use animated baits, which are most often artificial lures of one form or another. Perhaps it is because in many areas of Britain we have restricted bank space and are generally unable to wander about casting lures, and do not have many sufficiently large enough waters for a great deal of boat fishing.

Anyhow, whatever the reason, we English have developed pike fishing with sea deadbaits into a method that has accounted for a great many very large pike.

But it must be said that what has become very noticeable over the years of pike fishing with all methods is that sea deadbaiting is usually the slowest form of pike fishing, with not as many runs coming to the baits as would come to livebaits and lure fishing. Even more noticeable is the fact that sea deadbaits definitely tend to select the biggest fish.

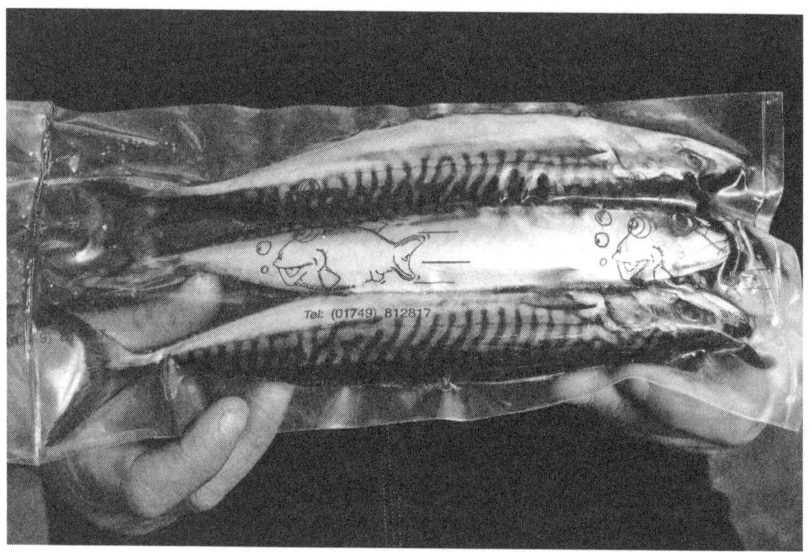

Frozen marine species deadbaits can be bought pre-packed from most larger tackle shops.

Obviously, no one knows for certain why this should be so, but I don't think it is difficult to work out. As pike grow bigger they must find it more difficult to conceal themselves in order to ambush their prey. They will also be slower, having lost much of that incredible burst of speed that took their victims by surprise. This being so they must then begin to rely less on their visual and vibratory senses and more on their sense of smell. So, much of the time they seek food by sniffing it out; by detecting the scent that emanates from dead and dying fish.

Which leads us to the next fact: marine species give off the strongest smell. Not only that, many are also very oily, and these oils seep into the sub-surface currents and lead big pike to their source. And this is why the oiliest, smelliest fish are the best pike deadbaits, the top four being mackerel, sardine, herring and smelt. Mackerel and sardine are very oily, herring is very smelly, and smelt has a unique odour that is reminiscent of cucumber - but only when fresh. That is the most important thing with all deadbaits, especially sea species, they must be as fresh as possible. Pike do not like decaying fish.

Methods

Legering is essentially the best way of fishing a deadbait, for that is the most likely place a dead fish will be found! On waters with clean bottoms a plain and simple legered bait takes some beating. The bait is cast out and left to lie there, giving off its scent and oils, while you hope the pike pick up the trail that leaks into the currents and follow it to its source. Many times, particularly with mackerel and herring, I cut the head off the bait to allow more of the blood and oils to escape into the water. When you do this, though, you must be prepared to change the bait more often - every two to three hours, say - for the leakage rate will be faster and therefore the bait will lose its vital scent and oils so much more quickly.

On waters where the bottom is weedy it is best to fish the bait 'popped-up' enough to clear the weed. Popped-up deadbaits can be very attractive to pike anyhow, for they are easier to detect and easier to take into their mouths. When I fish two or more rods for pike with deadbaits I always begin with a bait that lies on the bottom and one that is popped-up. It is surprising how often the popped-up bait catches more fish, even on clean bottoms. One of the other advantages of using a popped-up bait is that you can slowly twitch the bait along without the hooks fouling the bottom. The twitched bait method can be very good when the pike are in a dour mood and a little movement is needed to attract their attention.

Deadbaits can be dyed and flavoured.

Deadbaits can be made to float off bottom by inserting into their bodies a length of polystyrene through the mouth or via the gills, or straight into the body cavity if using half baits. There are special instruments you can buy for this purpose, or a piece of rig foam can be cut from a block. Another alternative is buy a length of 12mm diameter balsa wood and cut off lengths to suit.

These can be sharpened and pushed into the bait through the mouth or gill. Deadbaits can also be dyed and flavoured, which can often tip the scales in our favour with pike that have become wary of the usual offerings.

There is no reason why anyone should not try a sea deadbait that is suspended under a float, for it is as likely to attract pike as any other inanimate bait, but I do feel that sea species deadbaits are at their best when lying on, or close to, the bottom.

Whichever method you use, try not to cast too often, for this will undo the good work a smelly bait does when it lies in one spot for a lengthy period giving off its scent and oils. You can liken it to fishing with a swimfeeder, in that casting a swimfeeder too often, and in too many different spots, simply disperses bait in all directions instead of it emanating from just the one area. Be patient and the pike will find the bait. And when using sea deadbaits it could very well be a very large pike.

Chapter 13

Roach

One of the UK's most loved species, The Roach, eulogised by Mark Wintle

Dorset angler Mark Wintle is a true all-round angler with a preference for float fishing, especially on rivers. He has co-authored three other books with Graham Marsden on pole, carp and barbel fishing for the Crowood Press.

He has written the definitive book on roach for Mpress, 'Big Roach'. Mark has a wealth of roach fishing experience, having caught numerous 2lb-plus specimens. That, and his skill as an angling historian, make him an outstanding authority on roach.

Roach have long been one of the British coarse anglers' favourite fish. Indeed, for many decades, if not centuries, roach occupied the no. 1 spot, only pushed off in recent years due to the inexorable rise in the popularity of carp.

Mark with a fine 2lb 8oz roach.

The wide distribution of roach in all of lowland England plus parts of Wales, Scotland and Ireland, its ability to survive in a diverse ranges of waters, and the fact that even a novice can catch small ones, all combined to cement its popularity. It's found in almost all English rivers, the majority of stillwaters from the smallest farm pond to the biggest lakes, and had little problem colonising our canal network, surviving even moderately polluted waters.

The vermillion fins, delicate mouth and silvery scales with a blue sheen set off a handsome fish. A pounder looks big and one over two pounds is still rightly regarded by many as a fish of a lifetime, and one over three pounds often little more than a pipe dream. I doubt whether 1% of Britain's coarse anglers see a two pounder in their angling careers yet some specialists rack up tallies of hundreds. Little wonder that pleasure anglers, youngsters and the keenest of match anglers and big fish anglers all relish catching roach. Catching a few small ones is easy but as it grows so does its cunning and the big ones can challenge the most skilful of anglers, as does a sizeable match-winning bag.

Many methods were developed over the centuries just for roach fishing. Not for nothing was the pole originally known as a 'roach' pole. Floats like the stick float owe their origins to hardened match anglers trying to conjure a few small roach from a semi-polluted Lancashire canal, and the same goes for the development of casters and bread punch. The need for finesse in the tackle used, great bait presentation and careful feeding have been central to roach tactics for centuries. Before the technique to 'draw' gut to achieve fine diameters emerged in the 1870s, keen roach anglers used a single horse hair as hooklength, and even in those far-off days contests were held to determine who truly held the title 'England's Greatest Roach Angler', with heavy wagers on the outcome between anglers from the Nottingham and London 'schools'.

The roach record has been one of the most coveted down the years, and sometimes the most controversial. Unlike other species there has been far less movement in record sizes in a hundred years from the 3.10 of Wilf Cutting's fish caught during the First World War to the one that currently holds the record at 4.4 caught in 2006. The roach's propensity to hybridise with bream, rudd and occasionally other species makes it imperative to identify whether a potential record claim is the real McCoy and not a hybrid. These hybrids tend to be bigger than the normal roach. Graham Marsden has had a roach x bream of 8.4 and it's been shown that roach x rudd hybrids can reach five pounds in Britain. Although roach x bream are easily spotted the rudd variant is notoriously hard to determine.

The answer lies in DNA testing which is now a proven cost-effective method that requires a single scale (the fish soon regrows this) as a sample. Photographic evidence has proven difficult to decipher in telling roach x rudd from true roach (or rudd for that matter, as the hybrid often tends towards one or other of the parent species). The only clues are mouth shape, dorsal fin position relative to the pelvic fins, general body shape and colouration. These are all open to interpretation. Of six roach to hold the record, two have been arguably hybrids and another attracted unease over the details of its capture.

Whilst the roach is widespread, the waters holding big ones are less common. Many waters hold hordes of small roach, often stunted tiddlers, but certain environmental factors are vital to grow big roach. Clean alkaline water, plenty of the right sorts of food including silkweed and tiny snails and not much in the way of competition or predation are the main ones. This last factor has proved the most damaging in recent years with cormorant numbers soaring and destroying many good roach waters. Given the factors above though it is no surprise that the chalk and limestone rivers that stretch in a belt from Dorset and Hampshire in the south up through counties like Wiltshire, Berkshire, Buckinghamshire and Oxfordshire, Hertfordshire and eventually up to Norfolk and south east Yorkshire should all at one time have been renowned for big roach. The list of historic big roach rivers is a long one but the most famous ones include the Dorset Stour, Hampshire Avon, Kennet, Beane and Wensum. Many other rivers and stillwaters outside this broad belt have produced big roach at some time in the past (or still do) including the Taw in Devon, the Wye, the Severn, the Idle and the Ribble.

The immense demand for sand and gravel since the Second World War created many gravel pits that, once disused and flooded, provided many new fisheries ideal for roach. As many of these pits were in river valleys such as those of the Thames, Avon, Lea and Trent the good water quality meant ideal conditions for growing big roach.

The appeal of big roach stems from the species being a true anglers' fish. To catch big roach consistently demands subtle skills to handle relatively frail tackle, to be able to feed a swim without over-feeding and to detect and hit shy bites. For the river roach angler especially there are neither instant rigs nor shortcuts. Opportunity is an important factor in the development of a roach angler, and many that have been fortunate enough to grow up almost on the banks of a good roach river, as I have, get a head start on those living where opportunities to catch big roach are limited or non-existent, as is the case with Graham. It's no surprise then that many famous roach anglers had the cream of roach fishing on their doorsteps. Conversely, there have been those prepared to travel half the length of the country to sample outstanding fishing.

Apart from opportunity, an uncanny knack of consistently catching big fish and the right technical skills to make the most of the fishing, many of the big roach anglers have developed an obsession with catching them. Bitterly cold weather – often the best of big roach sport is in mid winter – or enduring endless blanks have failed to dampen their quest for the big ones. And despite catching many big ones, that desire continues to burn, often driven by the thought that somewhere in the dark recesses of the winter river is the giant that surpasses them all. Perhaps a three pounder, or a true monster, one over three and a half pounds, fires their dreams.

Such river roach over three and a half pounds are so rare that you can count them on your fingers. Even the mighty Hampshire Avon, a river that has yielded thousands over two pounds, has only produced half a dozen of this size, and three of those captures (the three biggest at 3.12, 3.15 and 3.15.8) were the same fish. Even the best stillwaters rarely fare much better. Linch Hill fishery in Oxfordshire is perhaps the best of them all. It has produced many roach over three pounds and at least one over four pounds. In the long past golden era of the London reservoirs only Bill Penney's 1938 record stands out at 3.14 though there were others over three pounds, especially in the mid 1960s. For the majority of successful big roach anglers, the three-pounder has represented the pinnacle of their career with some getting more than a few over this weight.

We are fortunate in that many of these fanatics kept dairies and wrote of their captures in magazines and books. Although I suspect that for every one that did many more did not, and details of their catches are lost for ever. So who were the giants of roach angling history? And what did they achieve and how? Catching a record, especially for such a coveted fish as roach when it was easily the most popular coarse fish, ensured a place in the history books.

Hornsea Mere, a large shallow water in East Yorkshire, produced a glut of giant roach from the time of the First World War through to the 1930s. Wilf Cutting set the record with a roach of 3.10, and had several others over three pounds. Other anglers had outstanding catches during this period, not least double National Champion Jim Bazley who had many big roach though fell just short of three pounds with a best of 2.15.8. The curious thing about these catches is that the successful method was float fished lobworms on a large hook, a far cry from conventional roach tactics.

Cutting's record lasted until 1938 when London angler Bill Penney, an outstanding roach angler of his time, caught one of 3.14 from Molesey Reservoir. Penney's skill was in understanding when and how to catch the big roach. He developed methods and tackle to fish the deep reservoirs, and for many years averaged fifty over two pounds per season.

Angling legend Dick Walker had a soft spot for big roach despite being more famous for his exploits with other species, and caught a prodigious number of big ones. He found the big roach in the Hertfordshire Beane especially challenging and devised a special float to detect their shy bites. His perseverance paid off in the end when a long campaign of feeding maggots in a deep hole finally got them feeding. When the roach got fed up with maggots he switched to a cube of crust and caught his best ever roach.

In more recent times, the river Wensum in Norfolk provided some truly outstanding roach fishing in the early 1970s. A number of anglers exploited this rich seam, none more so that John Wilson and John Bailey. Both anglers caught prodigious amounts of big roach from this river and elsewhere locally. Their approaches were different, Wilson favouring float-fished maggots and Bailey legered bread, but then both methods are favourite ones of roach specialists and they both succeeded.

The Hampshire Avon and Dorset Stour, two very different rivers in many respects yet near to each other and both historically important roach rivers.

Terry Lampard with a huge 3lb 5oz personal best roach he caught from the Dorset Stour. Copyright Terry Lampard, thanks Terry for the use of the photograph - Graham.

The Stour produced a phenomenal new record roach in 1990 when Ray Clarke caught a 4lb 3oz roach that dislodged Richard Jones's old record from 1975. Other anglers are more famous for their overall success on the Stour, particularly Owen Wentworth who caught many huge bags of good roach whilst boat fishing at Wimborne in the 1960s when the Stour was a river brimming with big roach. In later years, Terry Lampard and Tim Norman had a succession of monsters from a stretch not far above Wimborne. On the adjacent Avon the first specialist to describe his methods in detail was Captain Len Parker, better known as 'Skipper' and landlord of The Bull at Downton for many years. Here he controlled the fishing and did much work in improving the fishing for his guests.

He did plenty of fishing himself though, catching many big roach and being one of the first anglers to attempt to correlate water temperatures with his roach angling results, publishing the results in his book *This Fishing* in 1948. Many other anglers have since had outstanding success on the Avon over the decades; from Ron Felton, Brian Mills and Dennis Sawyer in the 1960s and 70s through to the likes of Dave Howes, Dave Swallow and Ron Smith twenty years later.

Match anglers have cherished roach for as long as organised match fishing has taken place, which is as far back as the mid nineteenth century. Even in these carp pool dominated days there is still a hunger for 'silver fish' matches, which largely means roach fishing. The heyday of match roach fishing was surely the 1970s and 80s when 300 peg matches drew the cream of the country's best matchmen to the Trent. Nottingham was home to some of the best but Yorkshire's finest took them on for many peg-to-peg battles for supremacy that was all about catching roach with exquisite stick float and waggler skills, later supplanted by pole fishing. Nottingham Federation stormed to three Trent National victories in the 1980s proving their skills with an unmatched consistency. Their aces were simply too good for the rest, and names like John Dean, Wayne Swinscoe, Johnny Rolfe and Pete Palmer deserve to be remembered.

Despite the scarcity of big roach in recent years, their ability to bounce back from calamity is remarkable, and you can be sure that as long as there is angling and roach to catch, especially big ones, there will be keen anglers eagerly seeking them.

Chapter 14

Rudd

Captivating and colourful, that's the rudd

RUDD STUDY

Is the art of rudd fishing a dying art? I ask the question because there are not anywhere near as many rudd around these days as there were 20 years ago and more. Where most other species are thriving in one way or another, with the record for many species growing in leaps and bounds, rudd are either at a standstill, or disappearing rapidly. Roach are the bane of rudd. When roach move into a water they usually, sooner or later, become the dominant species.

Hybridisation occurs quite rapidly, particularly where spawning sites are at a premium, and before you know it you have a species of such doubtful parentage it is anyone's guess as to what the hell it is. Mine, and perhaps the next generation of anglers, are very lucky, for we still have big rudd in sufficient numbers to make them worth fishing for. We should make the most of it.

A big rudd is a truly beautiful fish, from a sparkling quicksilver to burnished gold in colour, and with fins so red they make crimson look positively tardy. Their distinctive protruding lower lip tells us they are built for surface feeding, but all regular big rudd catchers know that they can, and often are, caught on the bottom. There is nothing odd about that, no more odd than catching bottom feeders at, or near, the surface. I wish I had a pound for every bream I have caught 'on-the-drop', including very close to the surface. And bottom feeders don't come more distinctive than bream. Rudd don't like bright light, which is why the best time to fish for them is in the evening and into darkness, or early morning before the sun rises. If you can find a shoal of rudd feeding before full daylight, and clouds prevent the sun from breaking through, then you're in with a chance of them feeding all morning, all day even, on days when conditions are absolutely ideal. But such days are very rare indeed.

Location

In and around marginal reedbeds are the favourite spots to find big rudd, and most good rudd waters have such areas in abundance. A reedbed has the same attraction for rudd as a candle flame has for a moth. In the early morning and late evening, and often going well into darkness, the rudd can be seen priming at the surface along the edge of these reedbeds. This movement is usually accompanied by loud slurps and sucking noises as they vacuum insects from the surface. One of the peculiarities I've found with big rudd is that they appear to travel in only the one direction when they're feeding, covering a line of marginal vegetation and then disappearing, the next time they're seen being the next feeding spell, either morning or evening. On the other hand roach will traverse back and two, feeding in both directions. Very often the evening feed is frenzied in the first hour or so of this feeding activity, for this is when most insects are spent and lying in the surface film, making easy pickings.

The open water should never be ignored, however, for when a warm wind is pushing the edible flotsam across the water, the rudd will follow it, often for several hundred yards and in large shoals. You can easily see these rafts of dead and dying insects. They look like a large patch of surface scum, a dull patch on the otherwise bright surface, and if you spot one in the early morning or late evening, watch out for those tell-tale swirls and splashes of big rudd as they take advantage of these natural larders.

My first taste of surface fishing (other than dry-fly for trout on small rivers, which has always been my favourite form of trout fishing) was with rudd on a small farm pond. I was only a boy at the time, but I distinctly remember, following a spell of float-fishing for roach and rudd with my favourite home-made peacock quill floats, throwing in my bread leftovers for the moorhens to devour when I'd left, and seeing half a dozen or so hungry mouths attack the bread as though they were determined to beat the moorhens to it. That probably was part of the reason for the frenzied attack on the bread, for the rudd most likely knew that they had to get in first to stand a chance. What they wouldn't realise was that the moorhens would not make an appearance until I had moved out of earshot.

The other thing about that day that stands out in my mind is that although I had seen the rudd taking bread from the surface on many other occasions, it was only then that the thought entered my head that presenting a surface bait to them could be a good way of catching them! Fishing a slow-sinking bait was the nearest I had come to it before. I determined I would try it on my next visit, which was the next day as it happened. And the simple approach I adopted was to fish exactly as I had before, but with no shot on the line at all between hook and float. From that day I got better and better at catching those rudd off the top; finding the right length of bottom to use; the best hook size; timing of the strike; and how best to loose feed to keep them interested.

It was many years later, sometime in my salad years as a 'specimen hunter', when I went through my next spell of serious rudd hunting, this time on a Cheshire mere that was renowned for good tench and even better rudd. A good tench at the time was 4lb plus, of which the mere had a nice head of them up to 5lb or so, and the rudd went well over 2lb.

The big problem on this fishery was that there was only one short stretch of bank from which to fish, the remainder being a bird sanctuary and out of bounds to anglers. Not surprisingly, it was the far bank where most of the marginal vegetation grew and therefore where the biggest rudd spent most of their time. But when the wind was right they followed it towards the fishable bank; you could see them priming and swirling at the surface as they sucked in spent insects.

To catch the biggest fish still meant a cast of more than 30yds, which ruled out float fishing of any efficiency, and also meant that loose feeding with crusts by catapult was out of the question (Chum Mixer-type biscuits were still being fed to dogs and cats only; fish were yet to have the pleasure).

So the hookbait had to go out via Arlesey Bomb on some kind of leger set-up. And I had to find a way of introducing loose feed.

The rig I decided to use was pretty simple, no more, really, than a modified fixed paternoster. I knew the depth so it was easy to get the rig set up correctly without a great deal of trial and error. To this day I have yet to find a better method of surface fishing at long range, providing the water is no deeper than about 6ft. Any deeper and sliding/running rigs have to be employed, which are fine if there are no algae particles floating around, which can foul up swivel eyes and make hard work of everything.

The beauty of the rig is that it is so easy to fish the bait at any exact depth you choose simply by allowing the bait to lie on the surface, and then hauling it down by pulling on the line at the butt ring and attaching a heavy bobbin at the bottom of the loop as soon as the depth you wish to fish at is reached. The bobbin has to be just heavy enough to stop the crust from rising again - what carp anglers call critically balanced. That way the rudd have only to sniff at the bait and the bobbin will begin to rise. I think this is a very significant factor towards the success of this method, for if a rudd shows an interest in the bait, if only swirling close to it, the crust begins to rise towards the surface; in effect behaving very naturally indeed, and simply asking to be grabbed before a competitor snatches the morsel from under its nose. The bigger the bait you use (within reason) the more easily it is controlled and therefore the more efficient the technique becomes.

The method is equally successful with carp, although you need at least two Chum Mixer and some rig foam to make it work. Crust too, if you can find a water where the carp will still take it!

I solved the problem of feeding crusts at long range by enclosing dry crusts in balls of groundbait. The groundbait was mixed so that it dissolved at different rates according to how tightly you squeezed it into a ball. The idea was to make balls with different dissolve rates so that the dry crusts would be released over a period rather than all at once. Also with that in mind I packed as many crusts into the groundbait balls as I could get away with, so those that lay in the centre of the ball were released to rise to the surface sometime after those that lay close to the outer surface of the ball.

The bottom line was that it worked like a dream; both the method and the feeding technique, and I caught plenty of rudd to a little over 3lbs over a period of several weeks.

My first efforts at surface fishing for carp also led me to a method I still use to this day, only slightly modified from the original rig.

The conventional (or should that be traditional?) method for catching big rudd is to present a floating bait at the surface, or to fish with a slow-sinking bait that lingers at the surface long enough to give a surface feeder a chance to take it, and then slowly sinks to tempt the rudd to take 'on-the-drop', and, finally, to lie on the bottom appealing to those rudd that are feeding in that area.

I'm particularly fond of boat fishing for rudd, for this allows me to be highly manoeuvrable, and follow the rudd while they feed. When they are feeding on the insect rafts you can drift almost alongside the raft, casting to the rudd as you go. More than once I have used the fly angler's drogue to control the speed of the boat so that I drifted across the lake at the same pace as the floating food. When I haven't had a drogue with me, such as those times when fishing for rudd in the insect rafts has been an unexpected opportunity, I've lowered the anchor over the bows of the boat and controlled the drift by lifting the anchor just enough to allow the boat to drift to its next position, and then releasing it to hold position for long enough to have a few casts at the rudd.

Most often, however, the marginal reedbeds are by far the best places to fish, for this is where the rudd begin to feed no matter where the weather conditions force them to feed later. Very often rudd are found on those waters where the reedbeds have encroached on the water for several yards, and it is frustrating to hear them splashing and slurping at insects right in the thick of the reeds where it is impossible to cast a bait to them – or at least land one if you were lucky enough to get a bait to them without it becoming hung up on the reeds. You can only wait for the right light when they will venture out and feed along the edge of the reeds, or move out to open water if they follow the whim of the wind.

Fishing the edge of the reeds is difficult from the bank, for you are obviously restricted to where you can cast. You have to fish available gaps (each gap will usually have some kind of platform on popular waters) or make one if necessary, and it is only across the front of the gap and at each corner where you can fish. With any other species it is not so important, for it is possible to lay groundbait and loose feed and tempt them to linger in the gap. Not so with big rudd, most often they simply will not be tempted to linger in any swim for any length of time, no matter how well you've fed the swim. To make things worse, there is that peculiarity of big rudd I mentioned earlier, in that they appear to feed in only one direction, travelling along the edge of the reeds in the one direction, or across the open water when the conditions suit open water feeding, and then stopping feeding altogether. Very rarely do they backtrack and feed on the return journey.

None of which means it is a waste of time feeding the swim. What it does mean is that you have to feed the swim on the little and often basis, with the idea of trying to ensure that there is some feed trickling from surface to bottom all, or most, of the time. Food lying on the bottom will not always attract the attention of those rudd that are travelling along, and feeding, at the surface, so you have to catch their eye at the surface, and then they will often follow the food down to the bottom and feed there for much longer periods than they would at the surface. I use brown crumb groundbait with 25% crushed hemp so that it continues to burst and mushroom from the bottom long after it has settled there.

Again, a boat is a tremendous advantage, for this eliminates the problem of having to try and hold them in the one position. You can anchor out in the water and fish towards the reeds, making a whole length of reedbed available for fishing. And then the adjacent length as they move along, simply by upping anchors and quietly rowing to the next position.

The float rig for big rudd is simplicity itself. All you need is a waggler float that is buoyant enough to carry sufficient shot to reach the swim. The float is set deep enough to fish the bait laid on a few inches following the brief spell it spends at the surface, and the slow journey to the bottom. All the shot except one small dropper is bulked right under the float (or use a loaded waggler with weight built into its base) and the dropper, a No. 4 for flake, and a No. 8 for smaller baits set about mid-depth. Always feather and brake the cast to prevent tangles and to ensure the line from float to bait lies on the surface as straight as possible.

Rudd love to feed in and around reedbeds.

Variations of this set-up will have to be made according to casting distance and weather conditions. If there is a massive undertow, for instance, then the loaded waggler will have to be replaced with an unloaded one, the bulk shot set around mid-depth, and the dropper about a foot from the hook. This, of course, will fish the bait on, or close, to the bottom, but when the undertow is that fierce it usually means that there is an equally fierce wind blowing, which will drive the rudd from the surface anyhow.

Rudd have a protruding lower lip to facilitate surface feeding, but remember that this peculiarity also makes it easier for them to take popped up baits. So make this one of your ploys and try popping up a bait a few inches off bottom when conventional laying on is not producing as many fish as you think it should.

On especially calm days, and on some days when there is a warm breeze, the rudd will very much favour feeding right at the surface. The dropper shot is then removed and the bait fished right in the surface film. Takes can be absolutely savage and belie the size of the fish, so be very wary when fishing surface baits. Keep the clutch set and your reactions finely tuned!

I generally use a 13ft match rod, a small, 2500 size fixed-spool reel, 4lb main line, and a 3lb hooklength. Hook size is, as always, according to bait size, with a 10's for flake and two grains of sweetcorn, and a 14's or 16's for maggot, caster, and single grains of corn. Flake is an excellent bait, and can be spiced up when the rudd get wary by tipping it with small redworm, maggot or caster.

Flake is especially good because of its natural buoyancy, for it allows you to squeeze more or less air out of it to regulate the speed at which it sinks. For very shy rudd bread-punched flake can be deadly. And let's not forget all those imitation baits that now offer us an excellent alternative, either used on their own or in combination with a 'real' bait. The great advantage of imitation baits is that they are naturally buoyant.

Imitation baits can be great for rudd fishing.

Takes can sometimes be induced by twitching the bait across the surface an inch or two, and regular casting is much better than leaving baits to lie for too long. Flake and crust especially need renewing often to maintain their buoyancy.

Finally, remember that rudd can virtually disappear from a water in hardly any time at all - there one season, gone the next. So catch 'em while you can!

Chapter 15

Tench

Fascinating and a fighter, that's the tench

ABOUT TENCH

I hooked and lost my first tench from the Macclesfield canal where it runs through Congleton in Cheshire. It was to be a stinking hot day, and even at 6.00am I fished in a short-sleeved shirt. I was fishing a swim known as Astbury Wide, a spot where the canal broadened to allow the barges to turn round, and just a 15 minute bike ride from my home. I was fishing for roach with the usual crow-quill float and 1½lb line to a 14's eyed hook. Bread flake was bait for several reasons; maggots were not readily available, and we didn't have a fridge in 1951 to keep them fresh; it was so much easier to cut a chunk off a loaf for that early morning session before school, and the roach loved it. It was also the perfect bait to go with the home-made groundbait I used to crush from stale and oven-baked bread by rolling it with a milk bottle.

I remember the morning as though it was yesterday (which is another symptom of advancing age when you can remember events from around six decades ago but forget what happened in the last hour). I had cast my usual yard to two yards from the marginal rushes and struck at the first bite within seconds. I had forgotten to put the ratchet on the centrepin reel and caused a massive bird's nest. It was a bad one, for the end result was that this bird's nest jammed in and around one of the runners on the 10ft split cane rod. I was left with two choices, either to fish within a few inches of the rushes, simply dropping the float more or less below the rod end, or to go back home and prepare for yet another boring day at school. Anything was better than the latter. Where a bad day's fishing is better than a good day at work, a bad hour's fishing is infinitesimally better than even the prospect of school when you're nine years old.

So the bread flake was lowered in right by the rushes, and I sat back on my basket not really expecting to catch anything, for at that age you need some convincing that the best place to fish is not always in the middle, or at least as close as you can get to it. I hadn't altered the depth I was fishing and my float was lying half-cock due to the bottom shot now lying well on the bottom rather than being held up by the float. I had thrown all my groundbait into the far swim before the bird had nested in my rod runner and I thought my prospects of catching anything were about as good as someone running a mile in less than four minutes. Which of course Sir Roger Bannister did in 3 minutes 59.4 seconds on 6 May three years later, breaking the then world record.

Just as I was wondering whether to collect a pocketful of stones for catty ammo my float suddenly stood up and waved at me. I had my hand on the rod when the float disappeared, and then found I was connected to a mad creature that pulled at the rod like nothing had ever pulled on it before. How I even got it to the top was due more to luck than anything else, but I did, and for long enough to see the smooth, olive skin, the red eye and big paddle of a tail as it disappeared forever, taking my hook and a few inches of line with it. I had seen only pictures of tench before, now I had seen one for real. I cursed that bird's nest, but went home with my head swimming with plans to catch a tench. Now I knew when, where and how to catch a tench, which I did in that same spot a few days later.

Small beginnings, but a lesson learned that was never forgotten. Tench were best caught when the weather is warm, in the early morning, fishing tight up to marginal vegetation, with a bait that lay hard on the bottom. That holds good today, many years later, but obviously with the usual exceptions to the rules that make fishing what it is, a subjective rather than an objective sport. Perhaps the greatest value of the lesson I learned that day is that it may have been my first inkling that the best way to catch fish is to learn about their habits, particularly their feeding habits, and then to capitalise on that knowledge.

At one time known as the Doctor Fish, due to a mythical belief that their body mucous had healing properties, I have to rate the tench among my best-loved species. They are found in all types of stillwater, from tiny ponds to massive reservoirs and gravel pits, and in some slow-flowing rivers. Though I have to say they seem most at home in shallow, lily-dotted estate lakes. Not too difficult to catch, yet not too easy.

Beautiful to look at, yet as tough as old boots. It has a sleek, shiny, almost varnished, body, not unlike a polished carving from dark oak, although the colouring can vary from very dark brown, through green, to a very light, golden hue. When seen in the water it doesn't move, but glides, slipping through weed with the same ease as wire slicing through cheese and with the grace of a ballet dancer. That veneered body, however, hides coiled muscles that impart such power into massive fins you have a bare-knuckle fight on your hands that gives no quarter.

The male tench, one of the few fish whose gender can be identified easily by the layman, has even bigger fins; big spatula-like pectoral and pelvic fins, and a fighting tenacity that belies its size. Like all freshwater species the male tench is generally smaller than the female, and it is popularly thought that the ultimate size of the male tench is about half the ultimate size of the female in a given water. I think the truth is something less than that, ie, a water where the biggest males are around 7lb has the potential to produce females of 10lb to 11lb.

The male tench. Note the big fins that identify it as the male of the species.

Tench are lovers of warm water, in spite of the fact that a few tench are caught each winter. The upper 60's Fahrenheit, to around the mid-70's are best, but lower temperatures cannot be ruled out at the right time of year. As I have said so often before, it isn't the numbers that matter where water temperature is concerned, but the trend of those numbers. A rising water temperature in, say, the upper 50's, in spring, will encourage tench to feed far more than a falling temperature in the upper 60's in mid-summer.

Late April, early May, the water is seriously beginning to warm and the natural food begins to multiply. The early weeks are particularly suitable for tench to feed close in, where the water is warming fastest and the food increasing abundantly. At this time of year the water is very clear and therefore the light can penetrate deeply, so this usually means the early morning feeding period will be short on those days when there is no cloud cover.

Tench are a contradictory creature though, for I have made some of my best catches of big tench on a few waters around mid-day, when the sun was at its highest and therefore the light able to penetrate to its maximum. In spite of racking the old brain cells over the years, in the effort to try and find a pattern, I have never been able to. It would make more sense if, on those days when they feed on a bright mid-day, the water was cold and a rise in temperature was the crucial factor. Yet that is not the case, for it happens during a run of warm days, when the water temperature is perfect for tench. It happens during a cold spell. It happens when it is calm and when it is windy, and in whatever direction the wind is blowing. And it happens when the water is crystal-clear or coloured. I have even noted the moon phases when it happens and found no connection.

There are more waters, however, where the tench rarely, if ever, feed beyond that important dawn plus three hour period. Where they occasionally feed in the late evening and through the night. The general pattern also includes the fact that tench will extend their feeding period on overcast days, when the sun is not allowed to make an appearance. So when you are faced with a water you have never fished before, go for the early morning period, and then experiment from there.

Accepting then, that for the most part, tench are inclined to feed best in the early morning, from dawn until the sun rises high enough to have an effect beneath the surface of the water, and on overcast days, why are so few tench caught through the night? The light (or lack of it) is right, the water is at its warmest, at least for the first few hours of darkness, and all other bottom feeding species are inclined to be nocturnal. Yes, I know that tench are caught when night fishing - I've caught enough of them myself at that time. Yet compared to the number of tench caught in the early morning and late evening the night-caught ones are well in the minority. If, as we all accept, tench are generally not lovers of bright light, why are they therefore not inclined to feed more through the night, just as many other bottom feeding species do? I have heard many theories about this, but none that cannot be shot full of holes. It has been said that weedy waters, which are typical tench venues, give off too much carbon dioxide from the weed at night and therefore there is not enough oxygen to encourage the tench to feed. But that won't wash, for the other species present in most of them, such as bream and carp, feed through the night, and tench require less oxygen to thrive than either of those species. Theoretically, especially where the light factor is concerned, tench should feed more at night than any other time. But they don't. Of course, there are waters where tench are caught mainly at night, and waters where they are caught occasionally at night. But there are many more waters where only a tiny percentage of tench are caught during the dark hours, compared to what those same waters produce during the day.

Tench and weed go together like hair-rigs and boilies. Find one and the other won't be far away. Any kind of weed is attractive to them, but broad-leaved emergent plants are mainly used for shade and bottom weeds for food supply and cover. Where there are fairly tall marginal reeds, or where broad leaves

Tench thrive best in weedy waters.

on the surface grow from the top of a shelf - which is often the case - and cast their shade over a shelf where weedy larders grow from the bottom, you have an ideal environment for tench.

The natural food of mature tench are bloodworms, molluscs, such as snails, mussels and shrimps. Like all fish they will eat smaller fish when the inclination and opportunity arises, and have been known to take hatching insects from the surface. I have seen evidence of them eating soft weed (filamentous algae) but I'm not sure if this was deliberate or the result of taking it along with the shrimps, snails and pea mussels that live in it.

Tench are not loners. They roam and feed in groups of half a dozen or so, although they are not shoal fish in the strictest sense of the word. True shoal fish are like a regiment of soldiers who feed and move as one, whereas tench move and feed in small groups, but each appearing to maintain its individuality. When very large catches of tench are made it is usually because a number of groups have come together at the same time to feed in the baited area.

Tench are an apparently fearless fish in some instances and are greatly attracted to an area where the bottom has been disturbed and caused the water to become cloudy. No doubt they associate cloudy patches with feeding activity and home in to ensure they have some of the action. Raking a swim, an old trick used by tench fishers for as long as we have records, serves the purpose of releasing food from the bottom and causing a cloudy area. Most of the large catches of tench I've had have come from raked swims in weedy spots, when numerous groups of tench have homed in to that same area.

Many anglers are reluctant to rake a swim, especially when the target is large tench, for they fear that the disturbance will ruin their chances. I have never found this to be the case. In fact, on countless occasions I have had the first bite within minutes of the rake being pulled from the water for the last time. Even so, I have never yet had the courage to rake a swim again, part way through a session, when the bites have tapered off, to see if that would revive their interest.

Although I am never reluctant to rake a swim, I am not under the illusion that tench will tolerate any and all kinds of disturbance. They may be tolerant of rakes causing havoc for a few minutes, and only retreat while the commotion is taking place, but I'm sure the reason for this tolerance is solely because they associate the activity with food rather than danger. A careless movement against the skyline or a heavy footfall on the bank, soon causes them to take flight. I have sat close to the edge of a water float-fishing under my rod end, and seen tench scorch away in panic simply from the movement of the rod above their heads. Whenever I can, I sit well back from the water's edge and keep the rod out of sight. When I cast I overcast by several yards and then draw gently back to allow the bait to fall quietly through the water.

It has to be said, however, that where tench are concerned you cannot take anything for granted. The only real pattern to their behaviour in many instances is that there is no pattern. In this respect they are totally unpredictable. It is this factor, as much as anything, that I love about the species. Even on the most dire day, when all seems lost, you are always in with a chance.

TRADITIONAL TENCHING

In this day of hair-rigs and bolt-rigs, boilies and bite alarms, it is nice, sometimes, to simply enjoy a type of fishing that was being enjoyed long before even legering itself became popular.

Don't misunderstand me, I'm all for high-tech gear and modern methods, most of them anyway, but I also have an old fashioned streak in me that regularly needs sustenance, and while I don't go so far as to root out my Mark IV rod and Intrepid reel, and wear clothes that Isaac Walton would have been proud of, I do enjoy a simple form of fishing where electronics and chemical baits have no part.

To me, float fishing for tench from a boat is the epitome of this type of fishing. During the summer period, up to about mid-September, sometimes longer, I can catch tench pretty consistently with this method. As the year wears on, past those few weeks at the beginning of the season, tench fishing gets harder, but with a boat it isn't so hard as from the bank, for you can track them down and switch swims more easily, and although you do go through periods when the tench are totally preoccupied with a hatch of some aquatic grub, and emphatically refuse to accept any kind of angler's bait, before too long they're back on the prod, happy to snap up anything on offer. And in September, usually for a couple of weeks at least, they can feed as well as they do at the beginning of summer.

Where boats for smaller lakes are concerned I prefer a flat-bottomed punt, the bigger the better, to provide as much stability as possible. The one my pals and I have used for years is 14ft long and 4ft wide, made from wood, patched a score of times over the years with glass-fibre, and weighs a ton (almost literally). It has served us well, but now lies waiting for more serious repairs. In the meantime we have bought a 12ft long, 4ft wide, glass-fibre dinghy that, while not quite as good as the punt, is definitely the next best thing, and requires little or no maintenance.

We use our boat on two Cheshire meres, both of which have soft mud bottoms, and require a mud-weight to anchor the boat at each end. When legering from the boat, which is quite rare, we also stake the boat to give it the extra stability needed to prevent legering bite indicators from registering false bites all the time. When float fishing the stakes are unnecessary, for the slight side to side swing you get on the anchor ropes has little or no effect on the floats.

We have carpeted the bottom of the boat. Not because we like to fish in luxury, but because it deadens the noise that scraping feet and dropped tackle might make, which can be considerable, being as a boat is much like a floating drum. Furthermore, the carpet is kind to the fish we catch when we unhook them. It is a little luxurious too..........

Once we have established a swim we will often leave semi-permanent mud-weights in position. This involves leaving the weights on the bottom and tying a plastic, capped, soft drink bottle to the end of the anchor ropes, which will float and leave the ropes at the surface, ready to tie to the boat when we next arrive. It saves a lot of the disturbance that is inevitably made when anchoring, no matter how careful you are, and always ensures you are anchored in the exact same position each time. And this is important, for even with a marker in the swim, if the boat is turned a few degrees from the last time you fished, you can be fishing a slightly different spot which, if there are distinct hot-spots, can make a big difference to what you catch.

That covers the essentials of the boat, but before I go on to the fishing I must mention one more thing. Never act the fool in a boat; never think a water is too small, or too shallow to drown in; and always wear some kind of life jacket. I know you see lots of pictures of anglers not wearing life jackets, and I know that the chances of drowning on a shallow lake are pretty slim, but life is too precious to take any chances. I dare say you're the same as me and want to be fishing next year too.

Boat fishing for tench is hard to beat. Note the life jacket.

We always use a swim marker when boat fishing; a small block of polystyrene at one end of a strong fishing line, and a weight at the other, the line being a foot or so over-depth to allow for fluctuations in water level. The marker is essential, for there is no way you can precisely locate a swim that may lie 100yds or more from the margins simply by lining yourself up to objects on the banks. We use a marker simply for guidance, for the actual swim lies 10yds from it, therefore reducing the risk of fish swimming round the marker line. It will still happen now and again, but don't worry about it. If you do worry you can use a cane instead of the polystyrene, attached to the weight by a short length of line. If a fish goes round the cane it simply lies over and springs back into position when the line passes over the top.

Tackle up at home, or on the bank. That way you will be ready to fish when you reach the swim and keeping the chance of any disturbance down to a minimum. The first job when you reach the swim and anchor up is to use a catapult to feed some bait. We always lay a carpet of hemp, followed by a few pouchfuls of sweetcorn and a few pouchfuls of maggots. There is no need to bait heavily, for you can top up with loose feed as and when the tench require it. Little and often, as required, is almost always the best way of feeding a swim. This is one of the greatest advantages of boat fishing, in that every swim is only loose feeding distance away. That, and the fact that every swim is accessible.

I use a 12ft Specimen Float rod, which is that little heavier than the usual match rod, and has a nice action that is not too 'tippy'. Lines are 6lb on the reel and 5lb hooklengths. Floats are various wagglers, ranging from Drennan Driftbeaters to peacock inserts, in sizes according to wind and drift on the day. Hooks are eyed Carbon Specimen hooks.

When maggot or caster is the bait the hook may be as small as an 18's if the tench are being particularly finicky and a single maggot is needed, or the more usual 14's or 16's for a bunch of two or three maggots. A single grain of sweetcorn, or a single redworm, usually go on a 14's; two grains, or two worms, on a 12's. Bread flake or lobworm is presented on a 10's or an 8's. Any other bait is very rarely used.

I'm always intrigued at how often tench swap from one bait to another. You can go fishing one day and slaughter them on maggot, and two days later not get a bite on maggot but clean up on worms. It can happen to some extent on the same day too, in that the tench will be feeding quite happily on one bait and then suddenly stop feeding - or appear to stop feeding. If it wasn't for the bubbles and occasional line bites that give the game away you would be convinced there wasn't a tench left in the swim. But a change of bait, usually any bait, is enough to coax them into feeding again. Time and time again I've continued to catch tench simply by giving them a regular change of bait. I would never go tench fishing with just the one bait, no matter how good that bait had proven itself to be.

Finally, a tip on playing fish from a boat. When you hook a fish – any decent sized fish - just hold it on a tight line. It will invariably kite round in a big arc, which you should allow it to do until it is at the opposite side of the boat from which you're fishing. Now you can play it to the net away from the swim, leaving it undisturbed and allowing your mate to get on with his fishing, and not having to wait for you to net your fish.

TACTICS FOR TRICKY TENCH

Duffer's Fortnight was a term used to describe the first two weeks of the season (when we had a closed season) when tench are at their easiest to catch. the phrase implied that any duffer could catch tench during that period. Let's just say that it takes more than a duffer to consistently catch tench at any time, but it is true though, that tench are never more vulnerable to being caught than they are during those first few weeks.

I usually begin my tench fishing campaign around mid-May, for tench are in far better condition at that time than they are several weeks hence when they're bloated with spawn. My tench fishing is relatively easy for about five or six weeks, providing the water isn't hammered, for the tench soon become educated to what food (bait) bites back, and react accordingly.

Up till then I can get away with using pretty heavy tackle, no matter whether I'm legering or float fishing, usually with a 6lb reel line to a 5lb hooklength to a heavy gauge hook; the type and size of bait deciding the hook size. Bites are generally very positive, legering indicators smacking up to the butt ring, and baitrunners spinning wildly, or floats either popping up through the surface to lie flat, or disappearing beneath the surface in the twinkling of an eye.

All of which makes for bloody good fishing in anybody's book, and notwithstanding serious hindrances like family holidays, etc, you make hay while the sun shines.

The next thing you know bites are getting fewer, or you think they are, until you examine the bait and find the end of a maggot has been nipped, or even crushed completely; or a grain of sweetcorn shelled, and not an indication to show for it. You then hair-rig the bait and play around with bolt-rigs and other set-ups. Float fishing probably becomes the best bet, so that is what you do whenever you can, and maybe you begin to see, and hit, more bites. From there you experiment with different shotting patterns and try the lift-method, which is excellent, and probably the most sensitive float rig of all when set up correctly. But even that doesn't last, for as time goes on; as natural foods multiply, and the tench become more educated to what is dangerous, hooked fish become hoped for rather than expected, and your tactics change to fishing for bites rather than fishing for fish. Obviously, you hope one leads to the other, but you are well aware that that may not be the case. It becomes blatantly obvious that Duffer's Fortnight, or Duffer's Month in my case, has drawn to a close.

So what do you do? The usual first reaction is to reduce line strength and hook size, which may well bring more bites. But there is no need for such drastic measures just yet, for there are a few other things we can do to bring more bites. Or should we say convert more bites to fish on the bank.

The increase in natural food is the main cause for concern - initially - for it makes our baits that much less attractive. Where bunches of three or more grains of corn, maggot or caster, big lobworms and pinches of flake, and other big baits were taken confidently, they are refused, or played around with to the point where the bite becomes unhittable. To counter this increasing preoccupation with natural food we have to increase the amount of free feed we introduce, using a food that is small and plentiful, with the aim of preoccupying the tench on that; a food that is also a good hookbait, small, but not too small it can't be used on a heavy gauge hook of no less than a size 16 - which is usually strong enough to land any size of tench where there are no really bad snags.

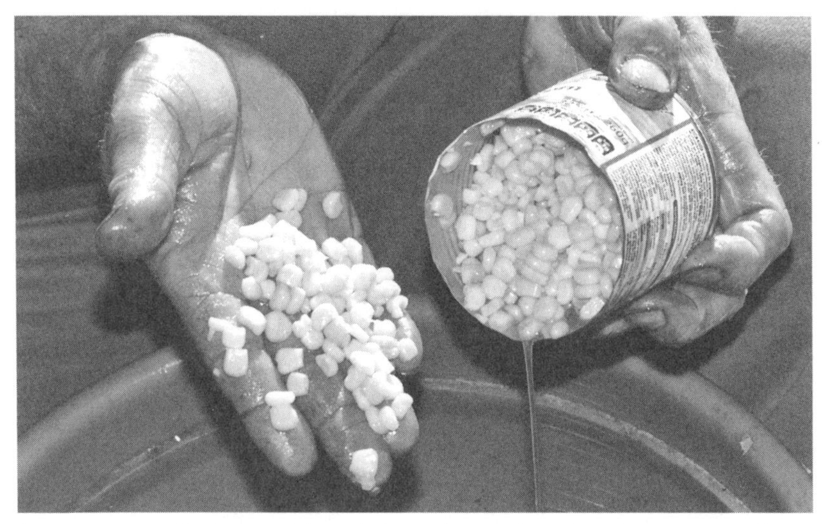

Sweetcorn, a great bait for tench in early season, but tench can soon become wary of it.

Sweetcorn is not a good bait to use for this purpose, unless you are fishing a water where the tench are numerous and always hungry (but then you won't have the problem I'm referring to anyhow). Sweetcorn is a wonderful early season bait, but as fast as the tench wolf it down in the early days they equally as quickly reject it when the education process is well under way. They reject it to the point where they will not enter a swim where it is present. I've watched tench on more than one occasion, slowly swimming along the margins in shallow water, stopping now and again to grub in the bottom, and on seeing a scattering of sweetcorn, pull up dead and veer off in another direction. I've only seen them do the same thing with one other bait, and that was white groundbait. You can sometimes prolong total rejection for a short spell by changing its appearance, by colouring the corn red or orange, but rejection is usually inevitable before too long.

The best baits to wean tench away from natural food are maggots and casters. I use hemp too, but I'm always a little wary that they may eventually react to it as they do to sweetcorn, but I have no evidence of any kind to back up my feelings. Casters are the best bait of all for holding tench in a swim. They are light enough to sink slowly and rest on top of weed and silt, stay there until they are eaten, and make excellent hookbaits. The dark, floating casters can give you an extra ace to play with too, in that they can provide you with a semi-buoyant hookbait - 'critically balanced' as modern jargon describes every bait that floats a bit. Maggots are the next best baits, but will crawl into weed and burrow occasionally into silt. Once you achieve preoccupation in tench with caster it is possible to make some really big catches, they love them so much. The big advantage with both maggot and caster is that the tench never seem to lose interest in them, or become wary of them as they do with sweetcorn. Boilies, especially mini-boilies, will probably do the same job if used on a large enough scale, and on waters where carp are regularly fished for, they could very well be the best bait of all. But I've managed without them so far, and will continue to do so for as long as I can. I don't like the idea of having to spend hours making bait, or paying high prices for ready-made boilies, when I can use something as good, if not better, and much cheaper.

The next step is to present small baits, preferably single items of the free feed you've been throwing in. If you've stayed with corn, then present a single grain on a 14's, rather than two on a 12's. Double caster or maggot is usually acceptable, but if you're still experiencing finicky bites, or have evidence (such as shelled casters or sucked maggots) that the tench are wary of the bait, then try a single. If you're careful, one caster can just about stand having a 14's hook buried in it. But don't hesitate to drop down to a 16's, or even an 18's if you feel you have to, using heavy wire hooks rather than fine or medium gauge ones.

The next stage, if you're still struggling to see bites, or convert bites into fish in the net, is to reduce the diameter of your hooklength, which does not necessarily mean you have to fish lighter. The following little anecdote illustrates exactly what I mean. For several visits last season a pal of mine fished for tench alongside me. We cast to the same swim and were using identical rods, reels, floats, lines and hooks, set up in exactly the same way. But I was catching by far most of the fish. On examination of his tackle, when it became obvious that there must have been some difference, we found that the only difference was that he was using a 5lb reel line direct to the hook; a very popular reel line due to its many unarguable qualities, including proven reliability. My hooklength was 5lb test too, but one of the new, supple, reduced diameter, copolymer lines. The difference when the two lines were laid together was glaringly obvious, both visually and to the sense of touch. My pal's line was like wire, stiff and uncompromising, compared to mine. From the moment he changed to a length of my line our catches thereafter were more or less equal.

The author caught this big tench on light float tackle.

There is only one thing left to do when you reach, or are still in, the same predicament, where convertible bites are at a premium. You have to go lighter. Lighter lines and smaller, finer-wire hooks, and certainly single, small baits. Providing there are no exceptionally bad snags it is possible to land big, hard-fighting fish on light tackle. Just make sure everything is balanced correctly. In particular you should ensure the rod is not too heavy for the line and when it comes to playing the fish, think of it as persuasion rather than punishment, encouragement rather than correction. Match anglers prove regularly that big fish can be landed on light tackle, and when it comes to the crunch; when you have to fish for bites to catch fish, and throw caution to the winds, you may as well go for it positively and confidently. There is no other way.

What I am against is fishing light for its own sake, rather than because it is a necessity. But when the choice is between no fish on heavy tackle, and an excellent chance on light tackle, I'm all for the light approach.

Chapter 16

Zander

Enigmatic and exciting, a species for the thinking angler

ZANDER

They were originally known as pike-perch, with many anglers under the impression that zander were hybrids of those two species. The zed, as it is fondly known by its hunters, is an alien that is steadily infiltrating everywhere.

Just 23 zander, transported from Germany's Lake Bothkamper, were stocked into the lakes at Woburn Abbey in 1878 and marked the steady but inexorable march of zander into an increasing number of British waters. In 1960 a number of mature zander travelled from Woburn to arrive in stock ponds in Bury St Edmunds where they spawned successfully. In 1963 one hundred small zander made the trip to the Great Ouse Relief Channel at Stow Bridge where the 97 that survived the journey were released.

Some three years later the real explosion began and the fall-out spread right across the East Anglian Fens resulting, in 1968, in the first British zander to make double figures at 10lb 4oz. A series of increasingly larger zeds were caught, with the British record being broken several times, culminating in the present record of 19lb 5oz caught from Norfolk's Middle Level Drain in 1998. Today, zander can be found in the rivers and stillwaters of several counties with more mysteriously appearing as each year passes. There is no doubt about it, zeds like the Brits and many of us like them. One thing's for sure, they're here to stay and although not the cup of tea of all anglers they're certainly a fascinating species to fish for.

I'm living proof that you can indeed teach an old dog new tricks. Not just one trick in the case of this old dog, but two tricks that were missing from my repertoire. Quite late in my angling career at the age of 60, I dipped my toe into the world of lure fishing following a lifetime of wondering what the hell anybody saw in it and found that the water was not only warm, but interesting. And not long after I ventured into another world that had so far eluded me; that of the zander. I caught my first zander (two of them in fact) on the first day I tried it.

Ever since zander fishing took off in the late 60's I have been promising myself that I would catch one. As an all-round angler they were the missing link in my particular chain and it hurt, in a way, to always have to say, "Zander? Never even seen one in the flesh, let alone caught one."

Distance was the one thing that got in the way. I was always too far from most zander waters where I stood a reasonable chance of catching one, and somehow every trip I went some way towards planning never actually made it. Then my old mate Stu Dexter told me about this local gravel pit near Leicester he fishes that has a decent head of zander. Now Leicester isn't excessively far away from where I live in a little village near Stoke on Trent, and my immediate reaction was, "when are we going?" But it actually took another year before we got around to it.

The first visit was a wash-out. Literally. It persisted down all day, non-stop. The rain thrashed on the surface for hour after hour and it didn't come as any surprise when we didn't catch anything. We fished with large and small smelt deadbaits we'd bought from the local tackle shop and small roach and hybrids that Stu whittled out on a short pole from the pit.

I knew nothing about catching zander, at least not from personal experience, but I'd read quite a lot as they always fascinated me. I'd read that they preferred a small freshwater fish rather than sea fish, but that it was worth fishing with sea fish if you had no other choice. I'd learned that, generally speaking, you fished for them with stepped-down pike tackle and that they wouldn't tolerate resistance. There were a few decent pike in the pit as well as zander so I decided I would fish with my usual pike tackle, except that the trace would be 15lb bs rather than 20lb or 28lb and the trebles would be 8's or 10's rather than 6's.

My running lead would be allowed to run rather than being stopped a few inches back with a couple of silicon float stops as is usually my habit when piking. I stuck with my drop-off alarms for bite indication, for after the initial plucking of the line from the clip the zeds would be free to run the line off the open spool.

We based our choice of swim on the local knowledge that Stu had picked up. It had margins about 4 - 5ft deep and slowly fell away to about 8 – 10ft some 30 yards out. Two rods each were fished, with a variety of baits being tried, one each in the margins and one each at distance.

Several times that day the lines were snatched from the clips, and several times nothing more happened. Each time we picked up the rod and felt the line for movement but there was nothing to be felt. On two occasions, on Stu's rod, a big flat spot appeared at the surface as something chomped on the small smelt and released its juices.

But still nothing happened to warrant a strike. I put it down to pike, that they were just not hungry but couldn't resist having a nip at the baits. I'd seen it before on waters where no zander were present. But I'd never seen it happen so often as this. And it bothered me. We arranged for a return visit four days later. In the meantime I would contact a couple of zander fishing friends for information.

Norfolk predator ace Chris Bishop told me that the pick-ups were probably zander and that they will kill a bait sometimes even when they don't want it themselves (he mentioned that there is a theory that zander will kill a bait for a fellow zander that may be too sick to kill bait for itself). Chris also contacted Dave Marrs, a very experienced zander angler who had actually fished the pit, and Dave gave us some incredibly detailed and valuable information. And Jan Porter told me that it was better to offer them as little resistance as possible, but what little there was should be consistent.

The second trip was different in many ways: we had more knowledge, it wasn't raining, and we felt a lot more confident.

We fished the same swim and almost straight away we both had bites. And we both failed to hook anything. Then I had a very slow bite that I felt when I picked the rod up and gripped the line between finger and thumb. Nobody was more surprised than me when a 2lb perch slid over the net, complete with a set of trebles in its mouth and the 4" roach it had spat out lying in the bottom of the landing net. Were they the cause of the dropped runs, I wondered?

The next fish was a pike of about 14 – 15lb that took a float-fished free roaming live roach. In between times we had experienced several pick-ups; obviously aborted strikes. It was frustrating to say the least.

I said to Stu, "I'm going to close the bale-arm and stand over my rods. The next time that line comes out of the clip I'm going to try to hit it with no delay whatsoever."

No sooner had I said it when my phone rang. It was Gary Knowles, still recovering from a recent bout of gastric flu. Following the usual pleasantries (you know, me taking the mickey out of his suffering, and him being equally as nice to me) we got round to talking about zander, what had happened so far, and that I was going to try to hit the next one from the moment the line was pulled from the clip. He said exactly the same thing had happened to him down the fens a couple of weeks previously and the advice off the Fen's zander lads he was fishing with had been to hit them on the first indication.

A 15lb pike was landed next.

That it was a mistake to feel for the bite following a pick-up as zander were so adverse to resistance they'd drop the bait straight away. Gary had been doing the same as me, which works so well for pike.

I had just two more bites and I tried to hit them as I'd said I would, standing over my rods and sweeping the rod back as soon as the line pulled from the clip. I hooked both and they were zander. The first one weighed 8lb 2oz and the second 7lb 7oz; not massive in zander terms but massive in my terms. It was my first zed, the first one I'd ever seen and if it hadn't had such an array of evil-looking teeth I would have kissed it. I was so overjoyed I would have kissed Stu if he hadn't ran off and I'm still not sure if he was scared of the zander or scared of me. Old Dracula was an impressive sight, a really evil-looking, prehistoric creature.

What a day! I'd loved it; a nice pike and perch, and not one, but two zander, a personal best of course and all in one day. Who says life begins at 40? I've started all over again at 60!

I've been back several times since with Stu and my regular fishing pal at the time, the late Dave Colclough, armed with lighter rods and reels. Those times I fished with closed bale-arms, a foot drop on the bobbins and ordinary bite alarms. We caught quite a few fish between us to just into double figures and it certainly paid us not to delay the strike once that indicator was on the move. Live and dead roach in the 4 – 6oz bracket were the best baits by far.

It has to be said though, that the solutions to catching zander on that particular Leicester gravel pit may not be the solutions to catching zander on your waters. Go with an open mind and if you experience difficulty in hooking them swap from one to the other until experience provides the answer.